Human Body Fengshui

An Almanac of Inner Daoist Cosmology

by

Dr. Wu Baolin

and

Austin Lane Muhs

with

Kevin T. Hill, Jesica Eckstein, Michael McBride,
Paulina Wierzbicka, and Brent Christopher Wulf

Three Pines Press
St Petersburg, FL
www.threepinespress.com

9 8 7 6 5 4 3 2 1

Printed in the United States of America
This edition is printed on acid-free paper that meets
the American National Standard Institute Z39. 48 Standard.
Distributed in the United States by Three Pines Press.

Cover Design by Diego Spitaleri

Library of Congress Cataloging-in-Publication Data

Names: Wu, Baolin, 1954- author. | Muhs, Austin Lane, 1986- author.
Title: Human body fengshui : an almanac of inner Daoist cosmology / by Dr. Wu Baolin and Austin Lane Muhs ; with Kevin T. Hill, Jessica Eckstein, Michael McBride, Paulina Wierzbicka, and Brent Christopher Wulf.
Description: First edition. | St Petersburg, FL : Three Pines Press, [2024] | Includes bibliographical references and index.
Identifiers: LCCN 2024013608 | ISBN 9781931483766 (paperback ; acid-free paper)
Subjects: LCSH: Feng shui. | Taoism.
Classification: LCC BF1779.F4.W779 2024 | DDC 133.3/337--dc23/eng/20240624
LC record available at https://lccn.loc.gov/2024013608

Contents

Foreword

This book grew from a class Dr. taught on human body Fengshui, attended by Austin Lane Muhs and Brent Christopher Wulf. Austin took careful notes and over time transformed them into this publication. Adopting a first-person narrative, the "I" used throughout refers to him since he is sharing his reflections and interpretations of Dr. Wu's teachings in his own words.

In time, however, Dr. Wu started a new class with a larger group that he still continues to teach to this day, titled "Wu Baolin's *Huangdi Neijing Yijing* Academy." This book represents their first collaborative effort. Upon completing the manuscript, Dr. Wu proposed that members of the Academy should review Austin's work and contribute to its improvement. Given Brent's attendance at the original classes, he was able to use his notes to further clarify a rather detailed account about the Daoist interpretation of the soul in the first chapter. This chapter employs a third-person narrative as to remain faithful to Dr. Wu's teachings on this rather important topic. While the remainder of the book is told in Austin's first-person voice. However, due to the involvement of other students in the revision process there are varied tones, subtly shifting the author's voice throughout the chapters.

Guided by Dr. Wu's teachings and with inspiration from the Daoist principle of performing good deeds, Austin has dedicated himself to the compassionate act of burying deceased animals, ranging from domestic pets to wildlife. Once, Austin encountered a deceased deer. Confronted with the challenge of its considerable weight and without assistance in burying a grave. He instead, adapted by mounding dirt over the animal, creating a respectful earthen memorial. This practice, rooted in respect for all living beings, has evolved into a mission of rescue and rehabilitation, with Austin extending his compassion to injured animals in need of care. Through social media and tireless journeys, he connects with those who have encountered injured animals, offering them a chance at recovery and a new life, only asking for donations to support his work.

Austin also spearheaded the formation of a peace coalition, uniting members from the United States, Israel, and Palestine, in a concerted effort to draw attention to the urgent need for intervention amidst the humanitarian crisis unfolding in Gaza. The coalition reached out to every member of Congress, advocating immediate action to assist those most vulnerable, the elderly and children, caught in the turmoil of recent conflicts. The coalition highlighted the dire situation of displaced individuals who had lost access to essential resources such as food and water, compounded by the harsh realities of being exposed to the elements during the initial outbreak of the conflict in winter.

This initiative resulted in receiving eight responses, a testament to the coalition's ability. Among these responses, a notable few indicated that certain congressmen were not only moved by the coalition's pleas but also prepared to advocate further for them.

Prologue

Standing on the front stoop of the Beijing Chinese Medical Center on March 7, 2024 at exactly 5 pm, I was compelled to raise my head and look northeast when suddenly I witnessed an unusually long and heavy lightning bolt hanging horizontally just above the small hill across the way. Immediately I found myself counting the seconds until reaching 22, the time when the thunder cracked and rumbled the ground beneath my feet. My first thought was, "Master Wu Baolin must be working on something very important" because the 22 miles northeastward from where the lightning came is the San Gabriel Valley, the place he lives.

As this occurred, I was called out onto the practice grounds to ride the wind, which was now blowing-in from the eight directions, spinning me like a compass needle in an electric storm. When the winds calmed, I retreated inside the clinic to then receive a phone call from my sister, as she was concerned for my safety after hearing reports of intense thunder, lighting, rain, winds and hailstorms coming down in the San Gabriel Valley. This was confirmation number two.

A patient of the clinic arrived a short while later and commented on the sudden storm and the gorgeous rainbow hanging overhead. In response I said, "You know, this extreme weather and rainbow was generated by Master Wu, by practicing Immortal Wang Chongyang's Dragon Qigong set." I followed her skeptic eyes into the treatment room where the digital clock was displaying 5:31 PM, which is both a Dragon number as well as Master Wu's address. This was confirmation number three. From then on, I kept the details of the event to myself.

Four days later on Monday March 11, 2024, on the day the 'Dragon lifts its head' (2/2 of the lunar calendar), Brent Christopher Wulf and I were summoned to the clinic for a five o'clock meeting. It was at this time that Master Wu Baolin began to explain his activities of March 7, when I interjected with, "It happened at 5:00 PM!" Confirming time accuracy with a nod, Master Wu proceeded to impart the mystery of summoning the Ninth Dragon from heaven and how that routine contains many curious qigong movements. Because of this he drew a fair amount of attention to himself at the local 24-hour fitness pool where he carried out the water portion of the ceremony. Following every written instruction to the letter, it took Master Wu two full hours to conclude before culminating in the powerful storm. This represents the highest level of human body fengshui.

—Michael McBride, Traditional Chinese massage practitioner, author and Daoist acolyte.

Chapter 1

The Soul-Seed

Everybody has a star in the universe, shining in the sky above. After a baby is born and lets out its first cry, it aligns with its corresponding star in the sky. This star harbors a soul, at the heart of which resides the "soul-seed" (*lingzi* 靈子), the core of the soul (*linghun* 靈魂). This soul-seed is very small, about the size of a pearl, and resembles a star. Each person is such a star, with a soul-seed inside them.

During the miraculous moment of childbirth, as a mother endures labor pain, a celestial soul descends from the sky or heaven to enter the baby's body. Moments later, the infant's first cry signals the splitting apart of the soul-seed. One part ascends back to the sky, appearing as a star, while the other remains embedded within the baby's body. Prior to birth, the soul-seed's presence is absent from the fetus.

Throughout the gestation period, the fetus is considered a living seed, but the soul-seed does not exist in the fetus yet. However, due to the pre-heaven combination of the parents' seeds (sperm and egg) there is the presence of a soul (*hun* 魂) in the fetus. Birth acts as a gateway for the soul-seed's entry into the earthly realm, where it combines with the fetus's soul to become the soul in the child's body.

It is important to note that the soul-seed enters the child's body in passing through the mother's womb first. Upon delivery, the umbilical cord is cut, severing the physical connection the baby has with its mother. In this moment the baby is sounding off its first cry signifying not only the physical disconnection from its mother but also its simultaneous division and detachment from its celestial soul-seed counterpart.

The division of the soul-seed can be seen as a literal splitting into two halves or as a duplication into two soul-seeds. This follows the Daoist principle of "one generates two" as Laozi says in the *Daode jing*. This bifurcation allows for one of the soul-seeds to ascend to the sky reclaiming its celestial position, while the other remains within the physical body on earth.

From the moment of birth, every individual is preordained to suffer tribulations. Everyone comes to this world to endure hardships. That is why, when babies are born, the first noise they make is cry: they innately know that they are here to suffer. It also pertains to the splitting of the soul and the distance felt between the baby on earth and its star in the sky. Simultaneously, it manifests in a mother's tears, shed in response to her newborn's plight. Her cries reflect a deep, intuitive connection with her celestial origin, as she too perceives the profound separation and ensuing journey of hardship her child must face.

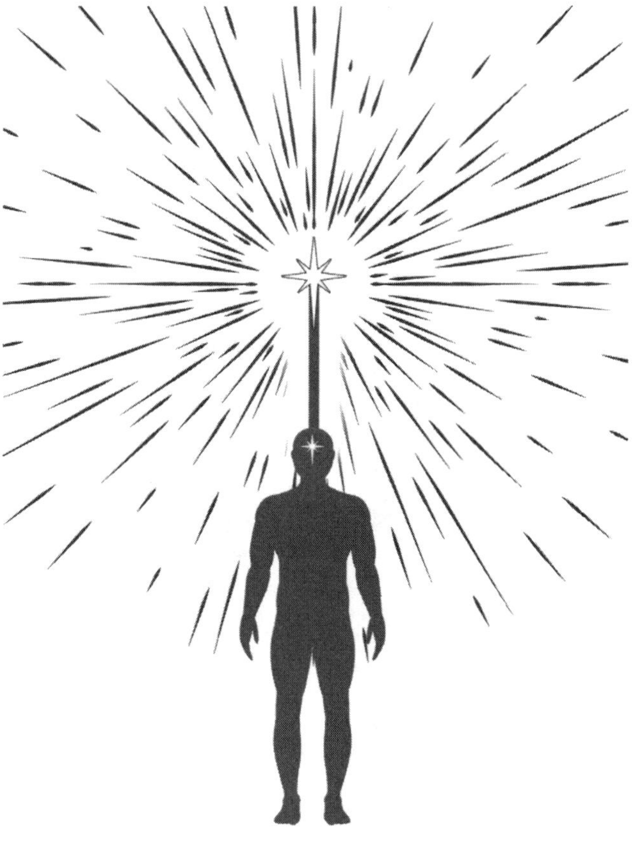

The *Daode jing* introduces the concept of nothingness, something invisible, referred to in Daoism as the "empty-nothingness seed." This soul-seed is the "empty-nothingness seed." It is invisible yet exists within the universe and the human form. The *Guanzi* has, "The righteous person seeks nothing; therefore, they can embody nothingness. Nothingness without form is called the Dao."

A baby's initial sound made at the moment of entering the world, be it a cry, a laugh, or any utterance, signifies its first day on earth. It heralds the onset of tribulations it will suffer in life. From that moment on, the duration of an individual's life, whether it reaches to a hundred years or stops at eighty, is predetermined by a specific tally. The trajectory of one's life, encompassing career paths, societal roles, marital status, offspring, and financial prosperity, is dictated by pre-heaven destiny, laid down prior to birth. This perspective is rooted in the *Yijing* (Book of Changes), suggesting that various aspects of a person's life are shaped by predetermined factors established in the pre-heaven phase of existence before birth.

The Third Eye

This life is just a stop on a short journey. Actually, a person's life on earth is like the sphere of *taiji*, it is circular. Everyone is like the curved synovial line in the middle of the *taiji*. The upper dot is yang, and the lower dot is yin, forming two yin-yang circles. Their convergence at the center represents the human being. It is a twisty path and everyone's life is just like that. Human anatomy mirrors this, with its moveable joints allowing the body to bend and flex.

The head reflects the near-circular form of the sky and the celestial bodies. From a Daoist perspective, the left eye is the sun and the right eye is the moon. Using Chinese characters to aid in understanding, between the two eyes, the sun (*ri* 日) and the moon (*yue* 月) come together, creating "bright light" (*ming* 明), the light of understanding.

Deep within the brain resides the pineal gland, the human being's third eye, which can see past and future. Therefore, Daoist practitioners cultivate this eye as it pertains to the pre-heaven state of the person. It stands in a direct relationship with the soul-seed star in the sky and also represents the soul-seed in the body, located in the pineal gland. This is the "empty-nothingness seed" of the *Daode jing*.

Many religions reference the concept of the third eye in various forms. In Daoism and Tibetan Buddhism, the cultivation and enhancement of the third eye form a significant focus. To symbolize its importance, many adepts mark their foreheads with a dot, positioned between their two physical eyes. While this dot is a physical, man-made symbol, it serves the deeper purpose of a visual reminder and a representation of the third eye, signaling the presence of a higher level of awareness and spiritual insight.

The third eye can be located through a specific triangulation method. First, identify the midpoint between the two eyebrows. Second, find the location known as the star gate in Daoism refers to the soft spot in infants. This soft spot is where the anterior fontanel meets the coronal sutures of the skull. It typically closes and fuses over as the child gets older.

Balancing Oscillations

Reaching the full potential in cultivating the third eye is a feat achieved by only about ten percent of people. A primary factor contributing to this is the prevalent skepticism about the existence of the third eye. Among those who do acknowledge its existence, successfully cultivating it remains a challenge. The cultivation of the third eye involves specific practices and methods. Without the right approach and understanding, achieving proficiency in harnessing its potential can be quite elusive.

From the moment a person is born, their soul-seed splits into two. To differentiate between them the one in the sky can be called the "celestial soul-seed" and the one in the human body can be called the "mortal soul-seed." Under normal circumstances the celestial soul-seed remotely controls its mortal counterpart in the pineal gland. For this to occur, its angle of deviation should not exceed 15 degrees. The celestial soul-seed can be compared to life's GPS, as the star in the sky guides one toward their destiny on earth. It is also called the Governing Destiny Star because destiny is determined by heaven. But how is it determined? This star, is analogous to an apple's core holding seeds. The soul-seed is generated by millions upon millions of information messages (packets) sent from the center of the universe.

Daoists support the concept that material things are determined by thoughts. Material things indicate matter and all concrete things and affairs. All substantive matter, the understanding is, comes ultimately from thoughts that emanate from the soul-seed, centered in the pineal gland. Cultivation practices such as qigong utilize thoughts mainly for the purpose of opening the third eye.

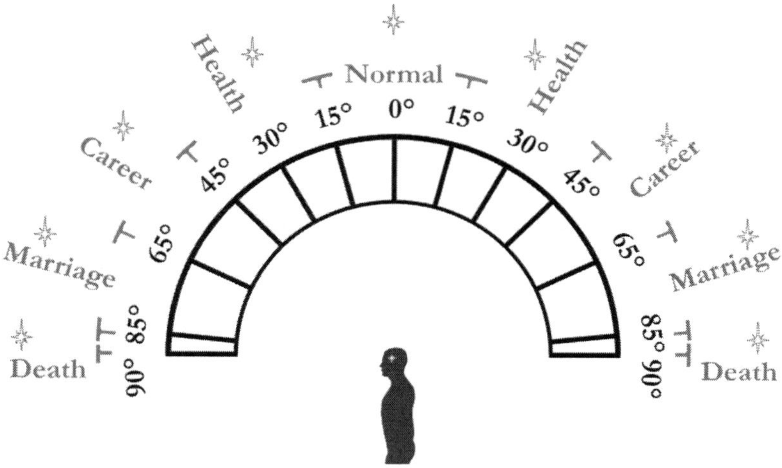

Maintaining an oscillating angle of deviation by 15 degrees between the pineal gland and the celestial soul-seed allows for the star in heaven to guide one toward destiny. When the alignment between the mortal and celestial soul-seeds deviates by more than 15 degrees, one will encounter trouble. Whenever there is such misalignment, something bad or problematic is likely to happen. For example, if it is between 15 and 45 degrees, the body will become sick. If between 45 and 65 degrees, one's career will have problems. If between 65 to 85 degrees of variance, one's relationships and marriage will be affected negatively, and if it exceeds 90 degrees, life will end.

Only by practicing qigong can one regain the soul's normal alignment, so that it can lead one toward their destiny. Taijiquan, yoga, and various other physical movements will clean the pineal gland, like polishing a crystal, and make the third eye's vision clearer. However, they will not adjust the oscillating movement of the celestial soul-seed to return to its normal range, which only qigong can do.

Upon death, the closing of the eyes marks the cessation of the pineal gland's function. At this moment, the soul, embodied by the mortal soul-seed, departs the physical body to reunite with its counterpart, the celestial soul-seed in the sky above. From there the soul undergoes the process of reincarnation, moving into one of the six paths of existence as based on their actions in this and previous lives. The totality of these actions determines the next life form: human, animal, or plant.

The Thirty-Six Categories

Existence in this understanding comes in thirty-six distinct categories, such as tribes, species, groups, and the like. For example, birds are classified under the feather group, while humans are under the pad-foot group. In terms of vegetation, trees form their own distinct category, contrasting with grasses and flowering plants, which are collectively placed in the flower group. Trees are considered yang and flowers, yin. However, within the tree category, tea trees are designated as yin.

The system further extends to include a ghost group and an immortal group. There are many different groups, and within them are sub groups. For example, cats, tigers, and lions, fall under the feline group; cows, horses, sheep, and lambs form a different group. This intricate classification system is structured hierarchically, with each of the thirty-six primary groups subdivided into thirty-six subgroups, which then further divide into thirty-six smaller groups, and so on.

One subcategory within the human body contains the five senses: the eye, nose, mouth, ear, and tongue groups. They are interconnected yet distinct. For example, the eyes and the pineal gland form one group while the ears and the kidneys form another. The same classification is also at the basis of the theory of organ correspondences in traditional Chinese medicine. It outlines the relationships between the organs and the five senses.

All these parts form the human body, which are is both the person and not the person. It is akin to a car assembled from separate parts. When the parts come together in the proper order and with the right alignment, they form a whole car. When the human body is viewed as separate parts, these parts—and especially the joints—can also be likened to the hexagrams of the *Yijing*.

Each individual part of the body, moreover, has a correlating relationship with heaven. Daoists also work with this in ritual. For instance, when celebrating a birthday, they might stand upright or lie down while holding a cup of "water wine." With this cup in hand, the first act is to thank one's eyes, followed by the nose, ears, etc. thus acknowledging the relationship each part has to heaven.

Intuition

All animals, including the feathered, aquatic, and mammal species, possess an inherent intuition or survival instinct. When people practice qigong, they seek to regain this intuition, which modern humans have largely lost. Today, people rely on logical thinking and psychological analysis, leading to various probabilities and deductions. Unlike animals, they have complex thoughts, but it is important to realize that animals too have their own language and way of thinking. However, animals prioritize intuition above all.

Human intuition does exist, as seen in phenomena like love at first sight, but it is significantly weaker compared to animals. The rise of modernity and the proliferation of electronic devices like phones, computers, and even refrigerators have further diminished it. Animals, not burdened by modern technology, maintain stronger intuitive senses even though they are also affected by factors like static electricity. For instance, animals can sense natural disasters like earthquakes before humans do, as evidenced by the behavior of rats and cats. Ants relocating before rain or dragonflies flying low are examples of animal intuition, often seen as a natural forecasting ability. In contrast, humans rely on technological tools and past experiences to make predictions.

This reliance on technology could be seen as either evolution or regression. While we have advanced intellectually, we have lost many natural instincts. Practicing qigong aims to reclaim these lost instincts. To achieve this, one must understand and align with the natural world, maintaining equanimity with animals and nature.

Interestingly, health can inversely affect this intuitive ability. Healthy people often lack it, whereas sick individuals, due to their altered state, may experience a resurgence. Children, for example, exhibit strong intuition, which tends to fade as they grow older. This is often attributed to maturity, but from another perspective, it is abnormal for humans to lose their intuitive abilities. From the Daoist viewpoint, children possess a unique feature atop their heads known as the "star gate," a soft spot that remains open for a certain period after birth before eventually closing. This is like having the sunroof in a car open. The pineal gland has a direct line of sight of star in the sky above, clear for all signals to go to and from the celestial soul-seed.

This opening is further linked to the navel. The umbilical cord, which connects a mother and her baby during pregnancy, becomes a source of potentially life-saving cord blood after birth. This cord blood, rich in stem cells, has significant therapeutic potential and can be cryogenically stored, much how sperm and ova are preserved for future use. In times of severe illness, this personalized cord blood can be reintroduced into the patient's system, potentially enhancing their innate blood supply. Despite its potential, the importance and applications of umbilical cord blood are often underappreciated in contemporary medical discussions.

Qigong practitioners will swallow air as *qi* 氣 all the way down to the elixir field (*dantian* 丹田) in the abdomen. Doing this, they restimulate sensory actions in the navel, where the umbilical cord was attached. Reactivating certain neurological sensors, they regain potentially lost information.

Children under the age of 9, and even up to 14, possess unique capabilities that are lost as they grow older and their brains fully develop. The diminishing loss of these natural abilities as one ages is accepted today as normal. However, it is not normal. The reason for the diminishing of innate abilities in people is their overexposure to electrical currents and other modern stimulations and the wide variety of processed foods they consume. Over time, these primal instincts have gradually diminished.

Bravery

To illustrate this with a simple example from behavioral studies, consider the concept of bravery, like charging forward in battle or facing challenges head-on. Bravery is universally praised, while its opposite, retreating or yielding, is often seen as weakness or cowardice. Bravery is associated with yang and retreat with yin. Common perception holds that bravery, as a manifestation of righteousness and justice, is commendable, especially since genuinely just people are rare nowadays. Acts of bravery, when they occur, are highly praised and reported on by the media, acting like a barometer of societal values.

However, throughout the long history of humanity, the number of brave people has been declining. This is attributed to a decrease in people's commitment and uncertainty about the correctness of their actions. People are bound by various moral and social rules, and these rules have their own logic. For example, perceptions change based on whether a person is married or has children. These are widely accepted as signs of human progress and experience, documented over thousands of years, that contribute to culture and society.

However, Daoists teach that every issue has two sides: positive and negative capabilities. As a result, assertive actions based on bravery and righteousness have become less common over time. A Chinese proverb that goes back to the

Analects of Confucius says, "To see what is right and act courageously" (*jianyi yongwei* 見義勇為). For example, this can involve recognizing an injustice and having the courage to speak out against it.

Society often uses religion and the prison system to manage or influence people's thoughts. Regardless of whether it is Buddhism, Daoism, Christianity, Catholicism, Judaism, or Islam, all religions promote kindness and doing good deeds. In short, these are righteous acts, representing a kind of comprehensive management system integrating logical thinking and psychology of the highest form.

The other method of control is the criminal justice system, which imprisons those who break the law. Incarceration for an offense like theft or murder is intended to protect others and, in this respect, it represents a form of positivity. However, it can also be perceived as unfair to the individual who is incarcerated, that is, a form of negativity. There is a saying that anything not expressly forbidden by law is legal. This suggests that areas not covered by law are automatically permissible, leading people to exploit legal loopholes. But this often leads to negative outcomes.

Consider the *taiji* diagram, representing yin and yang. The circle that encompasses both yin and yang is Dao, people navigate the curvy line between yin and yang. In terms of the human body, the head represents the yang dot and the feet represent the yin dot. In terms of the planet earth, the South Pole is yang, and the North Pole is yin, with the majority of the earth occupying the space in between. The surface area of the poles is tiny compared to the rest of the earth. Similarly, in human beings, the head and feet are just small parts, with the body occupying most of the space. This concept aligns with the Daoist principle of "one generates two, two generates three, and three generates all things."

Therefore, to find the backbone in all things, one must experience setbacks, make decisions, and then act with courage and dare to do it again. This is true bravery. What people seek is the heart, which is half in the sky as the celestial soul-seed and half in the human body as the third eye. It lets one know fear first, which is to have self-awareness of it. Then, based on this understanding, one makes decisions and then acts despite the fear: that is true bravery. Qigong practitioners cultivate this concept and adepts of human body fengshui also emphasize this principle.

For example, when a baby is born, its initial cry marks the soul-seed dividing into two parts, symbolizing the *Daode jing* concept of "one generating two." One part ascends to the sky residing as a star, and the other remains in the body. Two generates three, and three generates everything. This "everything" represents the entire journey of life, all the experiences one will go through.

Heaven and Humanity

The medical classic *Huangdi neijing* 黃帝內經 (Yellow Emperor's Inner Classics) cites the Daoist *Taishi yuantian ci* 太始天元册 (Book of the Ultimate Beginning and the Origin of Heaven):

> The great void is vast and empty, it is the foundation of the origin of generation and transformation. It is from which, all things derive their beginning. The five movements complete the heaven, spreading the *qi* of the true soul-seed, commanding the origin of earth. The nine stars hang bright, the seven luminaries revolve. This speaks of yin and yang, of the soft and the hard. Thus, the obscure (darkness) and the apparent (light) are in their places, cold and heat relax and expand. Generation after generation, transformation after transformation, the cycle of life and transformation of all things come into existence. (ch. 66)

This refers to the nine stars and seven luminants, relating to the nine palaces in the head and also correlating with the nine orifices of the human body. The latter include the eyes, ears, nostrils, mouth, anus, and urethra. Each of these nine orifices serves a distinct function and plays a crucial role in our interaction with the external environment. For example, the eyes enable us to see, the nostrils facilitate breathing, the ears allow for hearing, the mouth is essential for eating, the anus opens for defecation, and the urethra is essential for urination. The body openings thus serve as conduits for various physiological processes, bridging internal and external environments while also corresponding to the nine stars in the sky and thus reflecting unique aspects of our connection to the universe.

The seven luminants are the sun, the moon, and the five planets closest to earth (Mercury, Venus, Mars, Jupiter, and Saturn). In ancient Chinese, the word for the planets is the same as that for stars. The five stars are understood as representing the five phases in the sky, which thereby also correlate to the five inner organs of the human body.

The moon and the sun also have their bodily correlations, matching yin and yang as well as water and fire. Thus, the sun correlates to the heart, while the moon relates to the kidneys. This aligns with the medical concept of fire and water in the body, the heart representing fire and the kidneys representing water. Additionally, Daoists see the sun as the father and the moon as the mother.

The seven luminants are further connected to the days of the week as well as with the trigrams of the *Yijing*. Thus, Monday is associated with the trigram Qian ☰ (Heaven). In symbolizes the first among the five phases, which is the wood phase. This connection suggests a method of aligning one's dietary choices throughout the week to be in a harmonious relationship with one's "soul-seed" in the sky (Wu and Wulf 2023, 180-82; 2024, 60-65).

Qian represents initiation or the beginning of things. Similarly, wood is the first of the five phases and related to the season of spring. Each of the five phases match one season as well as a day in the work week.

The Five Phases in the Work Week				
Wood	Fire	Earth	Metal	Water
Monday	Tuesday	Wednesday	Thursday	Friday

The five phases fit in the work week, but what about the weekend? The eight trigrams can be linked with one of the seven days of the week and also aligned with the five phases, offering a cosmic way of understanding weekend days. Encompassing Saturday and Sunday, the weekend is marked by the number seven and the trigram Gen ☶ (Mountain), which represents the idea of stopping. Traditionally, Sunday serves as a day of rest for many, whether for religious observance or recuperation from the works week. This is in line with *Yijing* thinking:

Mon	Tue	Wed	Thu	Fri	Sat	Sun
Wood	Fire	Earth	Metal	Water		
☰	☱	☲	☳	☴	☵	☶☷
Qian	Dui	Li	Zhen	Xun	Kan	Gen/Kun

The Number Seven

The number seven plays an important role in ancient cosmology Among many other links, it is also associated with dogs, notably in the idea that a current canine companion may have shared a maternal bond with its owner in a past life, seven incarnations ago. In this case, it means the dog has an obligation to its owner. This is because to transition through the six levels and now the seventh one must transform. Thus, the roles in this life have shifted, with one being human and the other a dog. In the *Yijing*, the seventh level means transformation, and seven represents vastness, mountains, earth, and stopping. The highest number of conversion and change, it cannot be eight or nine when using the *Yijing* in calculating.

Eight represents "following the course," as in smooth sailing. If something goes smoothly, it will not get involved with seven, which denotes stopping. While acknowledging the eight trigrams and the nine palaces, *Yijing* calculation stops at seven. This mirrors the way a mountain disrupts flat landscape, indicating a point where forward motion or ongoing processes come to a stop. In this context, Daoists also embrace the notion that, when someone's life comes to an end and they die, their soul goes to a mountain in the north called Fengdu.

> Mt. Fengdu has been considered the entrance to the Daoist hells or earth prisons (*diyu*) since the 1st century CE; however, the first text in which Fengdu is mentioned as a place of the dead is Ge Hong's (283–343) *Baopuzi* (Book of the Master Who Embraces Simplicity). An entire administration of the universe's moral order is housed in this place. There are various courts and palaces. Records and ledgers of the dead are kept there. Virtuous individuals are sent on from Fengdu to the celestial paradises, while those who have done immoral deeds are sent to the earth prisons for punishment. The highest officials of this otherworldly bureaucracy were people of virtue during their lifetimes, whereas those who administer the punishments are often known only as "ghost soldiers" (*guibing*). From a cosmic point of view, the location of this mountain is in the northernmost quarter of the universe; however, various traditions place the entry into Fengdu at the base of Mt. Tai. (Littlejohn 2019, 85)

This principle extends further to fengshui and Chinese characters, where the arrangement of elements resonates with various states of being. For example, a door facing a tree suggests entrapment, as the combination of "door" (*men* 門) and "tree" (*mu* 木) forms the character for "difficulty" (*kun* 困). Therefore, one's door should not face a tree or a mountain because both signify a halt. Ideally, mountains should be situated behind a dwelling to offer support, akin to the spine's role in the human body, symbolizing stability, support, and something to rely on.

In urban settings, this principle translates to having a taller building behind one's residence, representing a mountain. This shows people how the gradual unfolding of fengshui between man and nature is understood. Just as the nine palaces correlate to the nine orifices of the human body, this understanding helps us interact with the universe.

There is a sequence in which these numbers came about. Yin and yang give rise to the four images, understood as lines arranged in pairs and made visible in major starry constellations in the four cardinal directions, envisioned as animals: the green dragon, while tiger, red bird, and turtle with snake (dark warrior). Moving on in numbers, from the four images arise the five phases and, in due course, the eight trigrams and nine palaces.

In concrete fact, the operation of change and transformation ends with seven. Even though cosmological numbering goes up to nine, the number seven is central, a key pivot point in the generation marked by numbers. Because the number eight represents smooth sailing, that is, a good and steady way of cultivation as well as normal and easy relationships with the world, the Chinese think of it as bringing good luck and like to use it in phone numbers, license plates, and house numbers.

Still, everything that happens in daily life should be calculated through the number seven. When the *Yijing* employs the number eight for calculations, it addresses scenarios that transcend ordinary life activities, concerning more higher-level matters in general. Essentially, events within the human experience, concerning day-to-day endeavors, can be calculated up to the number seven when using the *Yijing*.

The Phase Wood

Among the eight trigrams that form the foundation of the sixty-four hexagrams of the *Yijing*, the first is Qian which corresponds to the liver. This organ represents springtime, the season when all things come to life. It embodies the beginning of all things, their initial generative transformation.

The liver is of immense importance in the body. In traditional Chinese medicine, the heart is considered the emperor due to its role of governing all the body sections and organs. The spleen and kidneys are seen as vital because the body's innate or pre-heaven *qi* resides in the kidneys while the body's acquired or post-heaven *qi* centers in the spleen. But from an *Yijing* perspective, the liver as it is positioned between innate and acquired *qi* holds the utmost significance: it determines everybody's physical transformation from the beginning. This insight has been the subject of scholarly pursuit for millennia, notably since the era of Zhu Xi 朱熹 (1130-1200), a seminal Neo-Confucian thinker of the Song dynasty.

In addition, the importance of wood and the liver also relates to the days of the week. Here the first day corresponds to the liver, matching health and rejuvenation in the initial phase of generative transformation. Mondays are thus a time to honor and respect the liver by promoting a diet abundant in greens and plant-based nourishment, echoing the dietary habits of our ancestors at the dawn of humanity. This day is seen as an opportunity to abstain from meat and engage in detoxification, respecting the phase wood as symbolized by plants and trees.

Five Visceral Organs and their Correspondences to the Five Phases				
Wood	Fire	Earth	Metal	Water
Liver	Heart	Spleen	Lungs	Kidneys
Monday	Tuesday	Wednesday	Thursday	Friday

In China, the birth of a child is marked by planting a tree that serves as a living repository similar to modern "cloud storage," where information about the child can be stored. The person's soul divides at that time, so that the celestial soul-seed resides in the sky guides and the mortal soul-seed in the body. As they both combine to fulfill the person's, there needs to be a bridge or coordinate between them: this is the role of the tree. If you are aware of this, then you can plant a tree for your child when it is born or for yourself now, since you just became aware of its importance. For people who are not aware of the need to plant the tree, then the closest tree to their home ends up acting as their coordinate bridge between them and their star in heaven.

The same also occurs in other cultures. In Ireland and Germany, for example, trees are connected to newborns (Coitir 2023, 61). The Jewish tradition upholds a similar practice, notably in Israel (Cohen 1994, 79-82). In Japan, people plant a "princess tree" for every newborn girl (Japanese Mythology & Folklore 2014). Even the Christmas tree, traditionally topped with a star, subtly echoes this concept, symbolizing the connection between the tree, the star, and the birth of the baby (Jesus), albeit in a different cultural context. Today, many countries are advocating to plant a tree for every newborn to fulfill ecological concerns.

Modern science tells us that if there were no trees, humans could not survive. Where there are trees, there must be water. Birds will come and live on or near trees. And where there are birds, there is the ability to perform *Yijing* calculations.

Life Expectancy

Both modern science and the *Yijing* place the biological limit of human life at is 120 years, but then the Chinese divide this into five distinct phases of twenty-four years each. This reflects the five phases and also correlates with the Chinese calendar system of dividing the year into twenty-four seasonal divisions. Thus, from age 1 to 24, the wood phase represents the spring of life; from 25 to 48, the fire phase shows the summer; from 49 to 72, the earth phase matches the late summer of life; from 73 to 96, the metal phase stands for the autumn years; and from 97 to 120, the water phase represents life's winter.

Five Phases of Human Life				
Wood	Fire	Earth	Metal	Water
Spring	Summer	Late Summer	Autumn	Winter
1-24	25-48	49-72	73-96	97-120

The age of 21, historically viewed as the threshold to adulthood, marks a significant transition point in people's lives,[1] even though physical changes still happen after. A recent study, moreover, indicates that human brain development does not reach full maturity until around the age of 25 (Arain et al. 2013). Maybe one day science will discover the age of adulthood to be more in alignment with the *Yijing*, that is, at age 24.

Daoists promote the harmonious union of heaven and humanity (*tianren heyi* 天人合一). Studied through correspondences between heaven as the sky and each individual person, this extends to the ongoing topic that everyone corresponds to a star. Just as everyone has parents on earth, so the sun and moon also represent everyone's parents. Further examples of the correspondences between the human and celestial body appear in the 365 acupoints that each represent a day of the year as well as in the twelve meridians that correspond to the twelve months. The *Huangdi neijing* states, "When a person is just born, they first become essence," indicating the cosmic connection.

This principle suggests that at birth, individuals inherently possess a set of predetermined factors and aligns with the old Daoist belief that a newborn's life is preordained with specific parameters. These parameters encompass various aspects, such as longevity, marital history, career path, financial status, and number of children—all essentially preset at birth.

Yet, this destiny is not rigidly fixed. Rather, it is dynamic and susceptible to change. For instance, saving another person's life is said to extend one's life expectancy by seven years, demonstrating that actions and choices can influence and alter these predetermined aspects. Similarly, saving a dog's life is said to add four years.

It is important to note that the extension of life is not linear with each act of saving a life. For instance, while the first act of saving a life grants an additional seven years, saving a second life adds only five more years, not another seven.

---

[1] Traditionally this was when Americans were allowed to vote. However, legal recognition of adulthood shifted to 18 in the United States with the 26th Amendment in 1971.

This diminishing effect reflects a rule that every subsequent act of virtue adds ninety percent of the longevity granted by the previous act. This principle follows the many ancient numerical methods that are binary, hence the reduction of two years for each additional life saved.

Some say, I have saved several lives. For example, a veterinarian might say, I have saved many cats' lives. That means in the next life, that veterinarian might reincarnate as a cat. In the world of cats, it is possible to attain eternal life. Or it could be said that in a previous life, that veterinarian was a cat king. Therefore, in this life, the veterinarian has saved many cats. There are many other possible causes for the person saving so many cats in this life.

Chapter 2

The Flexibility of Fate

Embarking on our earthly journey, we are summoned to fulfill a profound purpose: the evolution and refinement of our souls. This quest, often overshadowed by the immediate demands of daily life—work, education, financial responsibilities—represents a deeper calling that transcends mere material achievements. It is an invitation to engage in soulful development, a process that enriches our existence and prepares us for the challenges and opportunities life presents.

Dr. Wu, drawing from the rich tapestry of Daoist philosophy, reminds us that the practice of spiritual growth is not a static routine but an ever-unfolding journey toward self-realization. Echoing the wisdom of Laozi, "When I let go of who I am, I become who I might be," he underscores the transformative potential inherent in each of us. This journey is unique for every individual, shaped by personal choices, creativity, and the pursuit of enlightenment. This path not only fosters our development but also serves as a beacon for others, encouraging them to explore their spiritual landscapes.

The pursuit of lasting happiness, deeply ingrained in Daoist teachings, challenges us to look beyond transient pleasures and superficial fixes. It calls for a commitment to cultivating our spiritual well-being, emphasizing the role of practices like qigong in harmonizing our inner and outer worlds. Through such disciplines, we learn to embrace life's uncertainties with courage and grace, navigating its complexities with a sense of purpose and fulfillment.

Our journey on earth, though marked by the inevitable ebb and flow of life's ups and downs, is ultimately a quest for meaning and connection. This path requires us to confront our fears, including the fear of the unknown, and to make choices that reflect our deepest values and aspirations. It is in facing these challenges that we discover our true strength and the capacity for profound change.

This exploration of courage and vulnerability is central to the Daoist understanding of life's journey. It invites us to view our experiences through the lens of spiritual growth, recognizing the interconnectedness of all things and the dynamic balance that sustains the universe. By aligning our lives with these principles, we open ourselves to the wisdom and beauty of the Dao, finding peace and contentment in the natural flow of existence.

In synthesizing these insights, we are reminded of the importance of maintaining a deep connection with our spiritual essence. The Daoist path offers a roadmap for navigating life's journey with mindfulness and intention, encouraging us to live in harmony with the natural order and to cultivate a deep sense of gratitude for the myriad blessings that life offers. This holistic approach to living not only enriches our personal experience but also contributes to the well-being of our communities and the world at large, embodying the true spirit of Daoist wisdom.

Success and Failure

Achieving success in our spiritual journey necessitates more than just the legacy of past good deeds; it demands our earnest spiritual endeavor in the present. Dr. Wu emphasizes the critical role of free will and personal effort in unlocking the potential forged by our aactions and the legacies of our ancestors. This challenges the conventional belief that spiritual or material wealth can be passively received without personal growth and diligent work. The act of honoring spiritual mentors and recognizing their trials is vital for acquiring wisdom and insights. Similar to statues, which are intricately shaped to attain their esteemed form, we, too, must undergo our own challenges to spiritually mature.

The teachings of the early patriarch of the Complete Perfection (Quanzhen) school, Qiu Chuji (1148-1227), exemplifies resilience, demonstrating that genuine spiritual achievements are the result of steadfast perseverance, going beyond the confines of our destined paths. As he says,

> I did not have bones of destiny (a significant amount of merit and deeds accumulated from past lives). [Thus] even though I have met an insightful master (Wang Zhe), I have not yet completed [my self-cultivation], [even though I have undergone] 10,000 sufferings and 1,000 harsh experiences. Danyang (Ma Yu) and Changzhen (Tan Chuduan) were predestined, and thus were able to rise and fly beyond heaven at will after ten or five years. Even though I have not yet completed [my training], the difficulties that I have undergone surpass those of ordinary people. (Eskildsen 2004, 47)

Stephen Eskildsen interprets this as a sophisticated understanding of destiny, integrating the concepts of fate and self-effort in the quest for spiritual enlightenment. Qiu's philosophy suggests that while some outcomes are preordained, the pursuit of immortality requires active engagement with life's challenges, viewing them as opportunities for spiritual refinement. This approach stresses the impact of past actions on one's current spiritual path, highlighting perseverance and commitment as vital for achieving spiritual milestones. It also underscores the importance of venerating our ancestors and mentors, acknowledging their contributions as foundational to our spiritual endeavors. Such a perspective cultivates a profound respect and gratitude for those who have shaped our journey, emphasizing the pivotal role of personal effort and humility in achieving spiritual growth.

The inheritance of challenges from our ancestors is not a burden but a catalyst for spiritual development, shaping us profoundly. Dr. Wu articulates that genuine spiritual progress requires more than rote practice; it demands a dedicated and continuous journey of self-betterment. Embracing this journey with sincerity often proves more straightforward than neglecting our shared responsibility to spiritually steward our planet. The focus lies not in deciphering the origins of our trials but in the strength to overcome them. Our rich cultural and spiritual legacy, bestowed upon us by countless forebears, provides the insight and resources necessary for this voyage. Placed deliberately in our specific era and location, we are called to discover and live out our unique purpose, encapsulating the core of our being.

Getting to be our best selves isn't about taking shortcuts. Rather, it is all about the hard work we put into growing spiritually throughout our lives. We wake up every day in the same place for a reason, telling us we are here for something bigger. Our bodies are gifts and tools for us to go beyond just living. Like ants tirelessly building, we are meant to push forward, facing life's challenges head-on. Dr. Wu points out that fate will not do all the work for us: we have got to put in the effort and shape it with our actions. Life is like magic, and we are the magicians, tasked with making the most of what we have got. So, if you are aiming for the stars, be prepared to work hard—there are no shortcuts.

Even though it might feel like everything from your looks to your life's path is set in stone, it is possible to change your fate with enough determination. Daoism says nothing is forced on us; we follow what truly calls to us. If we are curious enough to seek it, ancient wisdom has the tools to help us reach our goals, making life's journey our own despite the starting points we are given. Everyone's journey is unique, designed by the universe just for them, with guidance for those who are dedicated to their spiritual path. The endless possibilities in life show how amazing our existence is, pushing us to embrace the wide-open lives we are given. People all over the world overcome challenges meant for them, proving that beating the odds is a part of our shared human story.

Cradle to Grave

The moment we enter this world, the universe has already charted out fundamental aspects of our existence such as our potential partners, the wealth we may accumulate, and our life expectancy. Dr. Wu illuminates the inherent nature of adversity in human life, symbolically echoed in the instinctive cry of a newborn—a primal acknowledgment of the trials ahead. He notes that certain individuals are marked with distinctive signs on their bodies, found on the cheeks, below the waist, or at the navel, signifying a life path fraught with great challenges. These markers, discernible to those deeply attuned to the spiritual realm, serve as indicators of the preordained hardships some are destined to navigate.

Dr. Wu advocates a more profound spiritual engagement as a means to perceive and understand these significant markers and the struggles they foretell. He cautions against premature judgments of others, emphasizing our limited understanding of their previous deeds or the spiritual lessons they are destined to learn. Each person grapples with their unique set of challenges, contributing to the evolution of their soul across its expansive journey. This insight encourages a compassionate and empathetic stance toward one another, acknowledging that our current life is merely one chapter in the soul's extensive saga, urging us to foster kindness and comprehension as we all traverse this shared journey.

Exploring the principles of human body fengshui offers profound insights into our existential essence and spiritual trajectory, illuminating the intricate web of connections we share with the diverse tapestry of life. Dr. Wu delineates thirty-six distinct categories of earthly inhabitants, each branching into numerous sub-categories, thus highlighting the profound interconnectedness between humans and the broader kingdoms of flora and fauna, rooted in the narratives of our past life experiences.

This interconnection is poignantly illustrated through the notion that individuals incarnated as females in the present were canine entities seven lifetimes ago, with contemporary canines possibly echoing the maternal bonds from those bygone eras. Such perspectives underscore the absence of inherent human superiority, positioning humanity as participants in a broader ecological and spiritual ensemble, where roles are distributed without prejudice. The Daoist worldview of reincarnation posits that the bonds between humans and their animal companions span multiple lifetimes, necessitating extensive spiritual cultivation to facilitate the rekindling of these soulful connections in their corporeal manifestations.

Our planet is a repository of life in its myriad forms, from the tangible presence of humans, animals, and plants to the ethereal allure of spectral beings, mythical merfolk, and celestial entities. This diversity bestows upon our world a richness and complexity that captivates the imagination. Among these, legendary creatures such as unicorns and dragons hold a special place in the collective psyche, bridging the realms of reality and fantasy through their perennial presence in art and folklore across cultures.

Dragons, for instance, transcend geographical and cultural boundaries, featuring prominently in narratives from both Eastern and Western traditions. This universal fascination with dragons, alongside other mythical beings such as aliens, Bigfoot, and the Loch Ness monster, underscores the shared human propensity for wonder and the mystical. These narratives, irrespective of their factual basis, knit together the fabric of human culture, inviting us to partake in a shared exploration of the mysteries and marvels that pervade our world.

Animal Equality

Our world is a rich mosaic of life, with humans just one part of a vast community that includes animals and plants. In Daoism, every creature is seen as equally important, challenging the idea that humans are somehow superior. This belief is rooted in the understanding that we all play a crucial role in the balance of nature. For example, without plants and the food and oxygen they provide, humans could not survive, showing how interconnected we all are. The idea that humans have exclusive rights to the earth is questioned when we consider our shared space with other forms of life, including those in other dimensions.

Dreams show us that even our control over our experiences has limits. This realization should encourage us to live more harmoniously with animals and nature, learning from them and recognizing our shared journey. Our reluctance to protect natural habitats and work alongside other species highlights a broad human arrogance. Ancient Daoists, who integrated closely with nature through rigorous practices, show us a different way to live—one that is in tune with the natural world. Today, we often overlook the spiritual insights and environmental wisdom that animals and nature offer, missing out on the positive impacts we could have by caring for our planet.

Protecting nature not only aligns us with the cosmos but also helps balance the karma associated with our actions, such as cutting down trees. Modern science is beginning to uncover the rich emotional life and communication methods of trees, suggesting a deep, unexplored intelligence in nature. Recognizing this, we are reminded of the endless possibilities for learning and growth that come from respecting and understanding the natural world around us. Of course, modern science also points to the fact that even trees have complex feelings and communication modalities we just have yet to understand.

> Trees, of course, do not have eyes, ears, a mouth, or any other means to communicate. But trees can actually see, hear, taste and communicate. The sight of a plant may exist because they grow toward areas with light, meaning that they can sense the light with their leaves. Plants can also hear to the degree that they can even respond to human voices.
>
> Trees use their roots to absorb nutrients and to taste. They also have a wide arsenal of ways to communicate with one another, including sending chemical, hormonal, and slow-pulsing electrical signals and communicating through the air using scent. Trees even have senses that we lack, such as being able to sense gravitational changes, the presence of water, or even a block in their roots. (Bui 2021)

Throughout history, plants and animals have been eager to share their wisdom with humans, but it is rare to find those who are open and patient enough to learn from them. Asncient Daoists recognized this potential for knowledge exchange between species but realized society was not ready to embrace it, keeping many insights secret. The concept of universal equality among all beings highlights the essential role each plays in existence. According to the principles of yin and yang, every creature contributes to the ecosystem's balance, emphasizing the interconnectedness of life. Pollution harms all living beings, and despite their resilience, animals suffer from human-induced diseases.

Our evolution has been significantly shaped by animals like dogs and horses, which have played critical roles in human culture. Unlike modern technologies, animals provide an emotional connection that enriches our lives. Daoism encourages finding harmonious ways to include animals and nature in our lives, such as the creation of stringed instruments that blend the core materials metal and wood, symbolizing a balanced relationship with the natural world. This approach underscores the importance of coexisting peacefully with all forms of life in our technological age.

Chapter 3

Working with the Natural Order

Daoist thought centers on the understanding of how we interact with others and how we can create harmony in our communities. This idea goes back to ancient Chinese teachings, especially those of Confucius, who took Laozi's wisdom further by organizing society's rules. His ideas might seem old-fashioned today, but they were revolutionary in shaping a balanced society back then. Daoism teaches us to flow with life's ups and downs, offering ways to find peace at home and in the wider world. Dr. Wu uses these teachings to show us how to avoid getting too caught up in emotional storms, aiming for a calm approach to life's challenges.

Family issues are not new, but they are more visible now with so many marriages ending in divorce. Dr. Wu thinks our view of marriage is changing, becoming less of a must-do tradition. Daoists have seen cultures rise and fall, always finding ways to bring balance. They teach us to find harmony in ourselves and our relationships, helping communities find peace even when disagreements arise.

Human societies have always varied, from nomads to complex states. Today, we see more family conflicts, something many people have experienced firsthand. There is a clear need for stronger family bonds, which are crucial for a stable society. Dr. Wu shares stories from tribes with unique family structures, like children having nine fathers, to show there are many ways to build a supportive community. He also talks about family connections on a deeper level, suggesting that relationships are part of a larger spiritual journey that goes beyond this life. This might be hard to grasp, but it is a core aspect of Daoist belief, offering a new way to see our closest bonds as part of a bigger picture. China's history, filled with detailed records, backs up these ideas, showing us that life is interconnected.

Dr. Wu warns about the rise of robots and AI, which lack human emotions, challenging our understanding of love and connection. Love is central to who we are, driving us to great achievements. In an age where technology is everywhere, remembering and applying Daoist principles to our relationships can help us maintain our humanity and secure a world where genuine connections thrive.

Life throws many challenges our way, some as simple as crossing a busy street, which reminds us how unpredictable life can be. Daoists teach us about courage noting that unexpected moments are when we truly see how brave we can be. Courage is not just about doing what we have to survive but also about facing things that scare us or push us out of our comfort zone.

Imagine a person rushing into a burning building to save someone they love. That is a clear act of bravery because they are risking their life for someone else. But Daoists teach that true courage is more than just acting quickly. It is about knowing the risks and choosing to face them because one believes it is the right thing to do. True bravery means considering the risks and still deciding to face one's fears. It is not just a quick reaction to danger. Real courage means to stop, think about the dangers, and still go ahead because one cares about something bigger and greater.

Facing fear and then doing something about it is admirable. It is like knowing one has a big challenge ahead and deciding to deal with it head-on. This kind of courage includes facing big fears, even of death. One won't really know how brave one is until there such as test. That is why spiritual journeys or tough situations that test bravery are important. They help people see what they are made of.

Some might avoid danger, but others will face it and grow stronger. Daoists say that this is what courage is all about—finding out who we really are when faced with life's biggest challenges.

The Five Phases and Nine Stars

Exploring Eastern astrology involves delving into the intricate relationship between the nine stars and the five phases, a fundamental aspect of this ancient practice. This area of study is complex and multifaceted, representing a lifelong journey for astrologers. Even for those familiar with Western astrology, the concepts of the nine stars and the five phases might be new territory. However, gaining a basic understanding of these facets is crucial for anyone looking to explore the deeper implications of these theories, especially in the context of human body fengshui. This foundational knowledge opens up new perspectives on how cosmic forces influence our well-being and interact with the natural world. We can see some of the basic principles laid out in the text below:

> Daoist Nine Star Astrology is the essence of the all the Daoist practices and is based on the Pole Star (Yang), the Big Dipper (7 Points), and the Vega Star (Yin). All movement and energy patterns on earth are based from energy fields of these 9 points. Every 26,000 years completes one cycle of Light (Yang) to Darkness (Yin), and presently shifting the Pole Star (Yang) (Center of Galaxy) to the Vega Star (Yin), which there about 2,000 years after in this cycle before the shift. (The Professor, mantakchia.com)

Astrology and astronomy have determined that there are nine stars in the northern sky, closely centered around the northern end of the earth's polar axis: Polaris and Vega plus the seven stars that make up Ursa Major, the Big Dipper. They are responsible for the slight electromagnetic shift that occurs. Each star is integrally part of, and responsible for, each of the distinguishable electromagnetic phases.

(1) Vega (Yin) *							**(9) North (Pole) Star ***
	*(2)						
		*(3)					
					*(4)		
						*(5)	*(8)
						*(6)	*(7)

> When our planet is under the influence of one of the particular electromagnetic phases, one of the transformations phases or transformations mentioned earlier becomes accentuated, thus there are five fire years, earth years, water years, wood years and metal years with all elemental transformation phases represented within a nine-year cycle and each year is positive or negative (yin or yang). (The Professor, mantakchia.com)

In the nuanced realm of Daoist cosmic theory, the interplay between the nine stars and nature—and subsequently nature's influence on earth—presents a fascinating aspect not widely discussed. These celestial bodies, each with its unique energy, significantly impact the natural world and, by extension, human life.

For example, Daoist beliefs extend to the idea that each day of the week is under the governance of a distinct cosmic character, influencing various aspects of life and well-being. Consider Monday, associated with the numeral one, symbolizing new beginnings and the vibrant energy of spring. This day is linked with the liver, reflecting the Daoist understanding of how cosmic rhythms affect bodily functions. Accordingly, they recommend specific foods on different days to harmonize with these celestial influences, nurturing the body in alignment with the cosmic flow. This approach venerates the body as a sacred, spiritually attuned entity called "spirit" (*shen* 神), resonating with the broader universe's intricate patterns. This word also has a deeper meaning:

> *Shen* is the Chinese word for "god," "deity," "spirit" or *theos*. This single Chinese term expresses a range of similar, yet differing, meanings. The first meaning may refer to spirits or gods that are intimately involved in the affairs of the world. Spirits generate entities like rivers, mountains, thunder and stars.
>
> A second meaning of *shen* refers to the human spirit or psyche; it is the basic power or agency within humans that accounts for life, and in order to further life to its fullest potential the spirit must be grown and cultivated. A

> third understanding of *shen* describes an entity as spiritual in the sense of inspiring awe or wonder because it combines categories usually kept separate, or it cannot be comprehended through normal concepts....
>
> A starting point for an understanding of *shen* is the meeting place of heaven and earth, which is humankind. Heaven is the origin of the spiritual aspect of humanity and provides ongoing spiritual influences, while earth is the origin of the physical aspect of humankind. The ongoing harmonious interaction of heaven and earth in man is essential to maintaining life. In Chinese religious tradition, balancing yin and yang is important to provide organization of life and prevent harm to body and spirit. (Papazian 2019)

Heaven here represents a significant beginning, not merely a stroke of luck. It suggests the start of new endeavors and highlights the importance of embracing new phases in life with openness to growth. The universal adoption of a Monday to Friday workweek reflects a shared rhythm in human activity, suggesting a connection to a larger cosmic order. This consensus across cultures points to a deep-seated alignment with the cycles of nature and time, reminding us of our link to the universe's vast pattern.

Historical attempts to shift the workweek to nine days were met with resistance, underscoring the natural fit of the seven-day cycle for human societies worldwide. This shared rhythm, cutting across cultural lines, suggests a spiritual or natural order that humanity collectively tunes into. The nearly universal agreement on the seven-day structure hints at a deeper, possibly divine guidance in our perception of time. This shared understanding among humans worldwide hints at a profound connection to the natural and cosmic rhythms, inviting reflection on our place within the universal order.

The Twenty-Four Divisions

The ancient Chinese calendar with its twenty-four solar divisions offers a fascinating parallel to the cycles of human development, suggesting that the first twenty-four years of a person's life are marked by significant growth and transformation. This period of growth, deeply ingrained in the rhythms of nature and time, mirrors the agricultural seasons and transitions observed in the traditional Chinese calendar, each division reflecting a specific phase in the natural world and, symbolically, in human life. The passage below outlines that there are a few documented cases when growth happened at age twenty-four.

> Most of them attain their full height when they are 16 years old. Boys grow most between 12 and 16 years. During this time, they grow more than any other period in their life. Between 12 and 16, boys add at least 12 inches to their height and add 15 to 65 pounds to their weight. They tend to gain weight along with having hair growth on face, arm pits and chest. It is their puberty time

> where their voice also deepens as the vocal cords change. Many start having oilier skin which causes acne.
>
> As soon as they turn 18, the muscles and shoulders become broad and manly. It is before the age of 18 that most of their growth takes place although men continue to grow till they turn 21 years. However, in few exceptional cases they can grow till 25 years as well. It is at this point that they have reached their tallest height. Even their height stops growing, their muscles continue to grow. (Coveville.com 2022)

In the Daoist view, the first twenty-four years of a person's life are akin to spring, a time of growth and emergence. This period is part of a larger cycle that mirrors the changing seasons, reflecting the Daoist belief in the interconnectedness of human life with the natural world. Dr. Wu applies this philosophy in his practice, prescribing herbs and dietary adjustments in alignment with these "micro-seasons" to enhance well-being. This approach is reminiscent of the cyclical guidance provided by the Farmer's Almanac for agriculture, emphasizing the importance of timing in harvesting and planting.

Monks, who often live beyond a century, describe their long lives as journeying into life's "winter." This concept extends to the daily cycle, which is segmented into four parts representing life's seasons: from 3 to 9 am symbolizes spring, a time of awakening and renewal; 9 am to 3 pm denotes summer, a period of growth and activity; 3 to 9 pm signifies autumn, a phase of harvesting and reflection; and 9 pm to 3 am represents winter, a time for rest and rejuvenation. These time divisions serve as a guide for living in harmony with nature's rhythms, teaching that every aspect of existence—from the hours of the day to the years of a life—follows a purposeful cycle of birth, growth, decline, and rebirth. This perspective encourages a deeper appreciation for the natural cycles that influence our lives, offering a pathway to understanding and aligning with the Daoist concept of universal harmony.

These cycles have been studied for thousands of years. If you examine particular animals, you can clearly see this. The most obvious example is daytime and nighttime: daytime represents the world of life and the living, while nighttime is symbolic of the time of death. Some have even made references to sleep being the cousin of death. People sleep at night as well, further representing the rest time or wintertime of life. This is the time when people dream. These dreams then produce a new form of life for that person during the next day. Winter can also represent the long cosmic slumber in which the soul undertakes its journey back into incarnation.

This also corresponds to ancient knowledge passed down in the school of Complete Perfection, where the seasons are linked with the trigrams of the *Yijing*. The trigram Kan (water) is associated with cold and winter in nature and with the kidneys in the human body. "Among the eight seasonal transitions it corresponds to the beginning of winter. At the winter solstice inside the body, it becomes essence (*jing*)" (Eskildsen 2004, 63). Similarly, the trigram Li (fire) is connected to heat and summer in nature and to the heart in the body. "Among the eight seasonal transitions it [corresponds to] the beginning of summer. At the summer solstice inside the body, it becomes blood" (2004, 63). The ancient text continues:

> Essence is Nature (consciousness), and blood is Life (vitality). For a person to understand and master his or her Nature and Life, this is the true method of training oneself. A lesson says that essence and blood are the basics of the body of flesh. Real *qi* is the basis of Nature and Life. Therefore, it is said that those who have blood (i.e., all living beings) are able to produce Real *qi*. Those who have youthful and abundant Real *qi* can naturally for a long time bring together their essence and blood and constitute a shape. (2004, 63)

Stephen Eskildsen explains:

> The human body is described as a mass of *qi* that circulates and transforms into many different forms (such as saliva, essence, and blood) by the cyclical functioning of the liver, lungs, heart, and kidneys that corresponds to the four seasons of nature. Blood and essence (*jing*), generated out of the *qi* of the heart and kidneys, respectively, in turn generate the two categories of souls (*hun* and *po*) that give sentient life to the body by bestowing it with vitality (*ming*; Life) and consciousness (*xing*; Nature). The Real *qi* (*zhenqi*)—"Real" meaning primordial, uncorrupted, and everlasting—is the vital principle that creates and supports all life; it is the Real Nature viewed in its aspect as vital force. Terms such as *hun* and *po* or Nature and Life describe dual, differentiated aspects of it. Real *qi* is constantly generated and replenished if its dual aspects are nurtured and kept in harmony. (2004, 63)

Chapter 4

Classical Cosmology

People are born in the mortal realm to a set of parents yet regulated by the mechanisms of cosmic rules. They are sent not of their own volition but, for all their life, constantly influenced by the various star constellations and planets, each one serving a unique function and application. The Big Dipper for example has many duties, primarily regulating the flow of life and death on earth.

The Big Dipper is symbolized by the Chinese *wan* sign, better known in the West as the swastika, which for millennia has featured in indigenous art and religion. It did not become ubiquitous until the 20th century, when the Nazis sent emissaries to Tibet and appropriated what they could from esoteric Buddhism. They adopted the symbol for their own means, emblematically garnishing flags and uniforms from 1935 until the end of World War II. This is one example of the Big Dipper's role in regulating life and death.

Like the Big Dipper, many heavenly symbols are used in advertising today and clearly show influence on human beings. The Nike shoe company uses the ring of Saturn, commonly referred to as the Nike "swoosh." Saturn stands for meaning and structure, responsibility and discipline, all built into the ethos of this shoe company. If an army stood up using this ring of Saturn symbolism and harnessed its force to begin creating malice, would humans begin to fear this symbol like they fear the swastika? Daoist mystics understand the values of the constellations that govern us and use them for self-cultivation, appreciating how in nature every situation has two separate vantage points from which to choose wisely the positive way forward.

Historically, astrological symbols have been used among old-world tribes, established nation states, rising political parties, and business corporations—all trying to connect their interest with the stars. One example is the California Republic or Bear Flag Republic symbolically depicts the grizzly as a stand-in for Ursa Major, the Great Bear constellation. These symbols are generally neutral and like a sword can cut both ways depending on who wields it. In this case, the constellation's effect on California is life giving. In fact, California. the golden state, bodes the largest economy in the United States. Whether coincidental or by design, the successful alignment of concepts in the flag's design have shown to bear fruit.

Dr. Wu also notes that the Big Dipper or swastika corresponds to a death point in heaven, which gives it the meaning of duality, thereby present and prominent in all life and death scenarios. Utilizing this unique astrological symbol is a great responsibility. Still, other aspects of the Big Dipper remain. The Southern

Dipper oversees career advancements while the Western Dipper manages prosperity, fortune, and marriage. Although these concepts are prevalent in Chinese astrology, without a keen interest in the subject, they remain virtually unexplored by most. On average, when people think of astrology, they turn to their sun sign horoscope on the back pages of a newspaper, to the neighborhood Chinese restaurant's table mat, or a daily astrology app. Scholars and academics, however, have made concentrated efforts to keep the esoteric sciences current and evolving for reasons of divination and navigation.

Seafaring nations, independent explorers, and pirate republics launching expeditions around the globe have always used astronomy when setting course. Their navigating tools in concert with the mechanisms of the celestial bodies are set according to precision timing, especially in the ancient world when everyone followed the North Star. It is literally clockwork. Astronomy often is the gateway to astrology, which arouses intuitive communication or clairvoyance in some. This is similar to the right and left brains achieving harmony, the logical and the abstract complimenting one another.

As mentioned, humans are the earliest computers, organic machines capable of memorizing entire canons of historical literature. At the emperor's behest, these exceptional figures would divine annually, notably during the Mid-Autumn Festival, at Beijing's Altar of Heaven. At this esoteric intelligence gathering, a Daoist priest would predict the year's events, providing insights into the bounty or scarcity of crops, political affairs, international relations, weather patterns, natural disasters, epidemics, and so on. This generally provided sufficient enough time for the imperial office to prepare and distribute the proper resources or strategic maneuverings. Theoretically, if you could predict a rise in cold viruses for example then you could prepare the proper medicines in advance. Historical data, Chinese astrology, and *Yijing* numerical calculations played significant roles in this process.

Although these systems of astrology were multipurpose, their original intention was to keep human beings in harmony with nature. Long ago, across China, regional astrologers and tribal shamans would perform divination, seeking guidance from their ancestors during uncertain times. Their bestowed wisdom would inform the current generation on a way forward. The information was recorded and stored and became words to live by.

Eastern and Western astrology share similar aims but are characteristically different. Students raised in these schools of thought eventually form their own ideas and approaches to practice. The interpretation of knowledge is often based on the depth of its understanding. Some will add to the knowledge while maintaining the foundation; others begin a heuristic process but always at the risk of dilution. Cases in point: the multiple denominations of secular religions, medical philosophies East and West, and modern psychology where Sigmund Freud and his contemporary Karl Jung came to have their separate ideas and theories. These are outgrowths of the original seed but strong roots are the strength of any good tree.

Despite these inevitabilities, "know thyself" should still be at the heart of any astrology or discipline. The astrologer's most important duty is to guide others toward this end, for the purpose of finding destiny, true meaning, and purpose. According to Daoism, this information is accessible in the star seed. Making sense of the star charts in this context is imperative. Common astrology often misses the opportunity for revealing the significance of choices, which theoretically change a star's direction and trajectory. Poor choices lead the star away from the person, while better choices bring it closer. Good astrology presents an overview of where particular choices and actions lead us. Making decisions in life is challenging, which only the aspirant, not the guide, can make.

Everyone is born having the same level of difficulty. There is no easy road. If you are born wealthy, you may have more chances to evolve on the material plane, but psychologically, we all struggle from the beginning, crying, wanting, and needing. Some may be more intellectually advanced, but intellect does not guarantee or solve everything. Spiritual growth is not guaranteed to anyone. People must willingly choose the Siddhartha-road if it is to bring them peace. Astrologers strive to provide an objective perspective, i.e., help others reflect upon the path taken and bring to their attention reasons and why they should reexamine areas of their life so far unfulfilled. Practice without effort and effort without heart are both recipes for disappointment.

Chinese astrologers have a way of viewing the cosmos through concepts of spiritual psychology and fortune-telling. Their tools are steeped in a rich oral tradition as conveyed through the twelve zodiac animals (rat, ox, tiger, rabbit, dragon, snake, horse, sheep, monkey, rooster, dog and boar). Each creature encapsulates grand themes purposed for human life. For eons, Daoists have held the understanding that nature is the ultimate teacher, integral to human growth and advancing civilization, and thus integrated the animal kingdom into the pantheon for understanding our universe.

What would humankind do without the animals that not only preceded them but now support them? Oxen help plow fields; dogs stand by our sides as companions and guardians; chickens provide fresh eggs. No matter how far the boundaries of technology are pushed, animals remain essential, which is why the Chinese put an emphasis on their characteristics when pertaining to the human psyche and talents. Chinese cosmology serves as a reinforcement and subtle reminder of our evolutionary roots and whether or not we can exist without them. "No man is an island."

Animal Power

In the modern age, humans are among the laziest beings while animals that register lower intelligence are more adept at survival. If this is true, who is superior, humans or animals? Mother peahens carry their chicks one by one on their backs onto tree branches to be safe from night predators. Parent birds know how to break worms into small mouthfuls for their nestlings. Cows and sheep kneel to feed their calves. These displays of maternal love are easily on par with human love. With this observation, Dr. Wu challenges the notion that human love is superior to that of animals, especially when so many sacrifice themselves for the human race, often without objection.

Dolphins rank high in intelligence and in many areas surpass that of humans as, for example, in sonar communication. This is perhaps an unreasonable comparison since dolphins carry out different functions in the water, but worth noting none-the-less. Other examples are a dog's sense of smell, which is up to 100,000 times more acute than that of humans, while horses display greater physical power. The tiger's roar produces special responses in the mountains and jungles. Clinically, if a patient suffers from lung disease, the physician may ask him to roar like a tiger, because Chinese cosmology associates the white tiger with the lungs. The roaring vibration has also been known to reduce tracheal disorders. This is because roaring is akin to music, which lifts the human spirit, thus opening the chest and freeing the voice.

The Chinese see pigs as extraordinary creatures, believing that their essence lies in the eyes and head. In fengshui, wind symbolizes change and water stands for good fortune. Where does fortune reside in the pig? Its fortune resides in its head. Pigs are considered highly intelligent animals with a penchant for learning. In regards to humans, the boar's organs are the most compatible. Pigskin can be grafted onto human burn victims without rejection. Throughout the animal kingdom, only pigs' hearts are compatible with those of humans, utilized in heart valve replacement and more recently in heart transplants.

Many severe diseases begin with inflammation and infection but appear far less often in certain species. When given proper conditions pigs are not filthy animals as purported. This reputation partly comes from their appearance after rolling around in mud to cool themselves. However, when restricted to confined spaces, indoors or outdoors, this reputation is undisputed. Despite such conditions, pigs are particularly powerful and with stout immune systems.

Dr. Wu has researched animals since his upbringing in the White Cloud Monastery to include medical works and contemporary research studies. Published studies have shown sharks to be the most resistant to cancer. Cancer cells, after being injected, simply do not survive in the shark's biology. The second least affected by cancer are pigs and wild boars. Most are familiar with the rampant cases of cancer in dogs and cats. Cancer in humans is also on the rise. Many people practice disease prevention based on current science, yet in spite of this, disease mysteriously arrives uninvited.

Over many centuries Daoist monks have created animal-based exercise practices to promote health and longevity. They have sought to study animal characteristics and behaviors learning their secret healing skills of survival. Three Daoist martial arts practices in particular revere animal movements and breathing techniques: taijiquan, bagua palm, and xingyi boxing. The latter involves a twelve-part form and a set of martial moves that emulate the twelve animal zodiac signs.

By practicing these animal forms, Daoists have recorded well above-average lifes expectancy and remarkable resistance to diseases.

A horse trainer from a well-known racetrack was referred to Dr. Wu. Apparently, race horses were coming up lame, suffering fractures in training and during races. This is not uncommon except the frequency of injury was higher than normal. When horses are injured severely, they are generally put down as a mercy. To help prevent these injuries, Dr. Wu recommended acupuncture. Daoists at the White Cloud Monastery have been caring for horses since the Song dynasty when the patriarch Qiu Chuji returned from Snowy Mountain with Mongolian steeds he received from Genghis Khan (1158-1227). Acupuncture medicine was administered there to most any animal suffering from physical injury or disease.

Horses are similar to eagles in that they can renew themselves. Daoists say, "If a horse fractures a leg, do not put it down." Instead, place the horse together with another species of animal and innately the horse will reconnect its bones. It only has to be close to another animal to stimulate its inner knowledge of how to heal itself. As Dr. Wu has witnessed many times, the horse begins working, snapping the leg to reset the break. Conversely, horses provide healing for other creatures, including humans. Equine therapy is common place now, assisting war veterans and offering miraculous healing for people from all walks of life.

The monastery also devised ways to make horses stronger. Intentionally breaking the horse's leg where it is most vulnerable typically is done at birth while the bones are still soft and malleable. The leg heals back stronger and will be at much lower risk of injury for the horse's life. Chinese herbal medicines and herbal salves are prescribed to speed recovery. Some may call this cruel but if a mature horse breaks its leg, it could be put down before its time. Dr. Wu is not advocating the procedure but merely explaining what things were done to prolong life and health. Similar procedures are performed today for children born with physical abnormalities.

Birds and Felines

Eagles are another example. Monastics would cage an eagle with a chicken or a snake to promote health and longevity synergistically. Eagles can live as long as seventy years but in midlife, they begin to decline; their survival, most notably their flying ability, declines as their muscles atrophy and their wings deteriorate. The eagle then has two options: abandon flying and most likely perish or undergo and agonizing rebirth process. For the latter, it begins by using a hard stone and knocking off talons and beak. This is a very bloody affair, and they take some time to grow back fully. From here, with new talons and beak, it pulls out the feathers and waits for them to regrow in order to return to flying.

The eagle and other animals must be willing to pay the price of longevity. Humans are supposed to live to 120 years, and many disciplined Daoist practitioners reach 200 years of age, with the exception of the legendary Pengzu, who supposedly lived to 800. The *Yijing* notes that humans, under the right circumstances, can live for a thousand years. We are already surrounded by things that live this long. Ancient forests have trees that are 1000 to 4000 years old and still standing. In China, records of turtles with dated markings on their shell have surfaced after a thousand years, when discovered hibernating. There are records of massive immortal deer with old dynastic coins embedded in the antlers that were placed there in an earlier age. Daoists possess many special secrets of the body, such as the thirteen ghost points of Sun Simiao (581-682): when kept open and flowing, they prevent infections and inflammation, eliminating disease and increasing life expectancy.

Another important bird is the rooster, one of the twelve zodiac animals. Not to be confused with chickens in general, he is yang-masculine while hens are yin-feminine. In reproduction, the ratio of rooster to chickens is 3:1, one rooster for every three hens. It is called the "king of birds" as decreed by heaven. All birds, airborne or grounded, belong to the rooster category. Most presume this title belongs to eagle, especially since roosters do not fly particularly well. However, roosters were chosen for two important reasons: in a singing completion, with all the birds participating, the rooster sang most beautifully, winning first place. Second, roosters draw heaven and earth together, connecting night and day thus are a symbol of time.

The first sound on any day is made by a rooster, crowing loudly just before the break of dawn. This warning shot tells bad spirits to run and hide or be burned by the great yang sunlight. This takes great courageous and fearlessness in the face of danger. Subtle nuances such as these determine how animals are chosen to represent the will of heaven.

According to Daoist mysticism, cats were borrowed from the world of the dead and never returned. The invitation was sent to heaven by Judge Bao (999-1062) who was asked to solve a high-profile crime. At the time, a prominent family was losing valuables from inside the home. No signs of burglary or forced entry were discovered and everyone in and around the complex had been exonerated. Judge Bao was asked to investigate the mystery. To solve the case, he called upon his natural-born investigator, the cat. It was soon discovered that the thief was a rat obsessed with hiding shiny things. When the cat had completed the assignment, its usefulness became indispensable and to its dismay, it was forced to remain. As the saying goes, "The cat mutters to itself." This is an expression of its disdain for being stuck with foolhardy humans.

The other idea about cats is that they are heavenly creatures, which is why they climb and perch in high places. Daoists call them heaven's police force, bringing justice to earth. Impatient and steeped with boredom, the cat decided to begin teaching its mastery of taijiquan and yoga. It taught up to eighty percent of its martial skills to the tiger who is now known as the martial king. One day when filled with confidence, ambition and power, the tiger decided he was finally a match for his teacher and went in for the kill. Seeing rage in his student's eyes, the cat quickly climbed the nearest tree, well out of reach of the tiger's claws and said, "I did not teach you everything."

People soon came to revere the cat as an animal that brings wisdom, good fortune and money because when stalking, it makes absolutely sure to first track the rat back to its hiding place before extermination. "To the victor go the spoils." More importantly, the cat's permanent call to duty is because it controls and manages infectious disease. Besides thievery, the rat is known as the "king of disease," spreading contagions. This is why the small rodent can produce exaggerated responses of fear. However, the rat was also chosen as a representative of heaven, and for good reason.

If humanity were to cease to exist today, the rat would live on. Modern science and the public are well aware the infectious diseases rats carry but that is their deterrent. No one ever thinks of eating rats though they are abundant in nature and have a fast reproduction rate. Rats have survived droughts, floods, and ice ages since the beginning of time, which means they know how to survive and succeed in life where others cannot. They are masters of preparedness.

Their farsighted nature informs them of coming disasters, allowing them time to prepare contingencies such as food storage in naturally occurring refrigeration such as old hollowed-out logs. Many people look down on them but Daoists hold the rat in high regard and have learned the value of saving for a rainy day just like a packrat. They also studied the nature of infectious disease from the rat, making them more experienced physicians. Besides utilizing acupuncture and the thirteen ghost points to stay healthy, consider keeping a cat as a natural talisman especially in the year of the rat. It will minimize exposure to contagious diseased.

Another disease that is plaguing the world is diabetes. How is it treated at the White Cloud Monastery? Daoist monks attribute diabetes to eating habits as encapsulated in this statement, "If you eat too much and too well, it's impossible to digest it all." Treating this condition begins with increasing vegetable intake and decreasing meats and other rich foods. If a person eats three meals a day, that is taken down to two meals or even one. As a result, health improves. Diabetes is your body telling you that you have too much nutrition. It is a disease of the affluent. When you go from three meals a day to two or one, a small hunger is ever present and this is beneficial, a method applied also to working oxen in the fields. Diabetics are to avoid sudden drops in blood sugar so tapering down must be done gradually. Stimulating the acupoint Yinbai (SP-1) when massaging the feet in a mixture of soybeans and black beans is a simple Daoist treatment. Eating black beans is another known way to regulate glucose.

A tiger's strength is in its claws, which correspond to our wrists. We see our lower body and legs as vital and strong, but training our extremities lies in the hands and wrists. Doing one hundred push-ups can remedy many sicknesses because each pushup stimulates the Daling (PC-7), called the tiger's point on the inner wrists. Many Chinese soak their feet and get foot massages. However, Daoists soak their hands instead because the hands are closer to the heart. Soaking your hands in warm or hot water until you have a slight sweat around your forehead prevents catching colds. For this reason, wolves rarely catch cold: their wrist movements are stimulated by their endurance walking.

Acupoints

The five phases match the four seasons, which contain the 365 days of the year, corresponding to the 365 acupoints on the body. These are further reflected by the 365 points in heaven. This profundity is why acupuncture stands alone in the medical sciences. Everything in the body has a correspondence to something in the universe. For instance, February 1st has a specific corresponding acupoint that should be stimulated on the day. This is one of Dr. Wu's specialties, which in essence merges astrology with acupuncture to bring positive results. This concept is not covered in traditional Chinese medicine but is an extension of the Daoist model.

The ancients painstakingly studied the cosmic link between the human body and heaven. They observed nature in a way rarely conceptualized in the modern world. With these concepts in mind, bodily sensations or sensory experiences of daily life may well be a form of health messaging in alignment with this idea. The energy within the body follows the travel patterns of the meridians and complete fifty cycles per day, while externally, nature follows its own patterns. The goal of Daoist cultivation is to go along with nature and harmonize the microcosm with the macrocosm. To synchronize the 365 acupoints with those in heaven brings fortune, prosperity, and longevity.

Herbs are integral to this, since there are also 365 herbs to go along with the acupoints. Certain herbs are seasonal and prescribed during particular phases of the year. This is done to gain maximum health benefits based on synchronistic timing. Rotating herbs are added and subtracted to formulas in order to support the intended functions of the prescriptions.

The acupoint Zhongfu (LU-1) rules the lungs and is an example of how to stimulate one key point. It harmonizes the other ten acupoints of the lung meridian simultaneously. According to Dr. Wu, first stimulate the acupoint corresponding to the specific day of treatment to harmonize the patient with the specific timing of the universe, then prescribe the herb that corresponds to Zhongfu to further multiply force and effectiveness to treatment.

Many in the field of Chinese medicine never discover these esoteric techniques. In our current times, without concrete evidence using modern scientific scrutiny, traditional Chinese medicine runs the risk of having "the baby thrown out with the bathwater." It is a matter of trusting your physician regardless of the medical modality. The universe is vast and does not offer tools to measure these methods. Mainstream followers will have to wait for scientific proof. At times in history spiritual concepts did translate into the healing sphere of modern medicine. Hippocrates (460-377 BCE), the father of Western medicine is quoted saying, "A physician without a knowledge of astrology has no right to call himself a physician." There is precedence even in the Western world. Know thy history to know thy future was ever thus.

There are also distinct musical notes for each day of the year that may also be applied to the 365 acupoints. Many microtones and scales align in this system. Experiments involving nature's sounds have been conducted by Daoists for centuries. They aspire to reproduce the perfection of notes and scales taken directly from the natural world. For example, the sounds of each acupoint may be matched to a particular bird. As a healing modality, this warrants further research because in the sphere of sound the potential is certain. Daoists sing their favorite song every morning as a health practice to boost immunity.

Vibrations and sounds can affect mood positively or negatively. They have been shown to alter the formations of water molecules, depending on the harmony or discord of the vibration produced. People naturally gravitate toward sound and music. Sound therapy and sound baths are becoming common place, but have the recipes been perfected? Hopefully these concepts of sound do not fall on deaf ears.

People feel and innate pull when the star in heaven and the soul-seed within naturally gravitate toward each other. To produce this perfect alignment is gracious and beautiful, especially when done purposefully. To do this, one only needs to aspire. The applications of the 365-acupoint theory offer one option to close the distance. Connecting to any of the points in heaven is a milestone. This concept is universally applicable: there are no conflicting opinions in any personal or cultural beliefs.

Astrology is not new, but constitutes the original mapping system bestowed by nature. GPS programs are a wonderful addition to getting around, but the dependency leaves much to be desired. Laozi told Confucius, "Take three steps backward to reexamine your perspective on life." Laozi meant this instruction literally. The map has gone out of view. Acupuncture is a way to spiritually align the internal body with the external cosmos.

Astrology

Astrological systems of the past dealt with a segment of people who understood the need to examine both the external and internal worlds. More than a marker of coincidences, it served a purpose and also as a mechanism for survival. Just in the same way that the line of a master artist is different than that of one drawn by the untrained, so there is a difference in meaning.

A true artist knows he has to plot the steps of his work. Done by feel and with meaningful purpose, it is always supported by a sense of skill found and well cultivated. There is the confidence in engaging to one's highest ability. Chinese medicine follows and supports this endeavor for the benefit of its patients. This principle can also be applied in fengshui.

There are places to go in nature where people can find peace. Many have their secret spot or special place where rest comes easy. This is the aim of fengshui and acupuncture: finding general alignment. The special place is not limited to the world outside. It can also be found internally, in the heart and soul or in other places described in internal alchemy, such as the jade garden.

When searching for an ideal home, find a place where you can relax completely. Do not settle for anything less. The bare minimum should be somewhere that brings you a sense of peace. Humans find solace in or near nature. Many pay a high price to live on beaches or mountain properties because it brings that sense of peace to their lives. However, people should strive for more than the ambience.

The job of the astrologer is to help synchronize others with their life paths. Some astrology helps clients connect to their sense of purpose, but the deeper version of the science is to change fate when germane. Bearing in mind the starseed, it is no wonder the ancients had such an obsession with the meanings of the stars. As knowledge grew it became obvious the stars were a reliable way to track our personal fates.

Native Americans always revere the Great Spirit or the Grandfather when acknowledging the stars. The average American knows of shooting stars or the wonders of the Big Dipper and the Milky Way but little beyond that because in big cities they can barely be seen. This leads people to consciously remove themselves from nature. In order to experience the brilliance of the galaxy, you need to see it up close. Lifelong city people have never seen the brilliance of the stars due to glaring light pollution. Those that do make it to the country are forever changed when the sky give them a living painting to study: nature's museum of wonders.

Numbers and Their Roles

There are twelve months in a calendar year and twelve meridians in the human body, thought of as having an earthly and heavenly correspondence. The system is designed to remedy diseases and imbalances. Discovered and developed esoterically, it is also perfect for accelerating human evolution, enhancing the interrelations that move us beyond normal measures of reality. *Yijing* knowledge encompasses within the same system numerical significances, especially the number seven.

Seven is used to calculate anything involving the earthly plane. It relates to the realm of the present, the here and now. In contrast, number eight relates to heaven and good luck, i.e., interventions made beyond the mortal realm. In the *taiji* image, seven is the black yin dot inside the white yang portion. The number also represents an opening or doorway. Without the number seven, there is no way to calculate *Yijing*.

Seven marks the changing point on a land diagram and is the largest transformational number. The *Yijing*'s way of thinking about numbers is different from Western ways, e.g., the seven-day week. Most things in the *Yijing* revolve around the number nine, which is the number of completion and universality.

Numbers have meaning because nothing is without meaning. When you enter numbers into a calculator, there is a result, logical and fixed. The general consensus is that numbers are perfect and completely reliable as long as the calculation has no mistakes caused by the calculator, be it man or machine. However, Daoists do not look at numbers in only this way. They see numbers as a language communicating heavenly messages.

There is no way to avoid the concept of quantity when communicating. Counting is a way of keeping track. Even primal agrarian or nomadic societies understood the importance of a large herd of buffalo versus a few stragglers. A stampede is very different from a few lone buffalo strolling into camp. In this case, the numbers came to be about survival and calculation. It was a base-level skill.

People who used and studied numbers next began to see patterns. Patterns exist in all forms of nature. Even some key concepts of Western mathematics—the golden mean, the Fibonacci sequence, and the mystery of Pi's infinity—are instilled early in education. These are well-known examples, but even before modern mathematicians, people had studied numbers for thousands of years. What scientists call the birth of modern science actually came from the Pythagorean School of mathematics. The esoteric connotations of numbers have dwindled over time, but in the practice of ancient Egyptian religion, it was essential.

Arcane knowledge results from the ability to observe existing patterns. Numbers are involved in every complex technological convenience enjoyed in the modern world. In the past, people might have considered what we do with numbers today as some form of "black magic." The way cars run on gasoline might be considered an outgrowth of alchemy. These are examples of how science may have been considered evil, but curiosity is the mother of invention. Scientific projects using computers regularly make complex predictive calculations about the future. Although modern scientists claim that they are not interested in the *Yijing* or enigmatic numerology, their actions and technologies say otherwise.

Once upon a time, if a pattern emerged, a mental note or perhaps an investigation would ensue. Ancient civilizations were better integrated with nature. People were more accepting of the signs and omens provided by nature, using them as guidance. Numbers were a natural signal. Making things meaningful took less effort due to the close proximity to nature in comparison to modernized concrete jungles. This difference has made it challenging to find peace, happiness, and harmony.

When you work against the principles of nature, life is difficult. If farmers planted seeds in the dead of winter, would their crops yield in the same way as if had they been planted in the spring? Nature still reigns supreme over humans because without its rhythms we would starve. These are principles that benefit human life. Therefore, having a base knowledge of nature and its patterns helps our day-to-day life. We cannot escape the earth any more than fish can escape the ocean. That being said, we are stuck with what we have. Numbers are just one of the many subtle but powerful ways to interpret our life experience.

Changing Fate

According to Daoism, destiny or fate is fixed but also malleable with the right tools and information. Go above and beyond the call of duty during your life, and things may work out better than expected. Saving another human being from dying can earn you seven extra years of longevity. Save a dog and receive four more years of life, or three for a cat. If you can save a horse then you get five more years of life. Most other species will yield one year. If after saving these lives, you end up saving a second human life then that will bring you three and a half more years. Every time you save a person or animal, and repeat the same deed, the length of time that gets added on to your life is decreased by half.

This is how *Yijing* calculations are added and subtracted. This information is essential as it ultimately puts part of our fate in our hands. We are not helpless but possess the right tools to meet our spiritual commitments. Human beings are inundated with opportunities to succeed. For centuries, Daoist sages have debated about whether humans and other creatures are inherently good or evil. Everyone wants to help the world in the beginning and with enough good fortune keep the drive alive. Subtly, Daoists enjoy influencing this natural desire to succeed by helping people become cooperative in their communities and builders of thriving cultures. Turning lemons into lemonade is sometimes more valuable than being born with a silver spoon in the mouth. The gift of life is the ability to create change within and without, by the sweat of one's brow, the struggle for growth is hard fought.

How is this done pragmatically? How often does anyone come face-to-face with a life-or-death situation? "You may never know until you look. Just by being observant while driving with your head on a swivel, the opportunities to help others arise. Daoists encourage laying the dead to rest, burying any roadkill or the accidental chick fallen from the nest. If choosing not to participate in the burial practice, you may sometimes come across a mother animal that has for whatever reason abandoned her young. You may take the time to find them a home or call proper services. This is another way to rescue. There are many practical ways of applying goodwill, using thought and effort.

Daoists believe that any time a baby is born, a tree should be planted to assist in that child's development. That tree will have a special affinity with the child and serve as the child's record-keeper, storing information as it matures. Raising children and raising trees are analogous. The tree catalogs memories, keeping an eye on the child at all times, like a godparent or a protective talisman. The tree is to the child what the sun is to the stars, moon and clouds in heaven, a supporter. There are smaller forces that help govern humans as they grow to prosper. Ideally, you would plant this tree in your own yard, but if not possible, plant it anywhere it remains accessible so to check on it in the future.

The emphasis on trees is heavy within Daoism. They are key to human growth and potential. Anywhere there are trees, there will be water, which is also beneficial to humans. Without trees and water, it is hard to grow anything well. Look for places with the greatest volume and variety of trees and you will find a prosperous place to plant. If this tree is planted on your property, the close proximity will amplify the connection. There should always be at least one tree for every occupant in the household, otherwise the fengshui will be unstable.

The Secret to Manifestation

The spiritual essence of humans is often described as the soul, what Daoists call the soul-seed. Half of the it resides in heaven and is also known as the numinous pearl (*lingzhu* 靈珠) while the other part rests in the body. Both enters during gestation and split, but then the bodily section splits again, one half residing in the pineal gland or upper elixir field and the other half moving into the abdomen or lower elixir field. It is essential that these two parts, which represent yin, come together at the solar plexus (middle elixir field). This alliance allows dreaming to manifest fully. These body components must be in unison. This process is aided with guided visualizations found in Nine Palaces Qigong.

Before birth, the soul force enters into the ovum and is destined to become half of who you will become. This portion sprouting within eventually helps with decision making and assisting in other critical areas of your life. At first it is just pure force, but then the sperm, another carrier of soul force, and the egg unite at which point the soul takes full shape. This becomes significant for the willpower of the person. This Daoist schematic for the creation of new life could incite heated debate in terms of abortion law, were it to be accepted as viable. At the end of the day, Daoist practitioners have studied this for eons, so it cannot alter its findings just to suit modern culture.

These age-old studies may not sit well with some, but Daoism is of the notion that human life is precious. They do not recommend abortion and see it mainly as an avoidance of a spiritual responsibility charged to you by heaven. The parent is thought to owe that child something from a past life. Therefore, being the parent to that child is a form of karmic payment. This information may be a hard pill to swallow, but nothing in Daoism aims to offend. They are merely the findings of the ancient's observations on how to maintain equilibrium in life.

Daoists do not attach dogmatic penance to abortion. They do however recommend keeping the first pregnancy if at all possible. If after the first born, abortion is chosen on a subsequent pregnancy, this is more acceptable and any repercussions are mostly negated.

The soul force stays in the body until death, before returning to heaven for reunification. The soul force may indeed exit the body prior to death when you are either drunk, asleep, or elated i.e. when in extremely relaxing conditions. In these particular instances, the spirit temporarily leaves the body. When sleeping, it may surface and visit the other half in heaven given the time. Sleeping is essential and information gathered from dreaming can stabilize emotionality, enhance physical rejuvenation, and gain spiritual knowledge.

Through this night process the soul force is trying to align with the star in the sky. Another reason why fengshui is important is if the bedroom's fengshui is out of harmony, this impedes on the soul's likelihood to leave the body. As mentioned, if this alignment gets outside of forty-five degrees, danger is imminent. This type of misalignment can happen for a myriad of reasons, but Dr. Wu believes the most common reason is due to the interferences caused by electric and magnetic fields (EMFs).

Dao Teachings

Despite not reaching all segments of mainstream consciousness, Daoist teachings remain alive and well. This is largely due to the efforts of generations of monks and nuns who continually renew the religious canons and perpetuate the practices. Daoism mystically appears in the world, often in places where it has never been popular. One of my earliest memories is seeing a yin-yang image in second grade art class. Daoism is virtually unknown among the majority of the U.S. population, yet there it was rolling into my life. This is nature being all pervasive, reminding humanity of the root concepts of Daoist philosophy, albeit subtle.

Throughout the years, Daoist concepts have quietly seeped into popular culture in all forms of media and genres. Chinese films and television series still saturate their markets but the philosophies and storytelling, which have often fascinated the rest of the world, continue to inspire. One can surmise it is heaven's will that this information is in circulation, placed before ardent seekers who want nothing more than find their highest calling. The spiritual path, however, is not for everyone.

Daoists put no pressure on people to train as monastics. In fact, it is better for the lay person not to practice than to practice incorrectly or without heart. Internal exercise requires a level of aptitude and dedication to become proficient. One must practice solidly at the basic level: spiritual development takes effort and favorable conditions are not supported everywhere. People generally focus on material things as the means to survival. That is reality for many. Still, everyone can relate and aspire to the principles of nature, which are eternal. When people whole-heartedly realize that the spiritual world and the material world are interlinked, they more easily integrate ideas of self-cultivation into their lives.

It has been written that the blessings of the spiritually cultivated out-weigh those of a benevolent billionaire who gives away his wealth. The question becomes, D you "give a man a fish?" Or do you "teach a man to fish?" When you practice qigong, you help nature to grow and prosper, which includes the myriad beings. Think of it as projecting sunlight, a common denominator in generating life. It is a unique perspective and difficult to prove and not easily exhibited compared to philanthropy. Money may help civilization grow if you build a temple. But most people will not engage in these types of charity at least not without a mark of respect.

When we think of charity, we typically think of feeding the homeless, helping in the building of schools, and so on. After making a donation, however, few people follow the vision to its completion. Then perhaps it is more beneficial to promote energetic transformation. Daoist practices help remove obstacles and stagnations within natural energy grids by way of the ley lines also known as dragon meridians. They are unseen yet meaningful. When engaged in this self-cultivation you notice subtle shifts in light or rhythms or the goodwill of people and animals afterwards. Coincidental? You may have to do your own experiments to be sure.

Self-cultivation is key to accessing the root energy of the universe. Without energy very little of anything gets done on the micro or the macro. Energy, either naturally or artificially produced, has proven to be the greatest commodity on the planet. It fuels the modern world and wars are fought to control it. Human resources are energetically tapped as well and this is where the roads diverge. If desired, self-cultivation can help individuals gather and emit universal energy for themselves. We are solar panels in our own right.

Self-cultivation unveils life's mystery by increasing perception while enhancing personal experience. The value of personal experience is learning tacitly to your marrow, a tangible meter of truth and false, a road to self-reliance. To cultivate the validity of Dao is to do so experientially. Modern science measures what is tangible and observable, which creates limitations. If we use this as our guiding light, how do we explain something as simple as wind? You can feel and hear wind yet you cannot see it. Meteorologists can rarely predict from which direction the wind will blow. Nature is both a mystery and an enigma, best measured organically.

Nature is considered a constant and without a caste of people dedicated to cultivation and personal development, it will be hard for us as a species to evolve past our base instincts. *Qi* stagnation is impeding to the body and to nature. Bad behaviors and ill-advised activities work against health and good fortune. To unlock stagnation, aspire to nobility instead. There is no word for guilt in Buddhism, only cause and effect of moral or immoral judgments, since life is arduous for everyone. Chutes and ladders abound. Unlock the flow of *qi* to cultivate peace of mind.

Deciphering the causes of *qi* stagnation is imperative. It could be related to diet, poor decision-making, environmental factors, undue stresses, etc. These are factors we can change and control to varying degrees. "Heaven helps those who help themselves." When taking responsibility for personal actions heaven notices. When *qi* stagnation improves, circulation is enhanced and opportunities arise. The depth of the hole you have dug beneath you is relative to the rate of progression. If we do not take this upon ourselves, spiritual growth may become lost.

These practices are universally helpful, not only for longevity but also for learning patience, perseverance, and having the energy to meet our objectives. This leads to productivity and enhances the creativity of others. Never underestimate the power of good spiritual energy at play in the world. Great music can make thousands of people in a stadium erupt in elation, and one individual can help purify negativity, releasing stagnation wherever they may be. The silent path of self-cultivation is a viable one. If our energy improves, just as a smile or a yawn is contagious, so too are good vibrations.

Chapter 5

Human Motivation

There are very few motivations driving people. Decisions made are sometimes good and sometimes bad. The phrase, "Seven emotions and six forms of ambition" according to Dr. Wu describes greed. There may be millions of people per year passing through a city as big as Los Angeles, but there are only two: those seeking fame and those seeking money.

Keeping this in mind during daily life, both the good and bad sides of humanity become clearer. This is not to say people are evil for wanting. Everyone has a driving motivation and a need to attain something in life. We all work to survive but we also have the need to be understood. Attaining popularity at its core is a deep desire for our unique individuality to be understood. People deserve respect for what they do, provided they do it to the best of their ability.

When on the move, remember to look for those two things in a person's eyes. The human race is simple, but the vital feature everyone should know about is that we are diverse in attributes and skills. There is inborn talent in everyone. In terms of motivation, there are only two types: fame and fortune. Some wake up with a burning desire to make money; others want to be well-known and influence others. These people, some beginning from youth, hit the ground running, looking to make their mark on the world.

The Meaning Behind Money

In the past, when Daoist monks were running out of money, they would beg for food or alms, however, this is frowned upon in the modern era. Monks have developed other skills, a rice bowl if you will, to keep themselves viable members of society. They may accept food as payment when providing healing work or performing menial jobs, but they engage in gambling. Daoists have an interesting take on gambling, believing the act is stealing money from your grandchildren. They avoid the stock market for similar reasons. The difference between gambling and the stock market is that if your job involves making money through the stock market or supplements your income, be prepared to give away ten percent of those earnings.

Ten percent donated in mass benefits society. Although the market may not consciously support spiritual development, in the future these charitable good works will manifest in goodwill for all humankind. Donating ten percent long term, even if done for self-interest, deters misfortune brought about by the delicate scales of healthy wealth distribution. The *Yijing* has a theory on money.

Money is heaven sent, that is, "pennies come from heaven." It is given in order to help ourselves and our communities. This little seed is a humbling way to remain connected to the human experience.

In fengshui theory, money is akin to water and needs to keep flowing to maintain our health. If money sits somewhere for too long, it can harm its owner. Imagine stagnant pond water, which over time becomes gross and infested. Swamp waters are less than optimal fengshui conditions. Stagnant water produces turbid energy and acts as a portal for malevolence.

As we know, money is essential to living. Most people, in their quest to participate in life, to find love and start a family, or to live experientially, have varied interpretations of the ideal life. It is usually money, career, or success in love that drive us, but this can be a shallow orientation of reality, some left wanting more in the end. Is the concept of spiritual satisfaction and inner peace woven into those realities? Although money can reflect a type of spiritual accomplishment, this still might depend on the context in which you make it.

Fundamentally, there is a failure to examine the meanings and motivations behind making money. Some people might want to avoid working. Some want to enjoy the finer things in life while others seek adventures. Yet others are simply in competition to see who can make and spend the most. Perhaps innovation is at the root in some instances. No matter the reason, money is only as good as how it is spent.

Some believe that "money is the root of all evil" while at the same time, "money is the birthplace of everything high-minded and benevolent." This represents the duality of yin and yang. Even though money is heaven-sent, those wielding it with bad intention or through misappropriation spoil it for the rest of society. When used correctly and benevolently, money can help people and things to grow and flourish.

Water and money are also analogous to emotions; all require a measure of self-control. In fengshui theory, money is linked to water, the word *shui* being part of its name. Real estate properties located near water are generally better investments than those elsewhere. For example, the majority of wealth in the United States is concentrated on the West Coast and the eastern seaboard. To reiterate, water must be moving and alive; if left stagnating, it can have detrimental effects. Emotions are held to the same rule and best suited when they are flowing. To hold in emotions, to stew for extended periods of time, according to traditional Chinese medicine, eventually leads to disease. This takes contemplation to appreciate, but if you think about money as emotion, it begins to make sense.

What happens if people do not exhibit any emotion? Some people rarely laugh or cry, for a myriad of reasons having become jaded, hardened, or indifferent. This is not an ideal condition for interacting with money, since negative emotions have a way of influencing monetary transactions. On the other hand, positive emotions have a way of attracting money, but when things are not going right, emotions may spiral out of control. This can lead to unhealthy spending, but often the antidote to poor emotions is treating yourself to something nice, which can regulate the emotional body.

The compulsiveness of binge spending relates to emotional instability. One only needs to look at mainstream and social media to find plenty of case studies. This is where spiritual development becomes crucial to emotional stability and maturity. The desire for fame and fortune is part of being human, but without self-control to take it in stride with humility and appreciation, health, wellness, and money will deteriorate. Spiritual practices not only aid our cognition of reality, but also regulate the emotional body. Without the proper tools to move emotions in a positive direction, they culminate and stagnate. No one goes through life unscathed. Spiritual practices help us transmute these seemingly negative events into positive ones.

Balance is the name of the game. The process of managing wealth is stressful and, with so much to lose, there is a long way to fall. Having substantially less has its own challenges. It is a matter of inherent patterns and personal preferences. Great fortune or blessings? Security or peace of mind? Responsibility or nothing to lose? What are you willing to subscribe to? This is the inherent balancing of yin and yang. Quantum physics has proven that nothing is inanimate and everything has a mode of consciousness. This means that money has its own form of energy, too.

Water is associated with yin. Too much of yin or yang strikes an imbalance that is disruptive and potentially harmful. Those great sums of money accruing in the world today may affect the emotional body. One could surmise that fear and other dark emotions also generate money. Often negative emotions are at the heart of necrotic advertising, manipulative marketing and end of the world scenarios produced by industries: all are the implementation of concepts that induce spending.

There are many case studies on the effects of accrued wealth. Successful bankers and lawyers tend to appear reserved, stoic, and unyielding. This is the result of not spreading the wealth or donating enough to help bolster the community. They represent just an example; we are not making a blanket statement on specific professions. Although it is true that some people joyfully hoard their money, there may be unintended consequences for this behavior in the long run: everything has its price in life.

Benevolently channeling money into worthy causes can potentially enhance spiritual growth when it comes from the heart. Who says you cannot buy your way into heaven? Capitalist societies are market-based and thus benefit from keeping people on the back foot by using emotion to drive and fuel the system. When spiritually unfulfilled, the idea of spending money on material things brings satisfaction and temporary wholeness but, as mentioned earlier, treating ourselves to a new outfit or a nice haircut can be cathartic. These actions may shift our energies and influence how the world views us. When armed with the proper healing practices, emotional stability eases the burden of life and financial strife.

Greed is prevalent in modern civilizations. It is a race to the top. Not everyone who has climbed the mountain successfully is willing to give back. Perhaps no one is owed but there are people worthy of investment. Do some deserve to be poor due to their lack of effort? Absolutely, but good opportunities can make all the difference. Like any addiction, greed is harmful, a never-ending quest for pinnacle experiences. Many first experiences in life are joyful and make for wonderful memories. The soul finds joy experientially. Being open to what every new day brings as opposed to running after things, requires a childlike imagination that may diminish over time but should be nurtured.

"Money cannot buy happiness," but with spirituality and the reintegration of nature into life, unprompted joy returns even though the reconnecting requires effort. Most spiritual practices such as chanting, taijiquan, or qigong, inject positive energy into our life. They remove trapped emotions and turbid energies as the Chinese proverb has it, "The intelligent man learns something new every day, but the wise man forgets something every day."

"Every child wants to please their parents," is the beginning of humanity's need for recognition and fame. To get attention, children will often cry and pout, perform songs or do anything to get their parent's recognition. For parents, it is wise to realize that kids just want attention and interaction. "Hey mom, look at me," is a common refrain. Adults do not always have the time, focusing on day-to-day matters that require attention to detail.

Celebrities give the impression of having an ideal lifestyle filled with recognition, respect, and adoration. Some want this in varying degrees, while others simply want to be understood, yearning to be accepted despite their individual oddities. Fame represents the need for societal approval. Socialization begins immediately in life, especially in big families, and grows throughout adolescence. Inherent in this process is a need for popularity until we begin realizing that people who bring value to the world are comfortable where they stand. Spiritual values should not be confused with fame.

Popularity is traceable within the Western astrological system. As a general rule, famous people have Jupiter in their chart or Libra energy in their makeup. This is denoted by the presence of number-nine energies. Fame is not an arbitrary phenomenon, but predestined to a large degree. When prevalent, the number-nine energy mirrors other's energy back onto them. This makes them especially likeable because everyone can see themselves in them, even if only in small part. Jupiter on the other hand is the energy of attention and attraction. It draws people in like a magnet and is the planet of luck and good fortune.

The secret path to fame commonly overlooked is meritorious achievement. The registered accumulation of good deeds and their contribution eventually grabs the attention of the world. For the giving of person, fame is never the objective: heaven blesses unseen good works and grants notable distinctions to the deserving. One particular story involves a doctor who was trained by Dr.

Wu's grandfather. What he lacked in academic success he made up for in commendable actions. Eventually he became one of the most effective doctors in China. Those who perform in the face of adversity are certainly distinguishable.

Daoists believe virtue is a reward onto itself. Protecting virtue requires a continuous vigilance; without its pursuit, humans may not reach their highest potential. Doing the right thing, making sound and prudent choices, creates peace of mind and develops right *qi* (*zhengqi* 正氣) within. Internal satisfaction is as vital as anything in the external world. Fame and fortune are fleeting, and without striking the proper balance or setting reasonable parameters for how they are gained, they lead to eventual decline.

Although inane and hectic, today's world has made fame easy to attain. This is driven by the market, which has developed an insatiable appetite for content. Many online platforms have given almost anyone their ten minutes of fame, but for those driving the world, the engineers, the farmers, biologists, wordsmiths and problem solvers, merits and good character often go uncelebrated. Fiction is king and actors, however talented, influence the family more than parents.

It is truly a gift and a serious responsibility to garner the attention of others. Do not waste their time because life is precious. Everyone is uniquely special, but to be recognized for our individual contributions is a grace. Those who reach the greatest degree of influence in the world such as Laozi are still thought of in obscurity. In this sense, becoming famous is not a requirement of spiritual development. Samuel Goldwyn once said, "Success has ruined more men than failure." The two ambitions of fame and fortune are a challenge to the human condition. A subcategory of greed, is lust.

Lust in Society

Lust is rampant in modern societies and, because "sex sells," the pleasure principle, innate in all humans, is expedited into consciousness without filter or regulation. Due to early introduction of sexual themes and a barrage of hyper-sexuality in mainstream society, natural curiosity is piqued. In terms of wanton behavior, curiosity becomes dangerous. Lust drives people to do strange things, just as greed or fame might. Lust is often a learned behavior. The psyche is inclined to rapidly assimilate many concepts into the mind. The subliminal mind is constantly learning behaviors through the five senses as well as sensory proximity. When taken to extremes, it leads to overstimulation and becomes unhealthy. The mind must be trained.

Lust-*qi* is at the root of these behaviors and what the Buddhist call the "ocean of desire" (*yuhai* 欲海). People of all ages must be protected from the over-wrought exposure of disruptiveness. There is nothing wrong with the act of sex, it is procreation after all, but some of the intentions are obscured. Channeling sexual energy into more constructive endeavors is ideal, and an important component of self-cultivation. Some Daoist sects went a step further and developed dual cultivation, tantric sex practices where men and women engage in specialized sexual exercises to benefit health and longevity. The Indian classic called *Kama Sutra* has been widely proliferated in the world.

There are traditions that say having sex creates an energetic link or tether to a partner, which can last as long as five to seven years. This exchange of *qi* potentially affects individual chemistry, either positively or negatively. These matters are not mainstream but there are plenty of experiments conducted throughout the world to measure their effects. Perhaps these findings will one day be useful and help people to direct sexual energy more creatively. When we choose to express ourselves, however, the heart should have a say.

Physical attraction is a strong indicator, but a response from the heart, a jumpstart, is more profound in measuring whether someone is right for you. This can be an expression of joy toward another person. Other times the heart may hurt after spending time together. If there are improprieties, the heart will sense them and react accordingly.

French kissing can help gauge a person's heart because in traditional Chinese medicine the root of the tongue is in the heart. Making words and sounds relies on the tongue, so how people express themselves through words reveals their heart. When subscribing to the idea that energy links are created through intimacy, it behooves anyone to follow their heart and instincts before jumping hastily. This is simply being mindful of the Buddhist concept of cause and effect or preordained fate. The heart is a treasure. Treat it so.

Relationships are often easy to enter but difficult to end. Energy exchanged in sexual activity is not always beneficial or in balance. The act of intimacy can leave one elated or drained of vitality, depending on compatibility or intention. This may not be noticeable when young but, as *qi* begins to wane, the grounds of the relationship dynamic become obvious. Waning *qi* can diminish immunity leading to poor health conditions, listlessness, and fog, whereas waxing *qi* strengthens the immune system and improves luck.

From the Daoist perspective, it makes sense to preserve *qi* through diet, exercise, and spiritual practices. By remaining in balance, innate *qi* will shine through and lead to making sound decisions in life. Daoists warn against fox spirits, vampiric entities that create lustful scenarios using illusion, usually while their victim is asleep. Casting their spell, they quickly siphon essence from the victim's body, which may lead to premature death if continued over time, just like the actions of an incubus or succubus in Western lore. This type of energy-sucking demon is well documented across the world. It is one reason why Daoist and Buddhist monks protect and cultivate *qi*.

There is nothing new under the sun, and much of what is trending today is history repeating itself. The caveat is living in the information age, wherein lies new opportunities to grow exponentially as a species. A healthy society can be measured by its spiritual base but belief systems vary. As a general rule, Daoists believe in live and let live and following nature.

Same-sex dating and matrimonies are often the subject of heated debates in society, but common trends are analyzed differently by Daoists. They believe that people are attracted to *qi*. Whatever *qi* people lack they will seek in order to balance yin-yang within. If yin energy is deficient, there will be an attraction to the feminine; if yang is deficient, there will be an attraction to the masculine. It is energetic regulation. To add another vantage point, same-sex relationships, not procreating, are part of nature thinning the herd and regulating population growth.

However, even they may lead to unreasonable obsessions with sex due to lust-*qi*. Lust-*qi* can be absorbed through media content imprinting on the frontal cortex, sometimes with lasting impact. This is precisely why the film-rating system and other content evaluations were developed: to shelter young minds from exposure to lust-*qi*. Nowadays, without strict parental supervision, it is nearly impossible to avoid.

Daoists do not recommend watching other humans or animals during physical intimacy. They cite health reasons: a loss of vision occurs because you saw something you should not have seen; hearing loss happens when you hear something you should not be hearing; and so on. The participation and inclusion of lust-*qi* drives unhealthy curiosities. Religions all agree on setting parameters for acceptable levels, especially since the long-term physical and psychological effects can be devastating to society.

According to Dr. Wu, people enjoy sex and drinking because their effects soothe numinous energy (*lingqi*), allowing it to escape the body and thereby making people feel closer to spirit. Typically, the "genie" is not allowed out of the bottle until their separation at death. The French allude to this concept in what they describe as "little death," the profound feeling after orgasm when numinous energy is temporarily released into the ether. This approach to sexual activity makes it a spiritual experience. Redefining sexual expression from the social norms and the quelling of lust-*qi* is difficult and requires the restoration of a healthy outlook toward sexual partnerships.

Over centuries, Daoists have discovered practices specializing in the intentional release of the soul before returning to the body. For example, qigong meditations can open the meridians and, when properly directed alchemically, refine sexual energy into *qi* and then into spirit. There are both ascetic adepts as well as happily married priests, however, those in wedlock practice dual cultivation. Many advocate to undertake physical activity to expend sexual energy, while others encourage creativity as an outlet. However, these fail to address the deeper roots of lust-*qi*. Acupuncture, qigong, and taijiquan are effective ways for redirecting and transmuting it. Finding ways to vanquish undesirable obstacles is encouraged.

Sexuality is considered sacred to Daoists. They understand that humankind's distortion of nature is why heaven seals the third eye at birth. Based on research and observation, they conclude that other animals maintain direct forms of communication with heaven without any veil obscuring the complete reality. Thus, Daoists continue to learn from nature directly.

Looking at the internet as the bellwether of the species and the collective unconscious, lust-*qi* is perhaps the biggest challenge facing us today. There are varying beliefs on this matter, but it is valuable to consider that the desecration of human dignity via a distorted reality is probable. In essence, sexual energy is a powerful resource bestowed upon us by heaven in the hopes of achieving something great. It is the material building block linked to our spiritual energy and creativity. With it we can modify, restore or procreate to bolster the species.

In traditional China, lust-*qi* was less of an issue because men were allowed up to three wives, contingent upon their level of success. Polygamy was common in many parts of the world, since the birth mortality rate was high and the mean age of death well below today's thresholds. Monogamy is more widely accepted in the modern era, but could potentially be why there is a rise in lust-*qi*.

In ancient times, societies were preoccupied with surviving and improving living conditions. Sexual indiscretions were considered capital crimes punishable by death and taken very seriously. They were a direct threat to the family unit, and still are. Society today struggles to keep the nuclear family intact for a myriad reasons, but lust-*qi* continues to be an emerging factor, also deterring people from pursuing a conventional lifestyle.

Whichever way you view these issues, remember that these energies can be transmuted through spiritual efforts. If we do not properly cultivate them, inevitably there is stagnation. History provides some perspective. Here is a passage regarding the societal structure around the time of the Han dynasty:

> In traditional Chinese societies of extended families, men married not for romantic love but because their families wanted to establish connections with other families of their level or, most often, higher classes. All the wives in the family enjoyed the same status, with the first wife simply referred to as 'elder sister' by second and other wives. All children of the family (regardless of maternal lineage) had to regard her as their mother while children of concubines could only call their natural mothers *saijie*.
>
> As it was difficult to divorce wives with such influential backgrounds, husbands in such marriages of convenience often found gratification in concubines and mistresses (who are courtesans). A man with 'three wives and four concubines' was considered a very successful person in those times. Concubines were all women of lower classes bought with money, little better than maid servants. Still, they were better than the *mutsai* who had to give sexual favors without reward. (Wong 2003)

While the ancient system was rigidly structured, there were opportunities for upward mobility, such as when concubines were promoted upon the death of the first wife or when the first wife was barren and the concubine birthed a masculine heir, her status thus elevated.

Chapter 6

The Happenstance of Fate

Life's opportunities are the building blocks of dreams. Some people are born into beautiful fairy tale lives, raised in fine homes and surrounded by kind friends. They have strong roots that create a sense of belonging and purpose in the world, dedication to family and community. They are perhaps "born under a lucky star." Many aspire to attain similar fortunes. Standing on the outside looking in this appears random and unfair, but according to Dr. Wu, success is dependent on many factors.

A person's will to succeed and follow through with their actions is obligatory, indisputable and a reasonable recipe for success. However, actions in past lives contribute to shaping future existence. Past successes and regressions are major contributors to reincarnation. Previous performances create opportunities that might otherwise never manifest. However, "fortune favors the bold" and, regardless of one's background, success may still come from industriousness but may still rely on the past. Therein lies the enigma: fifty percent of human destiny is predetermined and the other fifty percent, although also predetermined, may be amended through discretion and sheer will. The question then arises: If life is predestined, why labor? Well, if we do not put forth effort, we can be sure nothing will ever change and life is wasted.

Life choices must be made within reason. Someone who grows to be seven feet two inches tall has a high probability of succeeding as a professional basketball player. However, if you are born five feet tall, despite being one of the top shooters, the odds are stacked against you and this option is not part of your fatd. Yet, there are many unlikely scenarios that come true. Some people possess a *je ne sais quoi*, the charisma to open doors or possessing a unique skill. This is the rice bowl that guarantees you a seat at the table. With the right amount of effort and perseverance, there is an achievable dream for everyone.

A person can be fabulously skilled and talented, but never catch a break because they have not accrued enough meritorious currency, the backbone of success according to Daoism. This is central to remember when cultivating. These words are not meant to discourage, but rather to give insight and solution to solving individual dilemmas and to inform on the continuity of time and conscientiousness. Often, people persevere and have major breakthroughs when least expected.

These are deep concepts to grasp, especially if one does not believe in reincarnation. The way in which Dr. Wu explains this phenomenon is that "all roads lead to Rome." Everyone is looking to advance their lives by moving to a thriving country or a city with abundant food supply and good schools, gaining a sense of security. Such is human nature. Not all reach their final destination but does that mean you should not try? This is the conundrum. Others are born there into ideal circumstances. Is it merely dumb luck or meritorious fortune? Perhaps it is both.

Every night the soul searches for a path forward in the state of dreaming, the subconscious hard at work. Good fortune *qi* may also be received from family members long past. The efforts of your ancestors play a significant role in your life, especially if they were good people, profoundly affecting success and karmic retribution.

Keep in mind that there is more to life than conventional or worldly successes. For example, spiritual hygiene is critical and, if realized, will find the support needed to live well. Good things happen to good people as like attracts like. According to Dr. Wu, to rise to the level of a president of a great nation takes seven lifetimes to amass enough goodwill, but without the will to succeed, we fall short of success.

Confucius stated, "If three walk together, one can be my teacher," indicating that the opportunity to attain spiritual progress is close at hand and clearly identifiable. One only needs walk through the open door. It is of significant historical context to note that these two concepts of karmic currency and determination are notably Daoist.

These two factors of a person's fate are important to realize. Parents play significant roles in the formation of a child's fate. Parents naturally want success for their children and to become dragons, but might not always understand the implications of their participation both at home and away. Wealth does not guarantee success either, and in many cases is the downfall as when children are spoiled rotten or in the shadows cast by their parents or siblings. We cannot look to bemoan our fate, merely fix the foibles of our ancestors and do better with our lives.

Drugs and Alcohol

Daoists tend to have a realistic view of the world. For instance, they do not criticize the use of drugs and alcohol but rather view them as medicine or tools. Wine and spirits take off the edge, allowing people to relax. When this occurs the human spirit temporarily comes out to play, becoming joyful. It can be especially helpful to the introvert who finds it difficult to make new friends. Alcohol in China was invented during prosperous times when herbal medicines were in development. In this sense, alcohol can be considered a tonic. The immortal and sword master Lü Dongbin of the late Tang dynasty was known for his ability to drink yet not get drunk, perfecting the method of alchemical transformation using alcohol as fuel, not unlike high-powered race cars. However, this secret self-cultivation technique is not recommended for the uninitiated.

There is good reason for the existence of all things, both conventional and bizarre. Spiritual outlets are few, and with the rise in insomnia and other sleep disrupters (noise, electrical current and voltage, Bluetooth, etc.), deep sleep is not achieved and the spirit remains locked in the body. In moderation, alcohol is therapeutic for releasing the spirit. There is also precedence for this theory in modern medicine, whose representatives universally accept that a glass of red wine before bed benefits heart health. Coincidentally, according to Daoist and Buddhist religious doctrine, the spirit resides in the heart, otherwise called the palace of blood. Always check with your physician first before trying even the simplest of remedies.

Nowadays in Europe and America, people are smoking marijuana in lieu of alcohol. Dr. Wu has commented on the medicinal effects of marijuana for pain, which correlates to Western medicine's application of the drug. The Chinese term for the plant is *ma*, literally "hemp," which also implies numbness. Traditionally, physicians applied marijuana topically, combined with other herbal ingredients, as a localized anesthesia during surgery. Just as the temporary release of the spirit is helpful during sleep or while extremely relaxed, conversely, an extended departure jeopardizes the spirit.

Aside from pain, other modern uses of marijuana include a fast-growing form of recreational spirituality surrounding the drug. Today's cultivation of the plant takes it far above the normal natural potency. Because of this extra strength, the time spent in altered states is extended, leaving the spirit vulnerable to evil *qi*.

Buddhists believe that there are six realms of existence and that the law of karma does not condone intermingling them. Monastic practices include policing these realms to prevent any breached entry. When creatures from other realms enter, they tend to attach and wreak havoc on human souls, causing disease. They are often mischievous and parasitical, looking to siphon off precious life force like the fox spirits. Similarly, humans eat animals, causing them to join the same realm. Humans also subjugate other humans for survival. It is a matter of perspective to understand the dynamics to surviving.

Lü Dongbin was reportedly admonished by Buddhists for his indulgence in wine: they considered him an impure eccentric. At the time, Buddhist schools and practices had attained great status and influence, which they used to preach abstinence. They also questioned Lü's sexual cultivation practices. Despite his critics he still succeeded in his spiritual aims. This reinforces the Daoist idea that many things can be useful when exercised within adaptive moderation principles. Darwin is cited saying, "It is not the most intellectual of the species that survives; it is not the strongest that survives; but the species that survives is the one that is able best to adapt and adjust to the changing environment in which it finds itself."

In the end, Lü Dongbin's training methods were praiseworthy. Daoists do not ban drinking spirits because of its many uses. It can drown sorrows and bring back one's inner nature if lost. Some people are born to be trailblazers. For example, Daoists are known to grant special leniency to people born in the year of the monkey, encouraging their spontaneous nature regardless of whether they succeed or fail. Their brilliance relies on following this unique nature.

The true Daoist secret of what makes a person successful has never before been revealed to the public. According to Dr. Wu, what dictates success is when the soul is unified. When the soul seated in the lower elixir field joins the one in the upper elixir field, the magic truly happens. It is similar to life taking off after meeting the right mate. This reunification defines success and failure. If the two forces cannot meet in the middle of the body, success always remains just out of reach.

Manifestation onto the external world emanates from this internal reconnection. Those who maintain balance and follow the natural flow of the universe reach this alignment while others who are discontented have more difficulties. There are many other contributing factors causing internal misalignment.

Although Nine Palaces Qigong is the highest form and optimal tool for internal balancing, nearly all Daoist practices lend themselves to this end. Purifying the body to more readily accept mystical energy is a consequence of Daoist cultivation. People wonder why Daoist practitioners spend countless hours practicing things like taijiquan or qigong. Why would they stand alone in nature practicing these arts, opposing the current trends of the day? They do this to make themselves whole, improve their lives and health, engage in the mystical, develop uncanny skills, and help lead others in doing the same. It cannot be the blind leading the blind.

From the outside, the path of Dao appears simple and carefree, but there is also struggle and bitterness to taste and swallow. If a musician practiced daily but did not see any improvement, he may quit. The same holds true for spiritual cultivation. Many start strong, then lose interest. Without instant gratification the Dao is lost to many. Although you drop the stone into a well and do not hear the splash, this does not mean nothing is happening, so stay the course. These methods would have disappeared long ago if they held no value.

Chapter 7

Daoist Ritual

During Daoist funerals, a series of rituals are performed to help the deceased person's soul or spirit move on to the best possible incarnation. Like followers of other religions, Daoists believe that the soul leaves the body after death. Dr. Wu witnessed this phenomenon on a number of occasions. The spirit appears as a white orb with a smokey, wispy quality that is very subtle. I have personally seen it after my dad's death. When he died, I was beside myself as I was quite young at the time. Then, before I went to bed that night, I noticed a white orb of light outside my window. It was quite bright, and it lingered for a moment before disappearing.

Many times, a soul or dying person will be granted one last wish. Often a person may hold back from dying for hours or even days while they wait to say goodbye to their loved ones. Similarly, their spirit may travel to loved ones after death and bring them good fortune, blessings, and heart-felt hope. This demonstrates that there is a sense of grace or mercy built into the regular machinations of the universe. Nature is not cold, but loving.

During Daoist death ceremonies, a special, tent-like room is constructed from nine layers of colored cloth which aids the spirit in leaving the body, allows it to be viewed more clearly, and keeps it temporarily contained. Having attended a number of these ceremonies, Dr. Wu has seen the soul of the deceased hover outside of the body while a group of monks chanted sutras to create a holy environment. The tent is important not only because it keeps the soul contained, but also because it prevents the messengers of death from taking the spirit to various other realms. The two messengers, one dressed in all white and the other in black, are responsible for capturing the soul and taking it to the underworld house of death for judgment.

Daoists apply their procedures to ensure that the soul picks the correct direction to exit the body. The direction in which the spirit travels after death plays a significant role in determining its future path. The eight directions or doors available to the spirit are represented by the eight trigrams and can be divined through the *Yijing*. It takes about ten minutes on average for a soul to choose its pathway: each lead to a different incarnation.

One of the doors available to a soul represents a more permanent death. This direction is rarely desirable and generally avoided. Therefore, during the ceremony, scriptures are recited by a group of Daoists to help the soul choose the most beneficial reincarnation. This is considered to be an essential and sacred ritual that helps the spirit to achieve its highest potential in future lifetimes. The death ceremony is only effective for the two-hour period following death. After this time, the soul will have already either left the body and chosen a doorway, or it will have been snatched by the messengers of death for judgment.

In addition to chanting spells, Daoists will also use talismans and the *Yijing* to calculate the fate of the person's spirit while observing their physical features at the moment of death. The eyes, represented by the Li trigram, are observed first, followed by the ears, nose, mouth, genitals, and anus. When the eyes begin to soften or the bowels evacuate, death is imminent.

Just prior to the death of a person who lived a saintly life with great spiritual accomplishments, changes in nature take place. This can include strong winds, flocks of birds or butterflies, unique cloud formations, the position of the sun and moon, which stars are visible, the humidity in the air, and any other abnormal occurrences. Daoists use this process to make records for their own use and to determine the future path of the spirit. Monastics will use funerary rituals and significant events to organize a chart for the deceased person during and immediately after their passing. Finally, the Daoist leader will select a student to speak out about the observations that were made and the implications regarding their reincarnation.

During the ceremony, the dying person is placed on a large scale, the size of a bed. At the moment of death, the scale will register a loss of anywhere from seven to twenty-two pounds, as the spirit leaves the body. Following the drop in weight, the smoky spirit will emerge, white and transparent against the background of colored drapes. Some spirits remain in the shape of a human, while others form a smokey ring or sphere. However, about sixty percent of the time, it takes the shape of a butterfly.

After emerging from the body, the spirit will either need to reincarnate, in which case it is sent away. It may also linger, and the Daoists will use a container to trap it for spiritual purposes. In either case, the spirit is brought into circumstances that are best for its continued growth and development. If the spirit leaves to reincarnate, it will float upward as monks and nuns play sacred music. People will leave quickly to prevent distracting the spirit from its journey. Large blocks of ice will be placed around the body to slow its decay, and seven days later, the Daoists will come back to observe any changes.

During these seven days, the spirit travels the earth, taking care of unfinished business by repaying good deeds, making up for past mistakes, and the like. For instance, Daoists view winnings from gambling as a gift from the ancestors or as a debt repayment from a deceased spirit. On the other hand, tripping and falling or suffering an injury can be caused by a deceased spirit seeking revenge for wrong-doings. Occasionally, the dead body will come back to life within these seven days because the spirit must accomplish a final task in physical form.

Love and hate never occur without a reason. When a stone is thrown into a pond, the ripples travel outward, and though they may not be visible, the energy of the wave continues to move through the environment. When they finally hit the edge, the ripples will bounce back, but this is a process that requires time.

The seven days following death allow the dying person's spirit to ripple out, repay all its debts, and diminish naturally.

After the seven days have passed, the body may be buried or cremated, depending on the situation. With cremation, there may be *sharira*, or dragon bones left behind: bright, jewel-like substances. These are considered sacred objects and they are placed in holy locations to be venerated. The body may also be put into a large container and buried for a period before being exhumed and reburied elsewhere. Bodies that rot quickly signify people that have accumulated bad deeds, but if the flesh has not rotted during this time, it is a sure sign that the individual has done a lot of good deeds in life. Their hair, beard, and ear hairs may even continue to grow after death due to abundant life energy. Finally, the whole, not yet rotten bodies are coated in gold, decorated in the shape of the Buddha or the eighteen warriors, placed in temples, and venerated in golden statues. Praying to them is believed to enhance the spiritual power of the devotee as he or she invokes the saintly force they contain.

The burying and exhumation practice is a specific ritual only practiced in Hunan and Sichuan as well as in some places in Tibet and Mongolia. The rest of mainland China currently practices a more traditional cremation ceremony. The relationship between the quality of one's deeds and the level of decomposition after death demonstrates that thoughts and actions are being judged from the moment are born. This instills a sense of personal responsibility that even children can recognize and forms the foundation of our sense of morality.

In Tibet and Mongolia, another form of funeral is practiced, known as sky burial. In this ceremony, the body is chopped into six pieces and sacred eagles and predatory birds are allowed to consume the flesh and organs. Eagles are considered the messengers of heaven: they can speed up the rate of reincarnation for the deceased. The best eagles for this type of ceremony are large golden eagles and those that that have undergone the process of rebirth which involves ripping off various body parts midway through life to stimulate new growth and increase longevity. This process of eagle rebirth and the ceremony of sky burial represent the mythical rebirth of the phoenix from the ashes, aiding the process of reincarnation.

Depending on circumstances and the moral quality of life, reincarnation can take varying amounts of time and involve various trials and tribulations, like the judgment described earlier. The stages of the afterlife are often quite difficult and disorienting, because they are experienced in a different form than we are used to, also making them hard to describe. The trials they entail are not meant to be traumatic or difficult; they are merely unfamiliar and unlike any previous physical experiences people encounter.

Just like living in a major city without having a car, if you do not have a physical form, the available options for spiritual progress are limited and restrict our growth. Without a body, we are obligated to follow the way that nature has intended for us and we must accept the options given. With increased spiritual progress, these options are enhanced and multiplied, allowing us to have greater control over our spiritual destiny. All healthy living beings fight for life. It is only through a complete lack of connection with nature that we forget what a magnificent gift we have been given in life.

Regardless of the trials and tribulations of the afterlife, our only option for advancement lies in the actions we perform on earth while alive. To die with no regrets, no diseases, and a smile on the face is both our best hope for a better future and a significant goal unto itself. By being the best person that we can manage, we can enter the afterlife feeling good and positive no matter what we may face.

Starting Reincarnation

Before a soul departs this world, Daoists and Buddhists do everything they can to help that person overcome obstacles and face death with confidence. This helps them secure the best possible afterlife and future lives. To this day, the Chinese are very, particular when it comes to finding the best possible plot of cemetery ground because they regard the afterlife and the journey of their soul to be of the upmost importance.

The first Chinese emperor, Qin Shi Huang, filled his tomb with thousands of guardian statues, the famous terracotta army, and an underground enclosure of copper depicting the land of his country with ever-flowing rivers of mercury to ward off evil. He did this because he feared being haunted by his past deeds and the spirits of those who he had wronged. A powerful leader, he made strong decisions that affected many people and gave numerous orders to his generals. These actions subsequently resulted in the death of many people and led to much ill will from others.

Revenge is real emotion, and after a person passes away, that energy must be resolved and surrendered before the spirit can continue on its journey through the afterlife. The emperor's main goal was to unite the country and, in order to accomplish this, he had to destroy any person or obstacle that sought to keep the regions separate. He understood the significant consequences of his actions that would manifest after his passing. Regardless of the cost, he accepted his destiny and, by the time of his death, had unified the seven warring states of Qin, Han, Zhao, Wei, Chu, Yan, and Qi under Qin rule.

In Daoism, it is considered wise to refrain from burying a body for seven days after death. During this time, the person can take care of any unfinished business in the earthly realm. This process not only helps the spirit rest in peace, but it provides good luck in various ways. The spirit of the deceased as well as the people he interacted with in life can benefit greatly from rectifying past debts. Daoists often consider good luck that seems to manifest without previous planning or attention as a gift from the ancestors or a deceased loved one.

Although our human form is lost in death, we nonetheless retain a bit of ourselves in the afterlife and beyond. The spirit is likened to the soil from which our personality and talents grow and develop. Without the original nature of our spirit, our passions, capacities, and character could not express themselves. There are many spiritual gifts that are recognized and employed both inside and outside of Daoism, and their foundation rests on the quality of our spirit itself.

By speaking with our deceased loved ones via prayers, dreams, or other methods, we can resolve lingering problems within the family. The dead are often disturbed when their descendants constantly fight or bicker about their issues, and they will make their displeasure heard from the other side in a number of ways. Many people do not even attempt to assuage their disagreements with others and miss many opportunities to be supported by loved ones who have passed. Though we often derive great joy and happiness from our friendships, our family is still more closely linked with our spiritual and karmic path. The actions of family members, living and dead, have a significant effect on our well-being, and therefore it is wise to understand them deeply and support them whenever possible, even if that means only a kind and loving prayer for their welfare.

Daoist funerary rituals differ depending on whether they are public or private, as illustrated in the following excerpt:

> Strictly speaking, Daoist funerals belong to the category of fasting or purgation (*zhai*). After the Song dynasty, the offering (*jiao*) was more widespread than the purgation. Purgations and offerings are held, whether the dead is a Daoist priest or a common lay person. When the patriarch of Complete Perfection Qiu Chuji died, his disciples conducted the Yellow Register Purgation Rites of Numinous Treasure (*Lingbao huanglu zhaiyi* 靈寶黃籙齋儀). In the thirteenth chapter of the *Honglou meng* 紅樓夢 (Dream of the Red Mansion), when Qin Keqing died, it was decided to keep her corpse for forty-nine days. One hundred and eight monks and ninety-nine Complete Perfection Daoists were invited to conduct the Offering for Renouncing Misfortune and Clearing Bad Karma (*jieyuan xiye jiao* 解怨洗業醮) over forty-nine days. (en.daoinfo.org)

As the above passage shows, Daoist burial rites, like those in other cultures, often include the participation of people familiar with the deceased and routinely extend to family members. This is because the actions of those who have died affect the lives of others, and their spiritual well-being must also be cared for. By performing good deeds and developing our spiritual awareness, we not only benefit ourselves but also those around us. In this way, we avoid the pitfalls of the afterlife and generate prosperity in the world of the living. The cascading effects of our actions leads many Daoists to extricate themselves from any type of politics of rulership positions. If necessary, they only occupy temporary advisory positions, or only chose to get involved only when called upon in a dire-circumstances that would negatively affect the lives of many innocent people. For instance, Sunzi, the author of *The Art of War*, wrote his famous text with the understanding that the information it contained was necessary to help good people defend themselves. One can be sure that Daoists would consult the *Yijing* to understand the will of heaven before engaging in such actions. It is not their goal to meddle with history and go against nature.

Due to the numerous implications of actions on our destiny and that of our loved ones, it is important to be able to listen to one's heart and understand our motivations. Daoists describe a fetus in the womb as a "human seed" or "baby seed," which carries the spirit that will live with the child from birth and throughout life. After birth, awareness focuses outward so we can handle the events of our lives. However, when we close our eyes, awareness once again turns inward and becomes one with spirit. This is why many meditative practices involve closing the eyes. This practice cultivates spiritual energy and develops awareness to ever-increasing levels. By closing your eyes while awake, we focus our conscious mind on our subconscious, heart-felt thoughts. Many other living creatures can be observed practicing this type of meditation. Turtles, for instance, often close their eyes while awake, which allows them to connect with the world on a deep and profound level.

After you pass away, you will once again be on the pathway to reincarnation. The soul has six different phases that it must pass through in order to be reborn. Depending on the level of spiritual development and past karma, it may take varying lengths to complete these phases. The actions that we take in life, and our level of spiritual commitment, can greatly affect the amount of languishing between incarnations. Furthermore, the amount of time that reincarnation takes may appear different from the perspective of living beings and purely spiritual ones.

Needless to say, a person who has had a significant, positive spiritual impact on society would have an easier spiritual transition. All of our behaviors have consequences, and the ones that remain unfulfilled in life will be accounted for after our passing because heaven sees everything. If we do what is right, good things will come to us down the line. The effects of our actions do not always reach us immediately, but eventually it becomes clear that the better we are able to develop our heart-felt spirit, the easier it becomes to pass through the process of reincarnation. Highly evolved spiritual beings reincarnate more quickly because the process has become easier for them, and those that are of the highest caliber reincarnate instantly. In order to benefit in the afterlife, we must be mindful of how our actions effect the lives and genuine, heart-felt feelings of others: trauma and healing both have effects that reverberate through our souls.

Meditation Times

Daoists believe that there are special points in one's life where it is necessary to take time out to rest and regenerate from life's trials, problems, and struggles. During these times, it is imperative that a person refrains from too many worldly activities and responsibilities, instead turning inward to heal and develop greater understanding. We must all work to earn a living and keep ourselves healthy, but by taking the time to repose and understand ourselves more deeply, we can elicit more and more help from heaven.

Daoists especially consider the ages of 66, 73, and 84 to be common "crossroad points" in life, where events seem to become slower and require a significant amount of self-reflection. They are also periods of personal regeneration that will dictate the course of the years that follow. Many people face complex issues at these ages that often require their full attention to resolve. This is especially true for spiritually dedicated individuals, such as monks and nuns, because by investing their energy in more beneficial future incarnations, they must take a deeper stock of themselves. It is often said that "time heals all wounds" and these times in life represent natural checkpoints where patience and understanding can heal at the deepest level. As we reach these bottleneck points and past issues move through us, the intense energy generated from their transformation changes their quality from traumatic to therapeutic and integral. Many significant effects can transpire at these times, but healing only requires our willingness to accept the present moment. By relaxing and accepting things as they are, heaven is free to manifest the best outcomes for all of us.

It is always beneficial to engage in peaceful activities during times of repose and solitude in order to increase their healing potential. In the past, masters have practiced mindful isolation for various lengths of time, from shorter periods of a single day or week to longer periods of twenty-one to twenty-eight days for more deeply rooted problems. To heal ourselves enough to benefit our future incarnations, periods of forty-nine days are common, and others have practiced for three to six months, a year, or even up to a decade. During these lengthy practices, adepts would meditate alone for nearly all waking hours, with only their thoughts and the universe to focus on. Free from distractions, the mind has the space and time to settle and readjust itself after a lifetime of intense activity and the demands of societal living.

Commitments such as these have always been taken seriously by practitioners. They would not leave the meditation chamber for any reason during their practice. This practice is held in the highest regard in the spiritual community, as it is the practice of using one's mind in the most efficient and beneficial way possible. Out of respect and honor, fellow disciples would regularly bring food, water, and essentials, such as freshly laundered clothes, as well as empty their chamber pot.

Each person's experience during these periods of seclusion is unique, but they all emerge with deeply profound insights. During these times, some have mastered sitting meditation, some extensively read sutras, while others practiced taijiquan or qigong. Masters sometimes use their time to coalesce various information and practice into new, more advanced forms. Their insights are regularly of a much more refined quality, and they never fail to become the most respected people in their chosen field(s). Martial artists have emerged from lengthy meditations with unique forms of combat, including taijiquan and swordsmanship, which have a profound effect on their life path and spiritual community.

The length of time that each person meditates must make sense in the larger context of their life. In Dr. Wu's case, his teacher, Master Du, realized that he was going to have a busy professional life filled with long hours of work. So instead of a single prolonged meditation, he advised him to periodically mediate for a single day at a time. Over his career, Dr. Wu too has devised many unique healing methods and come to a profound understanding of ancient Daoist medicine.

Water Cultivation

During reclusive meditations, Daoists eat very little in order to keep the body purified and unencumbered. Instead, they focus on drinking the highest quality water they can find, which helps to sustain their energy throughout the day. It also involves periods of fasting to further aid the detoxification process and allow the mind to settle more deeply. Drinking water is sometimes collected from special places, such as natural springs, but most often comes from local rivers. The special water contains a very high mineral content. To test its quality, a metal coin is be gently placed on its surface: if it holds an exceptional level of minerals, the coin floats. Only water of this quality is used for periods of fasting because, though it contains no calories, it provides energetic nutrition to the body.

People who regularly drink well-water live much healthier lives because of its healing and energetic qualities. For maintaining overall health, water that contains minerals and trace elements is best. Water that is filtered, either through reverse osmosis, or distillation, as well as alkalized waters are beneficial, but natural spring water contains unique *qi* from the earth, the sun, and the moon.

Daoists would often collect water by gathering the first snow that falls each year, allowing it to melt and saving it for later use. A uniquely pure type of water would also be collected by gathering the snow that had accumulated on the branches of pine trees. Seven days after this snow had fallen, it would be brushed off of each branch and stored in purified barrels. They would also collect water that had condensed on the leaves of a bamboo plant from the morning dew. This bamboo water has a unique, sweet fragrance and a subtle, pure taste that enhances and settles the *qi* of the body. The monks would use these special waters for tea and herbal concoctions or bury it to further enhance its quality. Most often, water would be collected with large porcelain or copper bowls overnight during rain or snow-storms.

Water, in order to be buried, must be sealed in a clay or porcelain container. The top must be covered with the same nine-colored cloths of yellow and red that are used in the burial rites. The container must then be buried for at least a year. After this time, the water is consumed, traditionally on the individual's birthday. While buried, it must not be dug up or otherwise disturbed, because this would interrupt the refinement process. The enhanced water greatly benefits health and longevity and increases overall well-being in many ways.

The rainwater from the previous year would also be used regularly by Daoist practitioners. This water would be gathered and stored in porcelain or clay pots, allowing its *qi* to be refined in a process similar to fermentation before being consumed the following year. This is yet another method of enhancing the water's energy so that it can be used for healing and mystical purposes. The practice of storing and burying water in this way dates back centuries. Like fine wine, bottles of water that have been stored for hundreds of years can still be found in some temples and sacred sites. This water has a naturally sweet taste and contains uniquely beneficial *qi*.

The practice of storing water inspired similar fermentation and aging processes used with wine. Today, we are blessed to have so many forms of water available to us. Not only have we developed plumbing and aqueducts to transport water over great distances, but we also have access to numerous natural spring waters that come from deep within the earth.

As water travels through the earth and over its surface in the form of springs and rivers, its quality and energy content are enhanced. Dr. Masaru Emoto demonstrated this by studying the crystal structures of various types of water as they began to melt from ice (2006, 154-68). The water that contained higher quality *qi* from natural sources always produced more symmetrical and complex crystal structures that could contain this energy.

Just as the ocean is always in motion, and clouds are continuously changing their shape, our thoughts are constantly changing. The most natural and healthy phenomenon in existence demonstrate this consistent impermanence and flexibility to changing conditions. In Daoism, clouds are often equated with passing thoughts, and the more purified and peaceful the clouds are, the more they are able to benefit the living beings they coexist with. Dr. Emoto and other scientists have extensively studied the relationship between water and human thought, especially in the form of prayer. They demonstrate the incredible and subtle power of the mind, lending further credence to the fact that the body, consisting mostly of water, responds to our intentions, moment to moment. This relationship also plays a significant role in our feelings, behaviors, and the circumstances we find ourselves in. As such, the spiritual health of a civilization can be assessed by observing the quality of its water.

Like a lake or ocean, our minds are in constant motion, and like our thoughts, water that is pure and tranquil can reflect heaven above. When the heart and mind are calm, we can see ourselves more clearly and more easily manifest our creative desires. Meditative practices seek to pacify the mind's activity for this very reason. These practices bring out more yang energy as they reflect the light of spirit. As the waves of the ocean become more intense and turbulent, they create froth and foam (yin) that prevent us from seeing reflections clearly. Similarly, a disturbed and unsettled mind forms negative thoughts that prevent it from seeing clearly. The calm stability of mountainous regions also provides this serene energy in a stable and long-lasting way, bringing strength and peace-of-mind to the living beings that inhabit them. Spiritually, even though the yin and yang are both revered and each serve a vital purpose, light, subtle, and peaceful yang energy provides spiritual constancy that forms a foundation for spiritual achievement.

Much energy is poured into fruitless social activities and novelty in order to do nothing more than escape our thoughts. Some people drink, others use drugs, yet others work long hours just to prevent themselves from feeling the pain of their past traumas. But at the deepest level, our spirits are constantly yearning for wholeness, healing, and integrity. It is not easy to address our spiritual condition, but the rewards are profound and enduring. Like the rivers of the earth, the body's meridians provide a channel for life-giving energy to flow. When this flow is unimpeded and the energy pure, the body is healthy and the mind is clear.

Being able to have clarity of thought and the unencumbered spirit of a child while inhabiting the body of an adult leads to joyousness and prosperity in life. Therefore, we should all recognize the importance of water and have reverence for the benefits it provides. Water, especially in its natural states in the form of springs, streams, rivers, lakes, and oceans, provides a vast array of metaphysical potential for all living beings in addition to its vital life-giving qualities. Without the vacillations of waves, whether they are thought waves, ocean waves, or the ups and downs of various circumstances, we would not be alive.

By drinking water, we activate the kidney meridian responsible for governing mind and brain. It is a form of receiving information from the earth and nature. As water travels through the earth, it interacts with various minerals, plants, and other organic substances, storing and even extracting the elements they are composed of. Scientist often refer to water as the "universal solvent" because of its incredible ability to dissolve any material if given enough time. Therefore, over time water begins to carry the essence of everything that it comes into contact with. This can be easily observed by watching the essence of tea leaves flow into the surrounding hot water when a tea bag is steeped. Water that has been stored underground represents the process of developing yang within yin. By sitting alone in a reclusive state, the water undergoes its own type of spiritual transformation, just like the spiritual devotees who meditate for long periods.

Water represents possibilities because it can take the shape of any vessel it is poured into. It represents the Daoist concept of "nothingness." When something is shapeless, it can easily become anything that is required. Since water represents thoughts and feelings, it can also be said to match the "mind of the earth." When oceans and natural water sources become polluted, the thoughts and feelings of all living beings are poisoned in addition to their physical structures; this breeds confusion, depression, and instability. As living beings, we rely on water to exist and function properly, and therefore the quality and quantity of the water in our environment is directly linked to the quality of our experience.

Today, many water runoffs, aquifers, and other bodies of water are inundated with pesticides and chemicals, largely from modern farming methods, as well as pharmaceutical and chemical companies, so it is vital to drink the cleanest water we can find. Traditionally, Daoists at the White Cloud Monastery, revered the water they collected more than any form of food they consumed. It greatly extended to their life expectancy by aiding them in their physical and spiritual regeneration practices.

The process of reincarnation takes varying lengths of time depending on the previous incarnation of the soul. It takes 500 years for an animal to reincarnate as a human being, while it only takes a flower 120 and a tree 100 years to do the same. By regularly engaging in spiritual practices during our life, we develop the potential to reduce this waiting period between incarnations. If we use all of our spiritual energy toward building something positive in this life, we can rest assured that we have done our best and mitigated the trials we must face in the afterlife as much as possible.

Chapter 8

Past Life, Present Life

2018 was the year of the dog, a time that allowed humanity to practice the concept of loyalty. While the cat is a symbol of independence and attracting good fortune, dogs represent the cultivation of fraternity and a higher standard of living. The energy of the dog assists us in remembering and regaining the virtues of our past lives. Therefore, dog years bring about an attitude of elevated living standards and an appreciation of the truly important aspects of ourselves.

Spiritually, dogs represent our mother from a past life. Within the previous seven lifetimes, all of us were dogs, and any significant dogs that come into our lives carry the spiritual energy of our past mother(s). Cats, on the other hand, represent the father and have a connection to the previous five lifetimes.

We all have karmic connections with the animals in our lives. They come to us as opportunities to repay past debts, undue wrongs, and develop future opportunities. Therefore, in addition to the obvious, unconscionable moral deficiencies that lead some people to beat or torment animals, these actions greatly compound the negative karma of the perpetrators. Similar consequences await those who kill random animals in nature.

I grew up in Texas, which has a strong hunting culture, usually and in most areas centered on deer. Deer are noble, spiritual creatures, and killing them in nearly all circumstances brings about negative karma. I remember my dad always saying that he could never kill a deer because he thought that they were too beautiful. So many people intuitively realize the negative effects of these types of actions without needing to be taught by others. Some members of my family would hunt birds, and I firmly believe that this brought about additional suffering for my family as a whole. Daoists do not eat deer, birds, turtles, snakes, and a number of other creatures because they recognize that eating them will eventually bring about misfortune.

In Daoism, killing is something that is usually limited to self-defense and survival. Although there are sects within Daoism that practice strict vegetarian diets, there are situations in which eating meat is necessary. In most cases it is simply not possible to get all the nutrients the body requires without eating meat. Therefore, it is wise to eat meat when necessary, bur do so mindfully and by maintaining an awareness of the consequences of killing of animals.

Many vegetarians often disagree with this information, but the Daoist research on this subject has been verified over centuries of trial and error. There are vital nutrients in meat that heal and nourish the brain and other vital organs which cannot be garnered through a strict vegetarian diet. Meat contains complex amino acids, proteins, and essential fats that are necessary, in limited amounts, for optimal health and well-being. Daoist do not promote the senseless killing of animals, but there are occasions when borrowing from nature is necessary. From another perspective, eating certain animals in a respectful and mindful way can help them reincarnate faster and achieve merit for giving their life to heal another.

To understand this perspective, it is paramount to realize that Daoists played a central role in stopping the age-old practice of sacrificing animals to the gods. They introduced the practice of burning red and yellow incense in place of sacrificing animals to appease the beings of heaven. Animal welfare and the protection of nature were early causes of Daoists and remain so to this day. They respect the animal kingdom because of the invaluable assistance they provide for humans and the environment. Animals are our friends and partners on earth: they should always be respected and honored.

Unlike many forms of qigong, the dog form can be practiced beneficially during all of the other eleven years of the zodiac. It is powerful because it unites the soul with the spirit, located in the head and near the stomach, respectively. This is accomplished through visualizations that combine various colors and shapes. Cats, unlike dogs, are more about attracting and seizing wealth, whereas dogs represent the cultivation of abilities and opportunities for securing good fortune. Cats, and the energy they embody, are an important counterpart to dogs, often studied together during dog years. They can often be viewed as a yin and yang pairing. Together, these two animals can help tremendously in the development of longevity, success, and emotional stability.

Everything in existence is living and, by practicing meditation and qigong, we can come to know this essential truth more deeply. Much of life depends on our ability to perceive, and those that can see beauty in any one thing will begin to see it everywhere. As we get better at seeing beauty in the world, life becomes lighter and more enjoyable day by day. We find our reflections in the world and the beauty that is outside is also within. Therefore, it is vital for us to clean up and purify our internal experience, so that our external selves can shine brightly throughout the universe.

Past-Life Family

These past-life connections to the animal and plant kingdoms are far-reaching tied to some of the most subtle and profound occurrences in our life. We have had connections to everything and everyone in previous life-times as well, because the entire universe has always been cohesive and reticular. By looking deeply, it becomes apparent that everything we see has some connection with us. The element of mystery within all things that many people feel intuitively is a recognition of this interconnectedness and the sense of belonging that comes with it. If every bit of plant life and every insect we see is part our distant family, any sense of loneliness quickly begins to dissolve. Feelings of loneliness, separation, and depression are only forms of spiritual misunderstanding. When our perception is clear, our true connection to nature is revealed.

If we want to make new friends, whether they are right in front of us or at the ends of the universe, we only need to learn how to communicate clearly with nature. Nature is always there, ready to communicate with us and comfort us when we are down. All of our problems are the result of our limited human perspective, and they can be overcome with greater spiritual awareness. Also, as a part of our spiritual family, plants and trees must naturally be intelligent and alive, otherwise they would not be able to interact with us and heal us when we are sick. Herbs have inherent properties that interact with our internal biology and that of other animals. Even human science and manmade medicines are based upon the observations of nature that our species has made over millennia.

According to the *Yijing*, while the numbers five and six relate to cats, while seven and nine connect to dogs and represent qualities that help us to recognize what is important and improve our circumstances. The relationship between animals and numbers is a vast subject that penetrates deeply into the functions of the universe as a whole.

> In 1994, a Chinese businessman paid 1.7 million USD for a car license plate with 9—a number particularly lucky that year because the Chinese word for "nine" sounds like that for "dog," and 1994 was the year of that animal. (Prettydarkhorse 2012)

As Iwan Suwandy says,

> The number nine is considered the luckiest number because all odd numbers are considered heavenly, and nine is the highest single digit odd number; and the Chinese word for "nine" sounds like the word for "long," as in longevity, or long life. [These homonyms only apply to Cantonese.] Nine also symbolizes the nine layers of heaven, and is associated with yang, male energy. Multiples of nine such as 18, 27, 81 (9 x 9) and 243 (9 x 9 x 9) are regarded as auspicious....
>
> The number seven can be regarded as both lucky and unlucky. It is sometimes seen as unlucky and associated with ghosts because, the Chinese word for "seven" rhythms with that for "certain death." It is often regarded as lucky because the word is also the same as that for "positive energy" and "life force." In northern China, you never see the price 250 Yuan. That is because to say "250" is the same as calling a person crazy. (2013)

In Daoism, the number seven represents an opening, or gateway, akin to a front door. This also has a fengshui application, leading to the principle that it is never wise to live in a place that has a tree directly in front of the front door. Seven is also a number that refers to one's earthly life, correlating it with the secular, fated aspect of existence. It incorporates the idea of worldly, cultural richness as well as the limits of systems and structures that arise from an established foundation. In *Yijing* theory, every number has a specific and multifaceted meaning.

The number eight represents divine luck. Many superstitious people prefer living on the eighth floor of buildings, or having phone numbers with many eights in them. While no life can be considered perfect, the pursuit of perfection in ourselves is nonetheless a worth goal. The hard work and difficulties encountered on the road to progress may be disheartening at times, but self-cultivation and spiritual advancement are well worth the effort. This is why the bodhisattvas swear oaths to continue returning to earth until all mortal beings have reached salvation.

Karmic Connections

Everything in the universe has a purpose and a destiny, and therefore they can also be said to have a life of their own. Recent discoveries in quantum physics have shown that even solid objects vibrate at a high frequency that is invisible to the naked eye. Anything a person creates takes on a life of its own because it is imbued with the purpose and intention of its creator. In many civilizations, people teach that having offspring is the only way to create a lasting legacy, but the objects and ideas that we produce also continue our energy into the future and benefit humanity. There are many ways that we as human beings can create provisions for others. Many great persons—Leonardo DaVinci, Nikola Tesla, Vincent van Gogh, and Isaac Newton—have contributed greatly to the world without being married or having children. The accomplishments of these individuals and many others like them have helped to advance our species and aided the personal growth of countless people.

During the year of the dog, many people are able to realize the benefits from the good deeds they accrued during previous lifetimes. They also can regain the energy of the things they had gathered and lost due to their passing. Personal experiences, opportunities, fortune, marriages, money and children are often the result of actions in previous lifetimes as well as those of ancestors. We each have a storehouse of unmanifested treasure waiting for us but to realize its blessings in this life we must exert our will as it is informed by spiritual understanding. Blessings are rarely bestowed without effort, though the effort required is often not as arduous or direct as we may first assume. Opportunities must be seized, and it is important to "strike while the iron is hot."

Everyone has certain opportunities, natural talents, and tangible assets in life, but nonetheless, fortune favors the prepared. The blessings bestowed upon us can be physical, emotional, mental, or spiritual, and each one enriches life in various ways. The gift of true understanding or enlightenment is often considered the greatest life has to offer. Aristotle, and Socrates before him, agreed that the best life is one of contemplation, self-examination, and open-mindedness. Yet truth can be difficult or even painful to face and accept. When the understanding arises that, from a larger perspective, there are no innocent victims in life, things begin to seem punitive. All the darkness and all the beauty of life go hand-in-hand; one cannot appear without the other. The ancient Daoist Zhuangzi had his understanding of destiny and fate. As Scott Bradley notes,

> To fulfill one's destiny is not to become or achieve something preordained, but simply to thankfully embrace everything that comes one's way. If this is doing, it is all that need be done. And yet, as Zhuangzi says, it is the "hardest thing of all." A parallel analogy might shed some light on this idea of "fulfilling." Guo Xiang, commenting on the relative size of each thing's fated givens, whether the vastness of Peng or the tininess of a quail, tells us that, "Since each fits perfectly into precisely the position it occupies, all are equally far-reaching and unfettered" (Ziporyn). "Fulfilling one's destiny" is fully occupying the totality of one's experience. This is true empowerment. (2012)

Fate is often defined simply as the things we must do. An intuitive sense arises when we are doing what we know we have to, as opposed to doing things that are optional or half-hearted. Spiritual practices were developed to help spur us along, giving us the added energy we need to face our challenges. To accomplish more, additional high-quality energy is required, and spiritual practices help us gather and refine it.

The circumstances we are born into are often based more upon the level of cultivation of the families and communities that we were a part of in previous incarnations. We find ourselves with our current family because we each have something to learn from, and provide for, each other. According to Daoist reincarnation theory, if you are male, your current mother must have been your girlfriend or wife in a previous lifetime. Similarly, if female, you must previously have been married to, or intimate with, your current father. While this may seem strange in Western culture, it is common understanding in many Eastern philosophies, based upon the knowledge of the *Yijing*. This is a manifestation of yin and yang which guarantees spiritual fellowship and reciprocity within family units and across lifetimes. Everyone we come across in life is significant and we have had previous interactions with them in some form. Meetings never occur by mistake: the balance of the universe brings us together.

Diligent spiritual practice mitigates many harmful and karmic past-life influences. Many atrocities in life can be traced back to the misdeeds of a past life, and therefore seeking revenge only propagates this energy, carrying it forward into the future. Everything in life has two sides, including the situations we find ourselves in and the stories we tell. If we reform ourselves and cultivate a spiritual life, our *qi* changes naturally and we can overcome obstacles with grace or avoid them altogether. So many things in life occur by being in the right place at the right time. Cultivating internal harmony through spiritual practice allows these synchronicities to occur with ever greater frequency.

Even the works of great artists are determined and inspired by the feelings and events that linger from previous incarnations. Through a deep understanding of their creations, it can clearly be seen that the past lives of visionary painters, sculptors, and musicians included profound and unique experiences. These individuals break convention and direct humankind toward beauty with the power of their spirit expressed through their works. Their unique perspectives from another time and place influence society and inspire individuals for generations.

The painters of beautiful landscapes, for instance, must have absorbed the beauty that surrounded them by spending time in the woods or by having lived previously as a tree. Having been a tree in the past, we deeply appreciate the beauty of trees in all our senses, forming an experience that yearns for expression. Whatever appears in the mind without planning or forethought has a direct correlation between the thinker and their former self. Humans, and all other forms of life, suffer karma.

Trees and plants are much closer to humans and animals than many people assume. Quantum physics has demonstrated on multiple occasions that plants not only register and respond to pain, but they also recognize and develop relationships with their caretakers. The energy of plants links to the person who waters and cares for them. With this understanding, it may be that on some level plants consider gardeners to be torturers or at least harsh teachers. A blade of grass may be lucky to be born in an open field rather than in someone's well-manicured lawn. The negative karma a person accrues for trimming plants may be negligible but, according to Daoists, chopping down a tree has significant consequences.

The sense of depth and connection that arises while looking at mountains or a tree on the street, evokes the emotional aspect of our relationship with nature. When we become aware of the consciousness of trees and natural structures, they respond in kind, based upon their characteristics. Just as an emotional response is triggered when we interact with a person we are attracted to, nature can evoke a similar response when we interact with it.

Trees can be male or female; they have their own way perceiving this emotional connection. When threatened, they have ways of trying to communicate their fear or displeasure in the hope of avoiding pain and suffering. On the other hand, when we admire a tree and treat it with kindness and respect, it will be happy and seek to help us. Trees have powerful *qi*, so it is unwise to underestimate or speak ill of them. Often an ugly tree survives longer and develops more energy than a classically beautiful or useful one. A tree with fancy wood or a long straight trunk is more valuable because it can be used to make an instrument or build a house, but it does not survive as long.

The wind also responds to our presence and appreciation. With a deeper level of spiritual cultivation, nature responds with ever more profound effects. Before practicing meditation, throw a feather in the breeze and note the direction it blows, then face this direction in your practice. The wind relays a message from nature, providing an example of the connection between the microcosm and the macrocosm, the individual and the universe. Similarly, to ask a deceased relative or spiritual guide a yes or no question during a relatively calm day, light incense before saying a prayer. If the smoke of the incense blows toward the west, it represents an affirmative answer; toward the east, represents a negative answer. This is an important element of human body fengshui.

It is difficult to imagine that everything in the universe is this sensitive, or that human beings could lack the awareness of the consciousness inherent in all things. Even famous paintings, objects, or works of art can embody the soul of a living being. Therefore, when artists say that they are giving birth to a piece, they are not far off. Each act of artistry or mastery requires conception, gestation, pain, and struggle before reaching its final form. Not every work is well-formed enough to become the vessel of a living spirit, but some works go on to change the world. It is often difficult to determine the degree to which the artist's skill is responsible for his or her great works, or the intelligence and spirit that they imbue into it.

Van Gogh created his famous painting Starry Night while looking out the window of an insane asylum. He suffered for most of his life with the pangs of creativity and at times they nearly drove him mad. Perhaps there were some unique and unusual spiritual influences coming through him at that time in such a strange place. All we can do as witnesses is meditate upon the beauty and complexity that this world brings forth for us to admire.

The World as Hologram

In the recent past, some have said that the world is a holographic computer program. The analogy makes sense superficially because with a computer, we can recreate almost anything in a digital space. But, with a deeper analysis, it becomes obvious that computers are based on finite codes that have nowhere near the depth of complexity that nature exhibits. Even with all of advantages of modern science, humans are not advanced enough to create something as seemingly simple and yet infinitely complex, such as a tree. We are not able to create organic spiritual life forms on our own. We can genetically alter things that already exist, but that process is not the same as creation. Consciousness like energy cannot be created or destroyed; it can only be changed from one form to another.

The spiritual energy that serves to inspire the world flow throughout the universe is not the result of a mere hologram. This would be a nihilistic viewpoint that only cheapens our meaning and experience as human beings. In my view, there can be nothing more dehumanizing than viewing life as strictly a series of arbitrary phenomena without meaning or substance. Even if our current reality is a stepping-stone toward a greater form of spiritual existence, it is not without meaning or reality. Everything and every movement in nature has some form of meaning in the greater context of reality. Only when we transcend this reality can we decipher this meaning for ourselves.

The symbiosis takes on many different forms, and energetically everything is dependent on many other things to exist. Yin and yang are concomitant throughout the universe. If there were no wolves, there would be no deer: their energies are interdependent, each one propagating and controlling the other. The full context of these vast and strange relationships can only be deciphered through the *Yijing*. It has been central since ancient times in decoding these very mysteries and in itself uses the workings of nature to decode all things in the universe. A far-reaching system of philosophy and divination, it produces insights much deeper and more eloquent than the human intellect can devise.

Chapter 9

The Building Blocks of Reality

In the universe, everything is unique while simultaneously being comprised of components that are shared with everything else. We are all made from the same material that forms the stars and planets. Our souls and bodies constitute an intricate system of vital energies, which can be represented by symbols, rich with meaning. The *Yijing* shows these universal energies in its hexagrams, composed of six lines stacked vertically. Each feature of our body is formed according to the energy of our soul, and this determines many of our actions and capabilities. But externally, it is the stars that have the greatest influence on daily life. After that, it is the mountains, which greatly influence weather patterns and divide the landscape, that are the most influential.

In fengshui, mountains are said to represent dragons. They come in two types: sitting and standing. Learning to tell the difference requires skill and intuition, but anyone who has spent a lot of time in the mountains knows that they have a strong, unique, and palpable energy. The energy of mountains is like a fingerprint: it cannot be mimicked or copied. Each type of ecosystem, from the oceans to the deserts, have distinctive qualities that attract equally idiosyncratic spiritual energies. Sensitive people and children can often perceive the more subtle differences of these locations, but most only notice the physical.

Land and environment give rise to various types of people and cultures around the world, not the other way around. Humans intrinsically settle near areas that contain abundant natural resources or beneficial geographic formations so they can prosper. These features are so important that these groups will readily fight for the right to inhabit the areas that surround them. Many wars have been fought over the course of millennia in areas like Greece, Egypt, and the like that have moderate climates, scenic views, and life-giving waters. All living beings want to live in the location with the best possible fengshui, but this is often understood in a different modality.

When given the choice between living on flat land or a hilltop, most people choose the hilltop. This choice is mostly intuitive, but there are also specific combinations of wind, water, and earth that bring about a sense of peace for inhabitants. Areas with better fengshui are intrinsically more beautiful because of the diversity of nature that gathers there. The preference of environment is largely due to the spirit of the individual. For instance, a person who dreams of living in a wide, open grassland most likely has the spirit of an ox or a horse.

There are many motivating factors that contribute to what we find enjoyable and preferable, which is why it is important to know ourselves and what brings us peace. While motivations may be unique and varied, it is generally true that most people prefer to live in places with good fengshui. The influence of nature is divine, and it is not to be underestimated. Nature maintains balance, helping all things to grow and develop, and we are intuitively drawn to the influences that bring us this balance and harmony.

Daoists describe the myriad beings in the universe as composed of various combinations of natural energy. For instance, water and sun combine to make male humans and animals; add lunar energy, and females take shape. Water and starlight create physical objects through influence and inspiration, while water and air give rise to trees and plants. The energy of earth, then, in the form of hills and mountains, creates an arena for all of these elements to live and flourish. Mountains are unique because they stand alone and independently, with the power to govern the flow of air and water.

On earth, the five phases combine to form life and everything in nature. For millennia, Daoists have studied these materials and their processes in order to understand the universe and themselves more deeply. Some even dedicated their entire life to studying just one subject or aspect. All human intelligence stands on the shoulders of these giants, and by seeing existence in their way we may come to realize the underpinnings of our development. It is one thing to learn from others, but it is a far greater task to discover knowledge for ourselves.

Water and Sunlight

Modern science has demonstrated that the negative ions created by the ocean and its movements greatly benefit all life and help form the atmosphere. The abundance of this energy is responsible for the calm, relaxed feeling people experience near the ocean. As these ions calm the body and relax the nervous system, the mind becomes tranquil in a feeling that is unmistakable and palpable.

It is a vital for human beings to be connected to the elements because of their healing, grounding, and harmonizing effects. All bodies of water, including oceans, lakes, rivers, streams, springs, and ponds provide these healing effects and beneficial ions. These water sources have been used by spiritual adepts for eons:

> Negative ions are present in the air we breathe in and they are also present in our bodies. The degree to which negative ions contribute to overall well-being and health is scientifically proven: they neutralize free radicals, revitalize cell metabolism, enhance immune function, purify the blood, balance the autonomic nervous system, and promote deep sleep and healthy digestion. On the other hand, in polluted cities, crowded areas and in confined spaces such as offices, industrial areas, schools and cars, you will find the highest concentration of unhealthy positive ions.
>
> The most important benefit of negative ions is that they clear the air of airborne allergens such as pollen, mold spores, bacteria and viruses. Besides they also clear the air of dust, pet dander and cigarette smoke. "Negative ions

> perform this function by attaching themselves to positively charged particles in large numbers and negatively charging those particles. As a result, these viruses, bacteria and pollen spores become too heavy to remain airborne and are thus prevented from entering your breathing passage where they can make you fall sick. In other words, negative ions form a protective circle around you." (Anderson 2014)

The same restorative energy is imparted by sunlight, scientifically proven to be a mood elevator. Some places, such as Seattle and Alaska, experience frequent inclement weather and clearly have higher rates of depression because people there do not get sunlight for long periods of time:

> Sunlight and darkness trigger the release of hormones in your brain. Exposure to sunlight is thought to increase the brain's release of a hormone called serotonin. Serotonin is associated with boosting mood and helping a person feel calm and focused. At night, darker lighting triggers the brain to make another hormone called melatonin. This hormone is responsible for helping you sleep.
>
> Without enough sun exposure, your serotonin levels can dip. Low levels of serotonin are associated with a higher risk of major depression with seasonal pattern (formerly known as seasonal affective disorder or SAD). This is a form of depression triggered by the changing seasons.
>
> A mood boost isn't the only reason to get increased amounts of sunlight. There are several health benefits associated with catching moderate amounts of rays.
>
> Decreased sun exposure has been associated with a drop in your serotonin levels, which can lead to major depression with seasonal pattern. The light-induced effects of serotonin are triggered by sunlight that goes in through the eye. Sunlight cues special areas in the retina, which triggers the release of serotonin. So, you're more likely to experience this type of depression in the winter time, when the days are shorter.
>
> Due to this connection, one of the main treatments for depression with seasonal pattern is light therapy, also known as phototherapy. You can get a light therapy box to have at home. The light from the box mimics natural sunlight that stimulates the brain to make serotonin and reduces excess melatonin. (Nall 2018)

Sunlight is critical to mental health, and this is one of the main reasons that Daoists avoid wearing sunglasses. People with sensitive eyes or situations that involve extreme exposure are exceptions, but in general it is beneficial to let the eyes adjust to natural light as much as possible. Another detailed and revealing book on this subject is Jacob Lieberman's *Light Medicine of the Future*. He points out that people organized "sun clinics" until the late 1800s, receiving nothing but sunlight for various conditions. Although not scientifically proven, the healing power of the sun has been advocated by Daoists, ancient Greeks, forward-thinking professionals, and qigong masters for thousands of years.

Lieberman goes on to state that many people can overcome PTSD-type symptoms through the use of different frequencies of light. In his clinical experiments, patients experienced powerful emotional reactions to viewing various colors of the light spectrum through specially constructed glasses. This also reinforces the Daoist emphasis of healing through the perception of color. Color healing has been practiced extensively in temples and monasteries for centuries to treat a variety of issues, especially emotional ones. Since the eyes are directly connected to the brain via the optic nerve, they closely connect to our mental processes and the subjects we choose to focus on. Another prominent researcher in this field also described the benefits of color therapy:

> Eventually, Dr. Ott turned his attention toward monitoring the beneficial effects of full spectrum lighting on certain human physiological conditions. Dr. Ott discovered that the color temperature of lights affects mental health, with balanced light reducing hyperactivity in classrooms and reducing negative behavior in prisons and mental health facilities.
>
> Dr. Ott discovered that even an individual cells' ability to properly reproduce in plants, animals and humans is affected by variances in lighting. Most importantly, he realized that light entering the body through the eyes controls and regulates our brain chemistry which in turn affects how we feel and function. (Ott 2014)

Sunlight interacts with us daily, and in this way heaven sees everything. The sun, being the primary driver of life, is central to all cultures and the most instantly recognizable phenomenon on earth. As the engine of nature, sunlight is one of the most highly regarded energies in Daoism.

Everyone knows the sun and its importance to life on earth, but it is also considered common and often goes unnoticed throughout the day. This gives it a humble quality: the sun is always present but never demands attention. Few people regard any form of nature as fondly as the sun, with few exceptions. Phrases such as, "everyone has their day in the sun," and "the sun will rise again soon," express the joy and admiration that people have for the energy that this celestial body provides. Without its constant presence, our existence would not be possible.

The sun represents popularity, exaltation, radiance, recognition, and success, all represented by the sun card of a tarot deck and deeply engrained in our psychology. Even though the sun may burn, it mainly gives life, and anyone who has endured a long, cold winter knows the incredible value of the sun's vitalizing energy. Also, sunlight is the primary driver of Nine Palaces Qigong, the most effective form of Daoist meditation. Harnessing this energy in our bodies imbues health, happiness, and creativity. Many pagan religions worship the sun along with trees and plants for the same reasons of rejuvenation. Humanity has recognized and appreciated the power of our most brilliant heavenly body for tens of thousands of years.

Daoists emphasize the importance of the sun's energy because of the amazing energy it provides, which allows us to enhance our spiritual nature through the practice of qigong. The vitalizing quality of the sun's *qi* is perhaps the most noticeable aspect of nature. Every living being loves the feeling of a crisp sunny day, and it's difficult to be unhappy when the weather is good. Good weather is definitely one of nature's most beautiful blessings. It allows for good health, more energy, and the freedom to perform more activities. People worldwide regularly pay hefty sums to live in climates with beautiful weather.

As humans, we are capable of overcoming many limitations, but without the prerequisite energies of the heavenly bodies none would be possible. Ideally, each of us should have a sense of reverence for our star. All living beings have to work and remain in motion to survive and thrive. Even earth, metal, and rocks must endure pressure and stressful forces to be transformed. In Daoism, everything is thought to contain life force and spirit to a certain degree and everything has to work hard in order to fulfill its proper function and contribute to harmony in the universe. The people, places, and natural forces that surround us every day assist all our spiritual efforts. No person is an island: we all rely on teachers and great people who paved the road for our success. Macroscopically everything works in conjunction toward further evolution and greater harmony.

Although all forms of life are important and have their advantages, it is nevertheless a rare and magnificent gift to exist as a human being. Our ability to think and feel deeply allows for remarkable self-awareness. Our levels of stress and sense of separation are difficult at times, but these are the sacrifices required to become heavenly beings. As discussed in earlier chapters, the wait for a human incarnation can be long but its benefits are majestic and awe-inspiring.

Qigong Practice

Most people live near sources of water, and the best homes are near oceans where negative ions are most abundant. Similarly, the best places to perform qigong have prominent natural features such as water, sunlight, wind, and mountains. Bountiful natural *qi* enhances the practice and accelerates spiritual evolution. Five Centers Practice relies on moonlight and nourishes yin-*qi*, whereas Nine Palaces Qigong works with the energy of sunlight and cultivates yang. The presence of water enhances both forms and sustains the body as a whole. The *qi* that comprises everything on earth and is fostered in qigong practice benefits both the individual and the surroundings.

By meditating in nature, we can help the trees to produce more oxygen. *Qi* helps trees to grow and release any negative energy they may harbor. Qigong nurtures this mutually beneficial relationship. Since Five Centers Practice is designed for nighttime and Nine Palaces Qigong for daytime, there is no wrong time to engage in qigong. The best times for sun-based practice are 8 to 9 am, 11 am to 1 pm, and 4 to 5 pm. Then yang energy is at its most important points in the daily cycle. Five Centers Practice is best done from 7 to 11 pm. However, sometimes the optimal time to practice is based on practitioner's zodiac animal.

We are all unique, and our age group, body type, interests, diet, and many other facets of personal experience contribute to our sense of self. By observing the ways apples grow and develop, we can more deeply understand how qigong practice can benefit us. An apple that grows on the north side of a tree, in the shade of the leaves, will not get as large, bright, and firm as one that grows in the full light of the sun on the south side. Similarly, qigong helps us to grow to our full potential and enhances our vibrancy and color. Through the practice of qigong, we can rectify any shortcomings in health, creativity, love, fortune, and other aspects.

Children ideally live happy and blissful lives because their growth and development are overseen and supported by adults who have mastered the skills the child is developing. Once children have expertise and enter the world of adulthood, they come across limitations that are more difficult to surmount. Similarly, as adults we can often become complacent in life and sedentary in lifestyle, and avoid wrestling with our limitations. Through the practice of qigong, we can go beyond our personal limitations, achieve goals, and develop new skills that we never realized were possible. Many times, qigong will take us past our limitations naturally and spontaneously. It isn't until afterwards that we begin to realize that we have developed into a much more capable individual step-by step.

In Daoism, a round, circular shape represents longevity. This could be rephrased to state that a well-rounded person can endure many things, and will therefore live a long life. Heavenly bodies exist for eons, are always roughly spherical, and move in rounded orbits. Similarly, qigong practitioners develop longevity by making their physical, emotional, and spiritual bodies as round as possible. Without these practices, we eventually become stiff, brittle, and weak in a number of ways. Without a well-rounded personality, people are likely to become unnecessarily stressed and jaded with life. Narrow-minded thinking is an example of a stiff, rigid personality. People like this expect only the worst outcomes, while nature clearly demonstrates that success is just as likely as failure. Nature supports people who have reverence for it and respect its power.

Spiritual practice creates change at a deep level. Qigong develops health by softening our internal biology and increasing the flexibility of our deepest tissues. Nothing is gentler than air, and qigong utilizes this energy through special forms of breathing to massage our vital organs and rebalance the body.

A compassionate heart is the only real prerequisite for these energetic spiritual practices. Qigong requires a good moral, spiritual quality, otherwise it is ineffective and can be potentially dangerous. Practicing meditation with evil intentions in the heart prevents growth and wastes energy. Of course, making mistakes can inspire us to alter our approach to a situation, but the ultimate lesson is to develop compassion. This is key with all things in life, because our intent is what helps us reach the right destination in the end. On our spiritual journey, we must strive to have the best intentions, backed up by positive actions, otherwise the mind remains focused on fantasy rather than integrity.

The Gaze

A kind, compassionate heart is the foundation from which many other skills can grow and develop. To be truly successful in life, these qualities must be exercised, supported by empathy. One of the most important attributes is a strong gaze. There are many things about a person's appearance that can be altered with cosmetics, exercise, surgery, diet, and habits. However, the gaze will always mirror the heart. The eyes are the windows of the soul and reflect the essence of the individual. Daoists often say that the left eye represents the sun, the right eye symbolizes moon, and the third eye combines these two energies to form the brightness of the stars. The human body is a microcosm of the universe, and in this context the eyes represent heaven.

The gaze is trained through observation, and just as looking closely at things, especially natural features, develops physical sight, visualization enhances the imagination. In Daoist medical theory, all illnesses are correlated with animal imagery. For instance, a contagious infection, such as influenza, would be symbolically represented by the rat, which is commonly responsible for spreading these types of illness. Therefore, with a strong imagination, a person could envision a cat during meditation to rid the body of its rat-like energy. Similarly, by looking at the stars, the ocean, or the mountains, we cultivate a stronger sense of self and get rid of limiting thoughts and beliefs. These practices not only develop the ability to visualize and sharpen the gaze, but they also change the appearance of the eyes.

Many animal lovers feel that zoos can be cruel institutions, but in addition to the rehabilitation that provide, they are also healthy for both children and adults since they help them create balance in their personality by developing their capacity for vision. There are always two ways to perceive all situations, and while the animals in a zoo are in a restricted environment, they are also accruing good karma by allowing humans to observe them. Visiting zoos can be seen as a form of treatment for many psychological and emotional conditions. Animals have metaphysical properties and abundant *qi* that affect their surrounding environment in numerous ways. This concept is easier to understand in the context of pet ownership. Owning pets is also a way to gain good karma, provided that you care for them properly. Developing a caring relationship with a pet can greatly benefit a person's character. Modern science cannot prove this, but Daoists and clinical scientists have come to understand these effects through centuries of trial and error and clinical research.

The quality of a person's gaze can solve many problems. People communicate a great deal through body language, and the quality of the eyes forms a large part of non-verbal communication. Sometimes a strong stare is enough to scare a misbehaving person into acting appropriately. Many parents have used this technique to get their children to behave. Spouses and romantic partners also communicate a great deal through looks. There are many instances where a gaze can convey a great deal of important information. Often it is easy to tell if another person would make a good friend, colleague, or partner with just a quick glance.

Most of all, people's gaze illustrates their level of mental acuity as well as the depth and quality of their thinking. With this information, it becomes possible to assess how much the person can achieve in life. The quality expressed in a person's eyes can be subtle and nuanced, but it nonetheless conveys a great deal of information. Many leaders in commerce, arts, and politics naturally have a deep, brilliant, clear, and determined look in their eyes. A deep, penetrating gaze is a sure sign of an intelligent person, and everyone who possesses such a stare surely has many unique strengths. These individuals can often realize their goals with minimal effort by leveraging their powerful intellect.

Each type of illness or condition can be mitigated by envisioning a specific subject, and viewing these subjects in reality with the naked eye can often be even more effective. To relieve depression and reduce stress on the heart, visualizing a small baby is often helpful. Mothers always look at a child with affection, and this energy has great healing potential. Therefore, looking at or imagining a small child in your heart will generate a sense of love which may not be readily available in daily life. This form of healing is cost-free and provides a sense of support both empowering and communal. By recognizing the subtle blessings that surround us every day, we can harness self-healing and make beneficial changes in our lives no matter what difficulties we face.

Often, when asked to imagine the happiest and purest things in the world, our minds immediately turn to newborn creatures of all kinds, be they babies, puppies, kittens, or chicks. These thoughts evoke the compassion that each of us has for life itself and the awe of how harmonious and supportive the universe can be. Innocence has a powerful energy that can heal us at a profoundly deep level.

Under the Sea

According to fengshui, the sunlight at sunrise and at noon has uniquely powerful healing potential. The light at sunrise can help treat eye conditions and greatly boost physical energy. Especially when there is a subtle mist in the air, it boosts the function of the liver and enhances the performance of the eyes. Cloudy days, on the other hand, are considered the best conditions for relieving various other types of illness. Fisherman are more successful during cloudy days because the low atmospheric pressure causes the fish to rise toward the surface of the water. Similarly, low air pressure causes invasive yin energy, which is responsible for illness, to rise to the surface of the body, where it is easier to treat. The atmospheric condition's effect of fishing is as follows:

> • Clouds: Clouds can prevent light from getting into the water. This is when most fish are feeding and will be found all over the area you are fishing in instead of congregating in one area.
>
> • Rain: Rain is perfect for fishing, and is one of the most ideal weather conditions you can ask for. The rain can wash more insects and different kinds of bait in the water, which creates a great feeding period for many fish. The rain in the water can also hide your line or lure easier too
>
> • Pressure Changes: When the barometric pressure changes, fish naturally become more active. If the pressure falls too low or becomes too high, then you may lose that fishing window. Similar to when there is too much sunlight, severe pressure changes can cause the fish to swim lower and even hide. (Karsen 2023)

Some fish hunt and graze on the bottom, while others stay closer to the surface. Daoists describe ocean eighty-one levels, each with its own unique characteristics. They also believe that the ocean reflects the vastness of the universe, that both represent infinitely expansive environments, and that human beings evolved from fish, and later, birds. Modern scientists often disagree with this assessment, but Daoists have a strong argument for such a proclamation. Fish share many qualities with human beings such as a central spine, pink flesh, and a rib cage. Then, flying fish evolved and developed the first primitive lungs. Thesy eventually made their way onto land and became the ancestors of mammals. Furthermore, Daoists also describe half-human and half-aquatic creatures living under the water, similar to entities like mermaids, still believed to exist today.

There are a handful of unexplained underwater civilizations that were discovered on the ocean floor, including the pyramids of Yonaguni island in Japan. The architecture here is akin to the Aztec structures of Central America, yet they are underwater. This site and others like it may be the remnants of ancient unknown civilizations that sank beneath the sea due to seismic changes; then again, maybe they were built by intelligent underwater creatures. Scientists regularly discover more about the high levels of intelligence and emotional capacity of whales, dolphins, and other sea creatures, and Daoists often profess that dolphins are more intelligent than human beings in many ways.

Mermaids have a long history in Chinese culture, and several texts describe their encounters with humans. For example:

> Chinese mermaids are called *jiaoren* 鲛人. Their appearance is the same as in Western tales, but in addition to their beautiful appearance, the Chinese mermaids are also outstanding craftswomen.
>
> According to the *Soushen ji* 搜神记 (In Search of the Supernatural), a compilation of legends about ghosts and spirits, whose author Gan Bao was believed to have lived in the 4th century, Chinese mermaids lived in the South Sea, spent their days weaving cloth, and if she cried, her tears would turn into pearls.

> The *Shuyui ji* 述异记 (Tales of the Marvelous), commonly ascribed to Ren Fang (460-508), describes weaving cloth in more detail. The cloth produced by mermaids was called "dragon yarn" (*jiaoxiao sha* 蛟绡纱). It was as beautifully white as frost and could never become wet, even in water. Some other legends say that Chinese mermaids sell dragon yarn to people, and the market where they trade is the mirage that mortal people see. (Sun 2015)

Many species still remain undiscovered yet are described similarly in texts of ancient civilizations that were isolated from one another. In addition to ancient Daoists, the Egyptians also depicted their deity Horus as half-bird and half-man. The famous Eye of Horus is a symbol of intelligence and the mastery of solar energy. While Daoists do not disagree with the theory of evolution, they also believe that certain nuances of it are still misunderstood. The histories and mythologies of many ancient cultures allude to our shared ancestry with fish as well as birds. Daoists believe that these connections will be understood more fully by modern science in due course.

Chapter 10

A Grain of Rice

A Daoist maxim states that the entire universe can be contained in a single grain of rice. This principle is exemplified in all living creatures and all natural features, as the smallest part of any complex system is a complete representation of the larger whole. Just as a single human hair contains the DNA of the entire individual, so too does a grain of rice contain vast secrets of the universe. Even a single intact cell contains all the information necessary to recreate the entire organism. This has been demonstrated through experiments with cloning. When modern scientists conducted studies on rice, their findings closely matched ideas by ancient Daoists.

> The two blueprints reveal that a rice plant probably contains more genes than a person does. Whereas estimates of the number of genes in the human genome lie between 30,000 and 40,000, indica rice contains between 45,000 and 56,000 genes, and japonica rice could have as many as 63,000 genes. (Graham 2002)

Although the physical body can be cloned to an exacting degree, the soul is unique to each individual. While the body may influence our decisions and represent current limitations, the soul is the ultimate basis from which decision-making capacity arises. Even clones do not share the same essence of being, and two souls cannot inhabit the same body. Scientists will inevitably explore the principles of cloning further for the benefit of all life, however, organic reproduction is always healthier and more wholesome. With organic procreation the soul and essence of the organism is allowed to form naturally and remains unencumbered on its spiritual journey.

While the body can now be produced in new ways, we still only have absolute authority over the organs and tissues we are born with, so we should use their faculties mindfully to achieve our fullest potential. We can only conduct ourselves properly if we cultivate good energy with spiritual practices.

While scientists are increasingly aware of how genes interact with cells to produce physical traits, they are still far from understanding how these structures determine a person's destiny and decisions. An ancient maxim states that "wisdom perfects art, and art perfects wisdom," and modern science is only beginning to understand that relationship it has with spiritual concepts such as the soul. In the past, many things that could not be explained scientifically were considered to be in the realm of the spirit or a form of witchcraft. However, with discoveries such as Heisenberg's uncertainty principle, it is becoming clear that there are aspects of reality that will never be fully explained by science and therefore the understanding of spiritual matters is necessary.

Just as priests in history considered scientists' work as be heretical and nefarious, modern scientists and materialists often see people of faith as ignorant and detrimental. This is the principle of yin and yang at work in the realm of knowledge. There will always be two sides to this discussion, and the ultimate truth must take both contexts into account. In order for us as a society to be healthy and function properly, we have to embrace things as they are, not as we would like them to be. Harmony within ourselves and with others requires us to understand the dynamics of these two modalities and combine them in all of our thoughts and actions.

Most humans are not capable of fully embracing these principles from birth, and so we must endure conflicts and struggles to attain them. Even people with abundant wealth and opportunities are often dissatisfied with life until suffering drives them to know themselves more deeply. Without shedding compulsive desires through spiritual effort, we cannot be fully content with our place in this world. We all arrive with past karma to be resolved, but this does not prevent the collective from embracing a more holistic perspective. The combined effort of many small good deeds and intentions ultimately maintains balance in society.

The laws of karma always place us in the perfect circumstances for our maximal growth and development as spiritual beings. Therefore, whatever our heart truly desires is achievable, if we are willing to make sacrifices. This is an ancient concept. Since the ultimate purpose of life is spiritual growth, if we do not willingly surrender our shortcomings, circumstances will force us to do so. Therefore, science and spirituality are not in conflict with one another, but complementary.

Many people only enquire about the esoteric side of life once they realize that ultimate happiness is impossible to attain through conventional means. As a result, many highly intelligent people eventually come to the conclusion that there must be something more to life than materialism. An "us versus them" attitude always fails to see half of the situation. We always make decisions based upon our current, limited understanding, and the truth is always larger than our singular perspective. We all have the potential to create more meaning in our lives, but this requires the wisdom to see past our limitations. Though each of us sees things differently, this does not prevent us from finding common ground or working together. No matter how vast our differences are, a noble intention can still bring us together in harmony.

Understanding the universe requires an awareness of both objective and subjective perspectives. The emotional, personal experiences of each individual are just as real and valid as the laws of physics, mathematics, and other sciences. If matter was lifeless and static, emotions would have no place in reality and our individual experiences would be illusory. Most people are chasing after an emotional high or peak experience. They are not looking to create a material structure just for its own sake but desire a feeling of accomplishment and meaning. Nobody can give your life purpose: this can only be cultivated in your heart. Thus, we appreciate rewards for nothing not nearly as much as for things we earned by our efforts.

The *Daode jing* states, "The Dao that can be spoken of is not the true Dao." This means that, while you can experiment and learn from others, the ultimate meaning in life lies in experiencing life itself and living by its highest principles. Similarly, if you want to truly understand the game of football, you must play it. You may know the rules and strategies, but you will never get to feel the emotional highs and lows that come from pouring your heart into the sport. Only those who play the game themselves obtain the meaningful, rich experiences that are at its essence.

Of course, our lives are not a game and there are spiritual ramifications for our actions, therefore the experience of life is not trivial. However, it essential to illustrate that we must participate in life on a deep, heartfelt level to fully experience and understand it. This is why we need to train our unique skill sets to live up to our potential and participate in the unfolding of our spiritual journey. Our fate is determined by cultivating innate skills and talents that would otherwise remain dormant. If we do not work at developing our abilities, we will not be able to grasp the larger meaning behind events as they unfold. But with proper training, we can begin to understand the events around us as well as our own feelings more deeply and continue to succeed. Modern society often provides many comforts, such as food, shelter, water, entertainment, and relationships, but without an active spiritual dynamic, most people will always notice something lacking in their lives.

The amount of energy and information contained in a single grain of rice is vast. According to Daoists, the smallest things in the universe are often the most significant, and they are always intimately related to the largest, most impactful events. Rice is an example of this because, although quite small, it fesds millions of people and animals. Small things such as rice, seeds, bees, earthworms, and ants all greatly contribute to the environment and make the existence of more complex life possible.

We realize all our greatest dreams and highest goals by taking many small steps. Anything worth achieving in the material world begins with a foundation of non-material elements such as morality, truthfulness, tenacity, and dedication. They are the fuel that drives us toward the realization of our goals. These correlations often go unnoticed, but it is clear that they are a significant part of our ability to manifest our desires. Spiritual cultivation and development are accomplished with these same methods. The power of our character and our spirit leads to further growth.

The Clouds Above

All of nature relies upon the interplay between light and shadow; heat and cold. Therefore, clouds play an important role in the integrity of various natural elements, such as water and crops. On cloudy days, people often experience joint pain, muscle tightness, and exacerbation of chronic issues. In fact, many can predict inclement weather because these issues will manifest as and when atmospheric pressure drops. This is often more accurate than the forecasts of meteorologists. Many animals have this ability as well. Cows, for instance, will lay down on the ground the day before it is going to rain. All things are connected, and by understanding the signs, we can accurately predict future events.

The body responds to these weather phenomena because it contains up to seventy percent water. Women and their menstrual cycles are also heavily connected to these types of phenomena.

> A synchronous relationship between the menstrual cycle and lunar rhythm was confirmed by investigative data: Among 826 female volunteers with a normal menstrual cycle, aged between 16 and 25 years, a large proportion of menstruations occurred around the new moon (28.3%), while at other times during the lunar month the proportion of menstruations occurring ranged between 8.5–12.6%; the difference was significant ($p<0.01$). (Law 1986, 45)

In Chinese, the term "monthly flow" (*yuejing* 月經) refers to the menstrual or lunar cycle and signifies female essence. Conversely, men's semen is considered male essence. The egg and the energy of menstruation are physical manifestations of a woman's life force, as is the semen of a man. Males and females can retain their essential life force through longevity training. When this practice is mastered, female practitioners can delay menstruation for an indefinite period of time. This potent energy is then recycled into the body to help it rejuvenate and regenerate. Life energy can be used to create a new form of life through procreation, but it can also enhance an already existing form of life through cultivation.

These methods of training have always been closely guarded secrets, een while they were practiced over thousands of years. A passage from the *Daode jing* is often used to describe the way people react to them: "The wise man, when hearing of Dao, immediately adopts it; the average man half believes it and half doubts it; while the fool, upon hearing of Dao, laughs." Nothing in life is achieved without sacrifice, and the principle of yin and yang guarantees that all sacrifices are rewarded in time. Not only do these forms of training frequently yield health benefits, but they also inhibit the process of aging.

Five Centers Practice

Five Centers Practice harnesses the energy of the moon and is usually practiced on the 1st and 15th days of the lunar month, that is, during new and full moon. This is because the moon's energy is most potent then and the ocean waves are larger and more frequent. As the moon's energy pulls on the water in the oceans, so it also effects the water in our bodies.

Everything in nature is cyclical, and these cycles govern our lives. Even our thoughts and feelings proceed in repeating patterns. At certain times of day, we may feel energetic and inspired; at others, our bodies require rest. Upon waking, many people feel groggy and unaware due to the slowing of blood and *qi* flow and the accumulation of yin-*qi* overnight. During sleep, the body is vulnerable to attack by outside pathogens and wayward energies. This is yet another reason why many cultures placed great emphasis on fengshui. Nearly every living creature intuitively recognizes the importance of having a warm, safe place to sleep. In the proper environment, sleep is rejuvenating and healing. As the body ages, it requires more rest in order to maintain its energy levels. Children wake up feeling energetic and excited because their energy levels are fully restored while they sleep. Elderly people, on the other hand, often wake up numerous times during the night and require more sleep to feel energized.

This is the Dao's way of spurring growth and development in the universe. As cycles begin to lose energy, new life is sown and new energy rejuvenates them. Understanding this concept helps us maintain balance in the face of adversity. If our lives do not seem to make sense, we may feel discouraged, but these disruptions are often precursors of the appearance of fresh energy and new life. We often become complacent and habituated to life's patterns, but when our career, relationship, pet, or friend is no longer around in the same way, our sense of peace is disrupted. By embracing whatever comes our way and not get discouraged by what we face, we maintain integrity and maximize the resulting growth.

All things have their time, and when their time is up, they go away only to reappear again later in a new form. Daoist immortality requires the ability to fully embrace these changes and leverage them toward further prosperity. Everything in the universe faces cycles of birth, growth, decay, death, and rebirth. These concepts are not unique to Daoism, they are also espoused by Buddhism, science and many philosophical ideologies. However, Daoist principles are based largely on this concept of constant cyclical change.

Through working with Five Centers Practice on the new and full moon days of each month, we humble ourselves before the heavenly bodies above and align ourselves with the cycles of time in a natural and ancient way. By meditating in this manner, we let heaven know that we are ready to honor the natural principles of the universe, create harmony in ourselves, society, and nature.

Right Timing

Understanding cycles can be used to great benefit by embracing the times of growth, and harnessing the energy of decline. In Chinese medicine, many doctors treat certain conditions only on specific days and at specific times. Called chronotherapy or chronological treatment, this is an invaluable tool for healing. Similarly, Chinese herbalists carefully choose specific times to harvest plants, since the healing effects of herbs are maximized when harvested during the correct season and right time of day. By understanding the precise moment when a plant is ready, its nutritional value and *qi* can be utilized to treat more serious conditions. Some herbs, such as winter melon, are even named according to the season in which they are harvested to emphasize this point.

The first tea leaves gathered each year are more expensive and have a superior taste because they were exposed to the fresh air and bright sunlight of early spring. Similarly, mulberry leaves are best when harvested at night during the fall because the additional moisture from the dewy air brings out their rich flavors. By adjusting our lifestyle to seasons and days, we can all cultivate extra energy and momentum in our lives.

Small advantages can accrue over time until they form great benefits to personal growth. When we have momentum, it is easy to see how we can move ahead and take advantage of opportunities, but without it, it is difficult to make headway. Stock traders, for example, are always seeking perfectly timed opportunities to earn extra profit. In one way or another, everyone wants to maximize their luck through timing—whether getting a good deal on a house or buying a car. Buying low and selling high is one of the foundations of capitalism and a prosperous economy.

Fishermen also rely heavily on the timing of daily cycles. Between the hours of 3 and 5 am, fish are most active and can be found in abundance near the water's surface. Chinese doctors similarly rely on sunlight cycles, known that at certain times of day a particular illness will rise to the surface of the body and is thus easier to treat. Then again, during the day abundant yang energy of the environment can be utilized to treat patients, making treatments more effective. Also, typically during the evening, symptoms grow worse and illnesses thrive due to the lack of yang-*qi*. Even Western physicians often agree that a fever will be at its worst during the evening. Statistically, just as illnesses become worse during nighttime, most people also tend to become ill or die in the winter. Both at midnight and the winter solstice yang energy is at a low while yin is high, matching their respective cycles.

Morning and midday are considered the spring and summer of the day, and abundance of yang-*qi* at these times allows improved health and increased physical energy. Changes occur more rapidly when energy is abundant, and the ability to make adjustments leads to success during these times. Conversely, situations that occur at night, such as late-night phone calls, tend to be negative or bear little fruit in the long run. This is true for both business and personal situations. When a new opportunity presents itself in the winter of the day (during nighttime), it may not have sufficient energy to come to long-term success.

Each season, daily and yearly, has its advantages and disadvantages. Abundant yang provides the energy to accomplish goals, but it can also lead to exhaustion; abundant yin energy allows for rest and balance, but it also lacks the power to fight off illness and negativity. It is up to us as individuals to adjust our lifestyle and habits to these environmental changes. Various forms of qigong have been devised to take advantage of these cycles and the benefits that each phase provides. By integrating ourselves and our actions with the cycles of nature, we can overcome limitation and cultivate ever greater levels of spiritual energy.

Scheduling for Weather

In addition to regularly timed cycles, the weather also plays an important role in the way Daoists schedule their actions. Sunny days are more conducive to certain activities than cloudy or rainy days, yet the same principles apply. Sunny days produce a much higher amount of yang energy, while rainy days contain an abundance of yin. Therefore, sunny days are great for physical activities, exercise, and healing. Cloudy days, on the other hand, lend themselves to nourishing activities, rest, and reading. In this way, the weather is a message from heaven directing us toward actions that are currently needed. By not going outdoors on cloudy or windy days and sleeping during rain-storms, the body can adjust to environmental changes and grow in longevity.

The human body is at its weakest during inclement weather, partly because the low atmospheric pressure increases stress on the heart, so during these times it is best to avoid stress or exertion. Cloudy days are also days when emotions rise to the surface to be processed and dealt with. By sleeping then, relationship friction with loved ones is reduced and the subconscious mind can process emotions effortlessly as it engages in dreaming. When you combine sleeping during bad weather with meditation during clear skies, emotional health improves greatly. The sunshine that appears from 8 to 9 am is pure gold, and this light has the ability to lift our emotions, reducing depression. Similarly, the light of a full moon from 8 to 9 pm also reduces depression, allowing positive emotions to thrive without being inhibited by limiting beliefs.

In Daoism, sunshine symbolizes mental clarity and happiness, whereas cloudiness represents distraction and emotions of all kinds. This is one of ways nature uses to signal the best strategies for maximum growth on any particular day. Sunlight also represents success and financial gain. While water represents money itself, sunlight represents financial literacy and the ability to manage money well. On busy retail streets, shops on the side that receives more sunlight, especially during the morning hours, often have as much as forty percent more business than those on the shady side. This is because people always want to be in the sunshine, either consciously or unconsciously, especially when the weather is drafty or cold. The sun provides that extra few degrees of heat and clarity which makes us feel at our best.

By following the cycles of nature more closely, it becomes apparent that the people who live the longest generally have a solid, regular routine. They rise with the sun and go to sleep when it sets. Many people who achieve great longevity have a regular routine, but beyond this many aspects of their lives are similar to those of their peers. Of course, some people work at night and prefer to rest while everyone else is busy, which has its merits, but in general, sleeping at night is a good plan. In the modern world, many people use artificial light in order to work extra hours, thereby burning the candle at both ends. This is not necessarily detrimental, however the nighttime hours should be used properly by meditating, deepen our spiritual connections, and preparing for the following day. When the rooster crows, it is a sign from heaven that yang energy has arrived and the active phase of the day begins.

Wind and Thunder

Wind surrounds us at all times, and it always seems to have a mind of its own. Just when it appears to blow one way, it switches direction and moves in another way. Daoists consider the wind to be the messenger between heaven and earth. The wind communicates a great deal through its movements. Even music and expressions of love and emotion are carried through the air in the form of sound. Although love as much as thoughts and feelings are invisible, they are often expressed through sounds and words. In the same way, heaven communicates its love for all living creatures through the dynamics of wind. It may be easy to believe that we are alone or forlorn, but the same wind touches everyone just the same. Thus, heaven reminds us that it cares about all beings the same way.

The same can be said of rain and other natural forces. While we should protect ourselves against cold and dampness, rain is a benevolent blessing for the earth. Lightning, on the other hand, is the result of extreme cold, dampness, and wind; it represents a form of anger and displeasure toward humanity. Some people can survive direct strikes by lightning, but these individuals are often changed dramatically by the experience. Lightning does not always represent a form of punishment from heaven, but it should definitely be viewed as a warning. Sometimes heaven will use lightning to strike down animals that have acted inappropriately. All creatures have certain advantages over others, and when these powers are greatly misused, heaven will punish them for their transgressions.

Modern people tend to disregard the power of shape-shifting as folklore or superstition. Daoists and indigenous people believe it to be quite real and take it literally, yet consider it unethical and amoral from a heavenly perspective and proceed to punish its activation. Many temples and monasteries offer lectures by elders to which disciples and nearby animals listen carefully. Some exceptional creatures may understand the instructions and develop supernatural abilities. Some of them might use their skills inappropriately, and heaven would strike them down to prevent them from interfering in the human world. These exceptional animals have often had past lives as human beings, but in one way or another, their actions prevented them from being reborn in human form.

Thunder and lightning are also bad signs for negotiations. If it begins to storm when you are on the way to work or a social engagement, the best course of action is to turn around and go back home. These are signs that signal a redirection and a complete turnaround of the current course of action. If thunder and lightning appear during a date, they often signal that heaven does not approve of the relationship or that important matters between the couple must be discussed. Conversely, if it starts raining during a date, that this usually a good sign. It is often a way heaven uses to encourage closeness by inspiring the pair to huddle together under an umbrella or awning.

Even though modern society and some individuals choose to ignore the omens that nature presents, the universe continues to communicate. The wind has a long legacy of expressing significant information to those who have the willingness and wisdom to listen. Dozens of current and ancient civilizations recount stories, mythological and otherwise, on the spiritual nature of wind. From ancient Romans to Native Americans and Renaissance pirates, many people have understood the blessing of wind. All creatures, including aquatic life, are affected by the changes in wind patterns.

While powerful gusts can make us feel uneasy, gentle breezes provide subtle comfort and reassurance about life. In Asia, instead of saying goodbye, many people will say, "Go with the wind." This is as a way of wishing them safe travels and encouraging nature to guide their actions. Wind is capable of communicating a number of things, but one of the most obvious is that it usually precedes rain. The wind is a blessing because it tells us what is about to happen. In Western astrology, wind a symbol of people born under the air signs, who are said to be strong communicators and intuitive messengers. In the tarot, the suit of swords symbolizes air and intellect. In these systems, the symbolism is not as expansive and concise as in five-phases theory, but the meaning remains the same.

In Western astrology, people born under air signs tend to be more focused on future developments or spiritual teachings. Wind encourages many things by stimulating change, evolution, and development. When we set the sails on a boat properly, the wind can carry us to our desired destination. Birds can fly because of the wind, and dogs can follow a scent carried in the air. In terms of fengshui, if there is no wind in an area, its inhabitants will stagnate in their personal growth and development. Therefore, an area no wind should be avoided just as much as a place with harsh winds.

As masters of the sea, the ancient Greeks understood the importance of wind in the achievement of their goals. Books like *The Odyssey* illustrate the great importance they placed upon the relationship between natural events and the outcome of circumstances. Their and other myths detail how much people rely on the winds and how these forces place them at the mercy of the will of heaven. Incredible bravery was required to set sail across the oceans in ancient times. So much was left up to chance that personal willpower and mental fortitude had to be highly developed in order to take on such great quests. Today, tools and technologies have advanced a great deal and we deal with different types of risk and stress than our ancestors. Yet, while intellectual knowledge greatly surpasses that of past generations, holistic wisdom still is only gained through life experiences to which all human beings, past and present, have always had access.

So many things in the world are accompanied by wind. It carries pollen, without which flowers and trees would stop growing and could not prude produce fruit. Daoists recognize that wind is produced when a baby is born or when a plant emerges from the ground. Similarly, when a business owner hires a new employee or engages in negotiations, the wind will increase to convey heaven's opinion. Air is also essential for engines to function properly. Paying attention to the patterns of wind during significant events will likely prevent heartache and difficulty.

In human body fengshui, if wind accompanies the arrival of a person, it signifies a highly successful and auspicious individual. Similarly, if a person walks on a dirt path, and their feet kick up dirt as they move it means that they are trustworthy and generally good. Conversely, if someone walks in a way that makes the sides of their shirt flap in the wind, it means that he is unreliable. Anyone who carries wind with them also carries an energy that potentializes everything else.

All things around us are connected, and by observing them clearly, we can intuit the cycles and patterns that are currently manifesting. Qigong practitioners are adept at recognizing significant signs that may appear as mere coincidences to others. Children that are adventurous, renegade types often become successful later in life. This is because their mind perceives and processes information differently from others, giving them an edge. Many famous and accomplished people have taken leaps of faith or traveled to far-off places in order to accomplish what they truly desired. This is a form of bravery that few people possess. It takes courage to go after what we really want in life.

Birds can migrate thousands of miles in the course of a year, and they rely on the wind to do so. We also rely heavily on the wind to carry us where we want to go in life. This is where terms like "winds of fate" or "acts of God" come from, which are even used in contracts and legal documents to describe unforeseen events and weather-related disasters. The wind contributes a great deal to events on earth, though it is often unnoticed.

Consulting the *Yijing*

Before performing an *Yijing* calculation, you must first find the proper direction using the wind. To do this, throw a feather into the air and observe which direction the wind carries it. This is the direction you must face while doing the calculations on that particular day. It is a sign from heaven, one of the most ancient secrets of *Yijing* as read by Daoists of the Complete Perfection school. After the calculations are finished, three sticks of incense must be lit to pay tribute to heaven and thank the spirits for their guidance. If the wind blows the incense smoke in the same direction that the feather went, the calculations were correct. This is a way to check the work of the *Yijing*, matching the principles of ancient divination as based on the movements of nature and the changes of the world.

When performing fengshui, it is important to take note of the trees in the surrounding area and observe how the wind moves through their leaves. If the leaves rustle gently, the area is auspicious and its energy is beneficial. These practices rely on timing and observing heaven's signals. By moving with the flow of nature, we can make the most of each situation, gathering the blessings heaven wants to share.

Success in life is achieved by developing ourselves internally at the level of soul and spirit. The wind assists us in this by showing us what will work for us and what will be detrimental. Although it seems simple and arbitrary, ignoring the signs of heaven leads to disappointment and missed opportunities. If you pursue things that are not destined for you, you lose precious time and energy that could be used to cultivate true happiness, success, and contentment. Although we may greatly desire certain outcomes, if they are not in accordance with the heaven's will, perhaps something far better is in store for us. Desire leads to suffering, and a lack of contentment leaves no room for peace and happiness. Humans have a natural, deep bond with trees, and any location devoid of trees or birds is detrimental to human development. Birds are also messengers from heaven, and they present numerous opportunities for humans during their lives. However, in order for birds to appear in any location, trees must be present as well.

Chapter 11

Rudiments of the Body

The hair of the body represents trees in human body fengshui. The hair that appears on the arms and legs, armpits, eyebrows, nostrils, and pubic areas, represents different aspects of the self. Nose hairs, for instance, represent various career opportunities, and the hairs on the feet represent the different paths one can take in life. They are called the five areas of completion. All orifices should be covered or surrounded by hair. A natural lack of pubic hair is a bad sign for a female, and men should be careful with their sexual energy around them. Armpit hair illustrates one's ability to hold onto wealth. While a lack of hair due to shaving is different than a natural lack of body hair, shaving nonetheless effects the *qi* and has consequences in the corresponding area of life.

Eyebrow hair represents how one does in love and the ability to make friends in life. Bushy and scattered eyebrows indicate sexual activity and many friends. Hair on the hands shows an ability to make a lot of money. Coarse leg hair, especially on a woman, signals a tendency to work hard and be industrious, thus showing a strong career and good potential for success. All these are good signs but not beautiful showing that the Daoist ideal of beauty is often not the same as that prominent in Western societies.

Every hair on the body is important and each one represents how many problems the individual will encounter during life. Many monks will shave their heads as a way to strengthen their connection with the moon and lunar energy. With practice, it is possible to viscerally feel the moon's energy. The hairs on the head protect the yang energy of the mind from external yin-*qi* which can come in the form of negative, distracting, and confusing thoughts. Some Daoists focus on cultivating yin energy, while others focus on cultivating yang, but in the end, they all follow similar principles and lead to optimal health and a purified spirit.

Hair under the armpits and in the pubic area is different from that of other areas. Rather than representing trees, like the hair on the back of the head, hair below the waist represents ocean plants. Hair on the back represents yang creatures, such as dragons and sheep, while hair on the front of the body represents flowers and plants. The front of the body is mainly related to yin energy, which is also associated with flowers and grass, as well as the moon. Similarly, the armpits and pubic hair are considered flowers, while the fine hair on the rest of the body represent trees.

In fengshui, if flowers bloom on a property, but the surrounding plants and trees have no leaves, it means the careers of the adults that live there may be successful at the moment, but won't last. It could also mean that the children's careers will not develop successfully. Conversely, if there are a lot of leaves but no flowers, the inhabitants are going through a tough time and are either depressed or stressed. Leaves are associated with the shoulders and arms, while flowers represent the face. If a person's facial features are symmetrical and have a healthy appearance, they will be able to easily achieve their goals and advance in their career. Symmetrical facial features also illustrate what type of career is best for the person.

Daoists consider the smallest things to be the most significant as, for instance, grass. Grass is a major factor in the success of the United States: the abundance of green vegetation has contributed greatly to the country's economic growth. Green represents growth, education, money, tranquility, and success. In Los Angeles and other arid areas, many people stopped watering the grass in order to conserve water during periods of drought. While water must be conserved, the lack of greenery also inhibits spiritual progress and economic prosperity.

The number and type of flowers and trees that surround a property contribute a great deal to the energy and success of its inhabitants. Most importantly, there must be at least one tree for every person living in a particular home. These trees can be planted directly in the ground or grown in pots. According to human body fengshui, the number of plants that surround a home should also correspond to the appearance and date of birth of its inhabitants.

The fine hairs of the body are related to the stars. Laozi said that there are 110,000 fine hairs on the body, while Shakyamuni Buddha said that there are 84,000. It is not important to know exactly how many there are, but in the past these numbers were gathered by completely shaving a body after death and counting each hair individually. Spiritual practitioners would do this to investigate more about the spiritual dimension and the dynamics of the material world.

To Daoists, human beings are like stars, flowers, and trees. A person younger than forty-five years is considered a flower, while older people are seen as trees. Just as a flower must be protected from strong winds and rain, younger people should avoid stressful situations and overwhelming psychological pressure. These conditions can lead to sickness, depression, or other negative consequences in younger people, but with age comes increased strength, confidence, and resilience.

Similarly, before the age of sixty, body and mind should be used to make money and develop resources, but after this time, assets should be used for nourishment and support. This is called *shi*; propensity or the natural flow of things. Before sixty, it is important to engage in moderate exercise to develop the body. After sixty, exercise should be more moderate and diet emphasized. After the age of twenty-two, physical growth ceases and health begins to plateau. Eating meat can be helpful before the age of twenty-two to aid in developing strength as well as after the age of sixty to support health and vitality. However, eating too much meat at any age can lead to sickness and exhaust the body's energy.

Human body fengshui, which closely resembles the ancient practice of physiognomy, emphasizes the correlation between various areas of the body. For example, the nose and lips correspond to the male and female genitals respectively. The ears have an energetic connection to the anus. It often goes unnoticed, but each part of the body is significant. All systems have both input functions as well as outputs. By receiving nutrients and beneficial energies, and expelling waste and negativity the body and spirit are nourished and purified. The quality and condition of superficial aspects of these systems, such as hair on the human body, illustrate the current state of these systems and how they may be deficient.

Plants and the Body

Each of the body's vital organs also has numerous associations in human body fengshui. The liver symbolizes trees and the wood phase in general, but pine and cypress trees are the varieties that come closest to representing this organ. The liver belongs to yin because it processes blood and emotions, although it functions as a yang organ because it has the ability to regenerate and governs cellular growth. Conversely, the pine tree is dominantly yang because it grows tall and strong and produces an abundance of oxygen, but it is also associated with yin because it thrives in cold climates and produces thousands of thin, elegant needles. In the human body, pines are symbolic of the hair on the back of the head, while cypresses appear in the form of male beard hair.

The liver is associated with willows, but mostly represented by various flowers, especially Chinese roses. The lungs are linked with chrysanthemums. Lilies, grapes, and lotus root mark the kidneys. However, lotuses contain a unique energy because their blossoms relate to flowers and plants (yin), while their roots connect to trees (yang). The *Lotus Sutra*, a major sacred text of Buddhism, contains prayers that invoke energy to overcome life's obstacles by metaphorically blossoming from muddy roots. This ability to produce beautiful flowers from muddy, turbid waters, makes the lots a major representative of many important concepts in both Daoism and Buddhism.

Oak trees and cacti belong to the stomach category, although the stomach is also represented by other tree species. It is one of the most powerful organs because it contains an abundance of both blood and *qi*. Therefore, it represents many things, including "bird of paradise" flowers, roses, vine blossoms, and jasmine. The ox is the zodiac animal that governs the stomach and spleen, and practicing qigong during the ox time (between 1 and 3 am) can heal and strengthen the spleen, stomach, and digestive tract.

Dates, dragon fruits, sunflower seeds, and peanuts, along with the plants and trees that produce them, all represent the human heart. Sunflowers are linked to the heart, while most of the other flowers are governed by the stomach and liver. The heart is often called the sun of the body, and thus related to sunflowers.

Furthermore, just like the energy of a healthy heart, the sunflower grows tall and strong; prolific, it thrives in the warm light of the day.

500 years ago, the master physician and herbalist Li Shizhen 李時珍 (1518-1593) compiled the *Bencao gangmu* 本草綱目 (Compendium of Materia Medica), which has exerted a major influence ever since and is still used as a key text for herbalists today. Besides medical information, it also contains descriptions of the esoteric and spiritual uses of various herbs and relevant treatments. By applying concepts related to the dynamics of heaven and earth, remedies, treatments, and their effects can be understood at a deeper, more profound level.

Li Shizhen outlines in great detail how plants, trees, and herbal formulas can be categorized as either yin or yang according to their properties. He also places human beings into these categories, thus allowing practitioners to better understand their personalities and decide on the most effective treatment. People of high yang nature share many qualities with the dragon, including benevolence, power, fortitude, and the ability to change circumstances. Conversely, those predominantly yin have the characteristics of tigers, including playfulness, strength, agility, and the ability to be highly adaptive.

By applying the principles of yin and yang to fengshui, we find that pines, which are yin in nature, benefit women and are best planted in the back of a property. Cypresses, on the other hand, belong to yang, and benefit men when planted in the front. Due to its potent yang energy and its deep black color, cypress ash is used to make ink, used not only used in calligraphy but also for drawing Daoist talismans.

From heaven's perspective and according to the *Yijing*, trees and humans share the same category. Therefore, to achieve a natural balance on earth, there should be at least one tree for every living human on the planet. Trees have a very potent and highly developed spiritual nature, equal to that of humans. Through the practice of meditation and qigong, it is possible to commune with trees and understand their intentions, qualities, and spiritual history.

> In 1983, two studies proved that poplars and sugar maple trees warn each other about worrisome insects. When one tree becomes infested, it warns others who begin producing anti-insect chemicals, to protect against attack. These signals are sent through the air. Even then, the splinter group of scientists studying this phenomenon were for decades waved away. Since the late 90's however, such researchers have proven that trees transfer carbon, nitrogen, phosphorus, and other nutrients, back and forth via mycelia. Today, though only a scant few people study it, the phenomenon is no longer in doubt. (Perry 2016)

More recently, Peter Wohlleben dedicated himself to the study of the inner life of plants and trees. In *The Hidden Life of Trees*, he describes may ways in which they convey messages.

> "Some are calling it the 'wood-wide web,'" says Wohlleben in German-accented English. "All the trees here, and in every forest that is not too damaged, are connected to each other through underground fungal networks. Trees share water and nutrients through the networks, and also use them to communicate. They send distress signals about drought and disease, for example, or insect attacks, and other trees alter their behavior when they receive these messages."
>
> Scientists call these mycorrhizal networks. The fine, hairlike root tips of trees join together with microscopic fungal filaments to form the basic links of the network, which appears to operate as a symbiotic relationship between trees and fungi, or perhaps an economic exchange. As a kind of fee for services, the fungi consume about thirty percent of the sugar that trees photosynthesize from sunlight. The sugar is what fuels the fungi, as they scavenge the soil for nitrogen, phosphorus and other mineral nutrients, which are then absorbed and consumed by the trees. (Grant 2018)

Modern science has known that plants communicate with each other for some time, but recently research has begun to uncover the deeper dynamics of this process. Studies suggest that plants are more conscious and aware than previously thought, showing basic emotions and intent. For instance, some plants help others reach sunlit areas, while others prevent neighboring plants from blocking their light.

Fengshui has only few rules and regulations for the placement of plants and flowers in and around the home. Within reason, the more plants and flowers are growing a property, the better, but the energy of trees is most important. By using intuition, we can choose plants and flowers that match our energy and uplift our emotions with their scent and appearance. In the same way we choose a pet, we should pick plants that we feel a natural affinity for. A strong intuition lends itself well to fengshui practice, and can lead to acquiring and cultivating quiet, peaceful environments.

Signs of Fate

XXX The human body contains many indicators for a person's future circumstances and life path. For instance, the eyebrows represent a person's ability to acquire money and manage their personal finances. However, there are only two facial features that continue to grow while other parts of the body remain the same; the ears and the nose. This becomes apparent in the appearance of elderly people, who often have large noses and ears compared to the rest of their facial features. The eyebrows also become thicker and bushier with age. As we acquire wisdom and intelligence, the ears begin to grow larger, therefore depictions of the Buddhas show them with very large ears. People with very round, circular ears have luck with money and finances because their intelligent with how they manage their resources. People with thick ears are lucky and fortunate in most circumstances because they understand risk and generally have a good attitude.

People with long ears have longevity because their kidney is strong, increasing their health and immunity. The ears represent both the moon and the kidneys, and in Daoist medicine, conditions such as deafness and tinnitus are due to an issue with the ear's ability to incorporate lunar energy.

During the first and fifteenth days of the lunar calendar, hearing and ear related issues can be more easily treated because the enhanced lunar energy fortifies the kidney *qi*. August fifteenth is an exceptional day to treat these conditions, especially for men, while women can be effectively treated for kidney and ear related problems during the third and fourth days of their menstrual cycle. This is because of the connection between a woman's menstrual cycle, the phase water (which includes the kidneys), and the lunar phases.

Human body fengshui principles have been developed and corroborated by observing similar correlations in animals. In the past, ranchers would sometimes have difficulty differentiating their young cattle from the older ones because calves grow quickly to their full size. To determine which cow or bull was younger, Daoists would place fresh grass in front of two fully grown cattle (mother and calf), and the youngest one would always be the first to run forward and eat. This practice relies on the understanding of compassion in cattle. The mother cow will always let her calf eat before she does. Similarly, to differentiate between male and female snakes of the same age (which can be quite difficult), two of them will be placed in a container with prey. On average, male snakes will strike at prey more quickly than female snakes.

Fruit of Heaven

As cultivators of spiritual energy, Daoists would always be mindful of their diet; eating only the freshest fruit possible. In most cases, they would eat various fruits, such as grapes, peaches, and oranges, while they were still hanging on the branches and vines. When older monks and nuns could not reach the fruit, they would have the younger adepts climb the tree for them and break off a small branch with the leaves and fruit still attached. If the fruit is eaten within ten minutes of it being removed from the tree, it is still considered to be alive. This dietary practice has been a major secret in Daoism, used to greatly increase the longevity of the practitioners. While it may seem overly simple, it is an effective and healthy dietary adjustment that anyone can try.

Many things change and require adjustment, but this ancient fruit consumption technique is a timeless exercise that goes to our roots as human beings. Even with all the advancements of modern technology, we still rely upon nature for sustenance. With this practice we develop humility and gain longevity simultaneously. Daoists strive to return to their original pure state of being, and by consuming fruit that is still alive and young, their energy becomes young and vital.

Many Daoist practices have not changed in thousands of years because they follow the principle of returning to the source, which is subtle and pure. Returning to the origin of nature is a straightforward act that does not require new methods and practices, only a letting go of unnatural thoughts and behaviors that conceal our character. In Daoism, eating produce that has been stored for days, weeks, or months, is akin to eating the corpse of the fruit because it lacks vital *qi*.

Eating fruit in this way preserves its original flavor and vital nutrients. Even though the modern organic and local food movements have provided us with fresher ingredients, this is still an inferior dietary in the eyes of many Daoists. Dedicated Daoist longevity cultivators pride themselves on eating only that which was going to secure them the longest life possible.

This is not only viewed as a way to cultivate superior health and longevity; it is a preliminary practice toward becoming one of the gods. This is alluded to in the Old Testament as well, when Adam and Eve are told that they will remain in paradise if they only consume the fruit of the trees, with the exception of the 'tree of the knowledge of good and evil'. (Gen 2:16-17)

Pre-Natal Education

In order to achieve longevity, we must detoxify our lifestyle and return to our pure original state. For this reason, Daoists have spent a lot of time and energy studying and learning about children and prenatal care. Childbirth requires a lot of time and preparation, and the birth of the spiritual self is no different. Mothers often do all they can to help their baby grow and develop in a healthy way both before and after the moment of birth. These efforts did not go unnoticed by Daoists, and they see these acts as a form of heavenly preparation for the new being about to come into existence. Compared to many other animals, human beings have a long gestation period. A human being requires nine-lunar cycles in order to reach fruition. Human beings are complicated and have a high level of awareness, and this level of refined development requires significant time in the safety of the womb.

In the White Cloud Monastery, there is a large statue of the goddess of maternity and fertility named Bixia Yuanjun. People who were having issues with conception or pregnancy would go to offer alms and prayers near the statue for a healthy child. As the Buddha of fertility, she is afforded her own courtyard in the temple dedicated to children and motherhood. Mothers are deeply respected in many religions and their efforts are sacred.

In Daoism, the symbol of the *taiji*, with the yin fish and yang fish, also represents the baby while it is still in the womb. This symbolism alludes to the shared origins of our two species and the importance of this sacred relationship. Fish are born in water, and the human embryo develops in amniotic fluid. The embryo represents the yang aspect, while the fluid represents the yin. That is why water in fengshui is so essential. All things, both yin and yang, come from a yin origin, just as all human beings come from a mother. Many aspects of human development within human body fengshui are the result of access to, and interaction with, water.

Daoists also have a whole series of methods and practices that are used to enhance a baby's soul while it is still in the womb. This prenatal education, includes singing songs and read ancient poems to the child. The most important method involves painting different colors and symbols on the belly of the expectant mother to help the baby learn, grow, and begin spiritual cultivation before birth. This method helps the child become healthier, more attractive, and more intelligent when they are born.

The most valuable result of these practices is an increase in the child's vitality and immunity to disease. Daoists have known for centuries that infants are born equipped with certain naturally-occurring antibiotics to protect their delicate health, and these methods enhance and fortify these immune functions by supporting *qi* and blood flow. Many children get sick immediately after birth because of their young, delicate state of health, but these cultivation methods strengthen the child and put the mind of the parents at ease. These Daoist practices are profound because they are non-invasive, easy to implement, and they have no side-effects.

If a baby is positioned poorly for delivery, Daoists will talk to the child through the belly (an encourage the mother to do the same) suggesting and encouraging it to turn its head down toward the cervix in order to have a smoother birth. In every known case, the baby has responded to these words, and naturally reoriented itself within the womb. This demonstrates that the baby is not only perceptually aware within the womb, but also intellectually cognizant. The developing tissues of the baby in the womb are comprised of yin energy, but when you paint colors on the mother's belly, speak to the child, or sing to the child, they become aware and imbued with yang.

This is the most natural way to balance the energy of the mother, her womb, and her developing child. The colors drawn on the mother's abdomen makes the child more intelligent and healthier, as well as happier and more emotionally vibrant. The pictures and shapes are not as important as the colors themselves, which should be vibrant and varied. The bright and vibrant hues communicate information to the baby within, and helps them understand many aspects of earthly life and spiritual cultivation.

Conceiving the child at certain times is also seen as significant from a Daoist perspective:

> [Someone] asked, "What do you have to say about the reason why there are ugly people and handsome people?"
>
> [Wang Zhe replied], "A lesson says that the properness (handsome quality) of one's appearance [occurs because] on the day [of conception] the father's and mother's two arouse and respond [to the] sun and moon before the *wu* (noon) hour and after the chou hour (2 am).

> "Thereby, [the child will possess] rectitude, honesty, longevity, and prosperity. His appearance will bring joy to the hearts of the father and mother. If conceived after the *wu* hour and before the chou hour, there will be [born] one whose appearance is not proper (is ugly) and may suffer from deafness or dumbness. His personality and intelligence will be inferior, and he will not win the hearts of people. His life span will be limited, he will not have prosperity, and his life will not be long. These are basic principles of creation. (Eskildsen 2006, 67)

Childbirth brings about a lot of change in the lives of the parents, and requires a lot of effort over the course of many years. Children have seven times as much energy as grown adults, and managing this difference can be exhausting. This is yet another reason that children have such an incredible impact on their surrounding environment in both obvious and unseen ways. There are many aspects of a child that have resounding effects in their life and among their peers. The above passage is not included to offend or be politically incorrect, but to illustrate the types of thinking that were commonplace in Daoist circles of the past. Recognizing that physically attractive people often have an easier time in society, Daoists, and many ancient people, sought ways to ensure the best possible future for their children.

Chapter 12

The Ideal Dwelling

When you purchase a house, make sure to consider its position and floorplan in the light of fengshui. Fengshui is the relationship of that house in proximity to the flow of natural energies (*qi*). This is an ancient study that has greatly impacted not only individuals' destinies but also the destiny of entire nations. Dr. Wu's previous book, *Lighting the Eye of the Dragon* (2000), goes into many of these culturally significant case studies in more depth, but in terms of its basic concepts, what is one way to prove fengshui's fundamental importance? People born in a thriving metropolis will generally have more career opportunities than someone who lives in the middle of nowhere. This is common sense, but it is also base level fengshui. Due to specific elements within nature, people choose to densely populate certain areas of the world.

Most civilizations were formed around the natural resources of a given area. High resource areas will attract more people and generate more opportunities for work, wealth and prosperity. If you live in a town with a hundred people, there might be fifty jobs in that town. But if you live in a town of ten million, there may be five million jobs. How do we explain this? Well, it is many times due to the complexities found within nature in those places. If you want certain things in your life to happen, you will usually have to be in the right place at the right time for that to happen. But you will also need to consider being where there is a higher likelihood of those chances. In fengshui terms, the more forces there are and the more varied they are, the more opportunities there will be in that place. This is significant for all human development, as fengshui runs deep, between practical logic, symbolism and higher awareness. The fengshui perspective is so all encompassing, its roots can be found in the Chinese linguistic system of characters

It is easy to see that Chinese characters are pictograms that do not rely upon the traditional alphabetization that English or Romance languages do. But there is a deeper meaning to these symbols. Each picture represented by the characters is a symbol. There are also many different characters that, when added together, produce different results. Why is it common knowledge in fengshui that you should not own a house that has a tree outside of the front door? It is because when you add the character for "tree" and the character for "front door" together, they create the symbol or word that sounds like "trapped." Words give form to objects, which are then represented by symbols, which then can be combined into new forms with new properties, good or bad.

Another example is the number four in Chinese, which sounds similar to the word "death." They are two words that sound the same that then create a connection in the mind. In the same way, you also would not want to walk out the front door and see a mountain every day. Who wants to imagine having to go out and climb a mountain every day of their life? That seems a bit arduous, wouldn't you say? The connection is there in the subconscious or intuitive mind. On the other hand, having a mountain behind your house is amazing; it creates a good support system, like an older sibling protecting you in the schoolyard from any bullies.

This also correlates with the human spine and your resilience. If a larger building or a mountain is behind the house, it can subliminally act as a booster for your spine and can then bring luck in terms of your health chi. No matter what structure is behind your house or dwelling, it is better if it is larger in size. That will work to help you live in harmony, with protection for your life path and earnings. Many of the concepts may seem non-scientific, but masters of these arts have been cataloguing their experiments and findings for thousands of years. Their data recognizes the connections between environment and personal perception, by tracking the results over hundreds of generations,

The Roots of Fengshui

When we look at fengshui, we look at two things: *feng* is wind and *shui* is water. They are the two principal factors at play when we are looking at a property or a place to lay our heads down. When looking for a property, you should look for an area where the wind blows gently and the water flows softly and smoothly. Of course, not every property will have water in or around it, but the ones that do not can be augmented with things such as ponds, mountain-shaped fountains, or even swimming pools to help balance out the *qi* of the property. The symbolism is enough to influence us. Ideally, one would live in some proximity to streams, rivers, or oceans for the absolute best fengshui, but scarcity or price does not have to be an obstacle. When you find a property, you are looking for what they would call a safe and hospitable place. This is a feeling that nature easily brings, but human-built changes can do the same, especially in our modern cityscapes.

So how do wind and water play into this whole equation? Water, when it is flowing gently, will both carry misfortune away from you while simultaneously bringing in money. Wind, on the other hand, governs luck or opportunity. These two are essential in the White Cloud Monastery practice of fengshui. Wind and water both are crucial. So, when you first go to a property, it is critical that you look at these elements. How is the wind blowing when you first get to the property? Is there any wind? Or is the wind too harsh and abrasive? There are many vast regions on earth where the wind is very strong. These are generally not places that you want to build. Many times, these windswept places have been the victim of over-forestation or other critical land development errors.

This type of human activity can create more wind because there are no trees to block and protect the local area. Again, when we look at fengshui, we are looking for balance; balance that might be harder to find than you would think. This is a serious issue, mainly because huhumankind has genuinely lost touch with the knowledge of this balance that the fengshui perspective values so fundamentally. fengshui is not a concept that is widely known. If people have even heard the term, it is vaguely associated with paganism or primitive magic. But really, if we look at fengshui logically, it is basic common sense about weather, environment and our human reactions to them. It is not to be feared. All animals use fengshui to build their nests or dens in the most secure place possible based upon their instincts. Are there any birds on the property you are looking at? If there are no birds, this is definitely not a good spot either.

Many people are also scared to move away from places they have lived their whole lives. Psychologically, it is a lot to ask to uproot someone and put him or her in an unfamiliar environment. When we think about when we feel our best, we usually think about spending time in nature, whether it is in the mountains, forests, or beaches of the world. As such, it would make sense to build houses in just such places. I would even conjecture that most towns which do not feature these types of natural elements, were originally formed around ranching or farming activities. Other than that, maybe those towns would not have been settled otherwise. Many nomadic tribes followed the buffalo on their migratory patterns, so perhaps this is in fact a form of fengshui. When you are camping, you will not place your dwelling in a place where a tree could easily fall on you in the middle of the night, just as the birds build their nests with instinctive logic

To reiterate, when we look at a dwelling, we are mostly looking for what we can do to bring harmony and peace into our lives. In some instances, a shoebox by the beach might be better than a palace in the middle of a windswept plain. It all depends on what you think will bring you harmony and peace of mind.

Correlations in the Body

As noted earlier, there are simple, logical human fundamentals at the root of fengshui. The will to survive and then thrive, in safety and prosperity, is the way of all life. This is the biological instinct that guides us, which is behind everything we do and desire. But the human body is the source of this survival instinct. Through the body, instinct is guided by the messages coming in from all around us, not only from the senses but also from subtle cues that trigger the nervous system and the emotions.

Ancient Daoists had an understanding of this that we are only just catching up to now in mainstream science and culture. For example, there are the five stars that interact with the nine body orifices in Nine Palaces Qigong. As openings to all heavenly information, the practice keeps these organs clear and active, helping the body to receive information from heaven. The five stars send information and different energies down to earth and someone who cultivates the clarity of their body's openings will be able to hear and make use of these signals. Sensing these signals leads to new opportunities and insight. In addition, the body has further cosmic matches. The sun is, of course, linked with the heart, while the kidneys are more akin to the moon. Liver, spleen, and stomach are all linked with the stars. The small and large intestines represent the clouds. The digestive tract, esophagus, trachea, and larynx are all related to the wind.

Paying attention to these correlations helps us harmonize with the greater universe. If these correlations were taught in schools, not only as ancient belief but also as active guidance for cosmology and medicine, we might all have a greater appreciation for human lives, starting in our youth. Right now, we live in an age where human life is not revered as much as it should be. Even though most people know that it is sacred on some level, on another level, trying to preserve the body itself is not truly a prime directive. Most people just use the body as they see fit, without reverence for how it is our only means to breed harmony from the inside out.

These concepts are furthered by putting them into the context of fengshui. Matching the body to a house, the eyes represent the windows, the door is the mouth, the nose matches the living room, and the ears correlate to the front and back yards. The left ear correlates with the front yard, and the right ear correlates with the back yard. Matching the owner's date of birth with the property further expands on this. If the owner's numbers do not match the property, it is a bad fit. That person then should not live at that residence. This is how seriously fengshui and *Yijing* are connected in protecting a person's safety and security,

Yijing Calculations

If you do the basic *Yijing* to reach a single number, that number, being yin or yang, should oppose what your natural number is. So, if your number is a yin number, such as 2, 4, 6, or 8, you will need a property with a yang number, such as 1, 3, 5, 7, or 9, and vice versa. According to Dr. Wu, these numbers should be calculated for the person who is the primary financial support for the family. Of course, if you have many people in your family, one calculation is not going to match with everyone. But if it does not fit with the primary provider, there might be issues for everyone else who lives in that dwelling.

Let us say you are born on 4-10-1978. 4 plus 10 (10 reduces to 1) makes it 4+1, which equals 5. Then you add up the year numbers. 1+9 equals 10, which when added becomes 0. Now add the 7 + 8 that makes 15. Then add the 1 plus the 5, which becomes a 6. Further add the 5 to the 6 to get 11. Now, 1+1 equal 2. Hence, your birth number would be a 2, which is an even yin number. This means that, if you are the main breadwinner in your household, you need a yang house. Determine if the house is yin or yang by using the number you get by adding up the address number until it reaches a single digit, as you have done for your birthdate. For our example, this ensures that the yin person is balanced out by a yang address.

The key to doing these specific *Yijing* calculations is to pair off all the numbers then add pairs together to reduce down to a single number. Add two numbers together and reduce to one. All of the calculations need to happen in sequences of two until you get down to a final single digit calculation.

Although we balance the prosperity for a family home by matching the yin or yang numbers of breadwinner and house address, a property cannot be totally yang or yin. It needs to have some of the opposite energy to level it out. This is where fengshui comes into the picture. *Yijing* calculations come down to a single principle, yin or yang. Fengshui is then used to help the person balance out the yin and yang within the property.

This can happen through changing the color of the house, remodeling the house, changing the arrangement of the furniture, the position of the bed, etc. Planting different plant life on the outside of the property can be a strong source of change. For example, flowers are yin, and many times can balance out a house, just with a few plantings. Bamboo should always be on the sides of the house and not in the back. A dwelling with no real vegetation outside may likely be fengshui deficient in one capacity or another. Everything in reality is about balance.

If a property is too yang, that can create issues. In the same way, a property that is too yin can lead to problems. When we look at properties that have too much yin, this can arise when people have died on the premises. This is just one example that most people would consider an undesirable trait even outside of the fengshui worldview.

To explain how fengshui works, we must look at the primordial forces of nature as typified by Chinese culture. First off, we can say that Dragons give rise to the clouds, while their counterparts, tigers, give rise to the wind. It is essential for to understand that things have both a physical nature and a metaphysical one. Some people understand and only work on the physical level, while others also work on the spiritual. This is the profound nature of Daoism. It serves as an intersection between the practical and the metaphysical.

If something is not practical, how can it be spiritual? If people cannot understand an idea on a basic, real-world level, how could it ever be a spiritual concept helpful to the common man? This is why the system of nature is orchestrated in its patterns. On the external level, we can look at nature and see it is beautiful, but where does this physical beauty come from? It stems from its deeper level of harmony within the greater system. Is a tree trying to be beautiful? Or is it just growing to try and reach its greatest height? It exists as it is, and is not trying to be anything it's not. This is what we perceive as the source of its actual beauty—its pure existence and the physical manifestation of its unique spiritual struggle.

No two trees are the same, no more than any two humans are the same. You do not have to understand a tree to appreciate its beauty, although understanding it can deepen the relationship you have with nature. There is no wrong way to learn about nature. Our senses, intuition, emotions, and imagination are all working all the time, even when we are not thinking about it consciously. As long as you make some effort to be aware of your surroundings, that is all you need toward deepening your connection to nature's messages and balancing your fengshui.

Fengshui at Home

Moving back to fengshui of the home, each of our senses has a conscious or subconscious response to the conditions in our living environment. The Daoists take this one step further and link the different parts of a house to the organs that are most influenced by these conditions. To start, the windows are the eyes of the house. The brightness of the windows based on their position is significant. This makes sense because, just as our eyes need light, so do the eyes of the home need some light as well. Windows need to stay clean outside along the property and within a house.

The mouth, or door, also represents the tiger. Any animal uses its mouth to kill and render prey. They always go for the neck first. The neck is considered your lifeline and is linked to your career. That is where the term "bottleneck" comes from. The throat represents the bottleneck and is the weakest spot in the body. In Chinese, there is a phrase that says that the neck is the "ultimate life killing point." As such, in fengshui, we strongly emphasize that the throat cannot be blocked. This is like cutting off the air to the rest of the body. The throat represents the neck. In the home, this throat is the front entryway into the house. This is why the entry area should be kept uncluttered and clean and the front door should not open directly to a bathroom. How are you going to get air into the body if your airway opens to a place that does not allow your body to get air? This is why this is such an issue in fengshui; the body of the house also needs to breathe to be healthy.

Once you enter the front door, that hallway that leads toward the living rooms is like being in the nose. We then can see that the nostrils are the bathroom and kitchen. The left nostril is the kitchen, and the right nostril is the bathroom. Patients with eye conditions need a house with an east-facing front door. This way, when the sun rises in the morning, you are able to see that sunlight. That action of opening your door and seeing the light is a type of treatment for the eyes. It is best if that morning light has just a little bit of cloud cover or morning mist. That is the absolute best type of sunlight for the eyes.

When we go back to a human face, anything dealing with the face above the eyebrows represents the sky. In terms of treatment, for treating ear problems, you look at the front and back yards. It is common for people who do not have a backyard at all to have right ear problems. People with a messy front yard may have hearing issues. The house is like the human body, with not only a respiratory system, but also a digestive system. Humans eat with their mouths and defecate through their backside. This is like the front and back doors of the home. This is also the model in hospitals. Patients come in through the front door, whereas the coroners will collect those who have passed away through the back door.

It is important in fengshui that the person who has the home has alignment with that particular house so that the house can also be in alignment with the universe. Our body is the microcosm of the universe and our home reflects the environment that surrounds us in this same microcosm versus macrocosm dynamic. Therefore, no matter the actual positioning, the house is given its set of directions, based on the location of its key features. No matter what direction the house faces, the side of the house with the front door is also always considered the south side of the building itself. The south side of the home and the property both need the phase fire, centered in the heart. This is because fire comes from the south. If a house faces south, it needs trees in the east. Trees represent dragons. In real terms, we cannot physically see the dragons living on the earth, so the trees represent the dragon energy. Why does a tree represent a dragon? This is because the definition of the dragon is that it is rooted in the ground, but can grow toward heaven. In addition, the east side of the house needs plants with round and thick leaves and tall trees.

South is how the bird flies. It should be vacant or empty on that side, not just the south exterior, but also the front door area, as the building's personal south side. The heart is sometimes known as the monkey or the bird. Some people are known for being indecisive, which is akin to the birds. This is not always a bad thing, because in the *Yijing*, everything is based on change. This would mean that if the person is bird-like, they could quickly change course to adjust to whatever is happening around them. The right side of the house is considered the west and is dedicated to the tiger that represents the roads. The back of the property is akin to a person's back. And the two legs are the fencing or the walls around the property. One leads to two, two leads to three, and three leads to all things. This is the core principle in all things fengshui.

The number 1 is the head. This gives rise to 2, which represents the 4 appendages. This means that you should always keep your front door clean. 1 head, 2 appendages, which leads to 3, which is a person's genital area, which leads to all other life being created. This concept of the creation of all things can also be thought of as the sun and the moon. Only when the sun and the moon are both present can all of the stars come into existence. These are the three heavenly treasures.

There are essence, *qi*, and spirit in all human beings. These are the three treasures of humanity. The earthly treasures are fire/water/wind. All of these elements are central to human life. Without them, we could not sustain life. All of these things are magical, and they in turn give rise to all other phenomena in existence. We cannot forget the importance of these treasures in our quest to understand life. They are the raw essence of all things; they give rise to all things. They are the keys to the doorways of true perception. When we value what we have been given, we can live a life based upon appreciation and happiness.

The decoration of the front door is like a 1. Generally, it is best if bathrooms and kitchens are big. This will help you a lot. Dr. Wu notes that bathrooms in the Middle East are often huge and sometimes have golden toilets. Although it might seem crazy to have a golden toilet, it is excellent fengshui. Gold can work to contain the bad *qi* of our human waste, which is why gold is used in this capacity. Often, we see that bathrooms are becoming bigger in modern houses as the design needs of the occupants change over time. Women specifically spend a lot of time in the bathroom getting ready, so it makes sense for them to have a larger bathroom where possible.

Bedrooms and Kitchens

In every house, there is an ideal placement for a bedroom. This is key when you are looking at a house, choosing a room, or building a house of your own. The better we sleep, the better we can rest and regenerate to face another day. The easiest way to determine the best placement is by looking out toward the front door. When looking toward the front door from the inside, the room on the left will be the best placement for a bedroom. This placement is generally the best fengshui area of the house. The bedroom should be a little bit dark, not struck with sunlight, as this is the place where you go to rest. This placement puts the bedroom in the area of the house that equates to the lower elixir field. This in turn puts it in the same category as the fertility sector of the body, which makes sense in that regard.

The bathroom and the kitchen definitely need to be separated by one partition or another. Dr. Wu equates this bedroom placement to being in between the two mountains. It should be a peaceful, dark space, just like a house in the middle of a valley. This is why he recommends many of his patients who live in Los Angeles relocate to Malibu. This is because being between two large mountains is an ideal fengshui placement for housing.

As a family, if you do not have a lot of family members, it is often advised not live in a big house. Normally, the size of the household should correspond to the size of the house. Living in too large a house for the number of people living there can diffuse the *qi*. However, if the bedroom is small, it is still OK to live in a big house with few people. As a general rule of thumb in fengshui, the smaller the bedroom, the better. As you sleep at night, your *qi* comes out. If the bedroom is too big, the *qi* gets dispersed. Since we spend so much of our lives in our home sleeping, resting, and spending quiet personal time, no other room is more important for consolidating and preserving one's *qi*.

According to Dr. Wu, a messy bedroom can lead to involuntary sighing, because that represents the state one's emotional affairs. In terms of décor, he recommends almost no furniture in the bedroom. This can help keep a person's emotional state healthy and happy. Emotionally, too much furniture can represent you being clogged up internally or just prevent the free flow of emotions. As in fengshui theory, emotions are represented by water. When thinking in these terms, water should not be dammed up and should be able to flow freely. What happens when water cannot flow? Well, just look at a murky or stagnant pond. Metaphorically, this can happen to you internally if your emotions are not allowed to move about as they should. This is a great example of how our environment effects our emotions, not only on obvious psychological levels, but also in subtle physical ways that are more subliminal. These subconscious elements then can turn around and impact real health related issues, such as poor sleep. Keep your bedroom in optimal position and condition to prevent a domino effect.

Kitchens in fengshui should be wide, as they represent the umbrella, the uterus of the female and the male prostate. This is a good way for women to avoid any serious long-term health problems with their reproductive organs. The cleaner the kitchen, the better off that person will be in terms of these issues. It is very easy to have a messy or cluttered kitchen due to hectic modern life, but this is just one more reason to keep things clean. Cleanliness is next to godliness, as they say, and in fengshui, this is equally true. We have all experienced the relief of having a clean house. It just makes you feel a lot better after you put in some hard work on cleaning something dirty. It is hard to say why this feeling happens, but it is definitely a reality of human life. Dr. Wu has also said that having a mess here and there is not bad. If things are too clean, to the point of being obsessive, that is not good either. But in terms of general tidiness, focusing on the kitchen and the bedroom is strongly recommended. Just as colors influence our mood, simple things like a clean and clear room are enough to make massive positive changes in fengshui theory. The ancient Daoists understood that even minor adjustments to what we see and interact with every day are enough to sustain a sense of peace and order and thereby preserve health and well-being.

Signs From Heaven

Thunder in the sky is a warning sign from heaven. In human body fengshui, this is represented by flatulence. Yes, as odd as this may sound, that is the human body's form of thunder. Especially in places like Los Angeles, where there are not many thunderstorms, it is vital to listen to the human body in their absence. The body is always talking to us. Understanding this is essential. An ache in our organs is their way of crying out to us, warning us, begging us for change.

According to Dr. Wu, flatulence is nature's way of warding off trouble from our lives. He says that most flatulence, especially during negotiations or critical talks, is a sign for you as a participant to end the conversation or negotiation and leave. It is important to remember that everything has a meaning. Our backsides speak their unique language of danger. Dr. Wu says that gas can portend all manner of smaller difficulties that one can go through. He said the most indicative or meaningful signs could come if you pass gas when you are looking at a property as a renter or buyer or when you are doing fengshui.

If you break wind randomly during your visit to the property, you should just pack it up and leave. Similarly, if lightning always strikes close to your property, this is a bad sign. It means that either animals in the area have cultivated to the point of becoming demons, or demons or other dark spirits have invaded the area, and you should not hang out there. This is an indication your environment is what we could call a bad neighborhood. If a harmless looking neighborhood has pockets of bad people or evil spirits, it is only a matter of time before something starts to go haywire. We have all seen a movie showing how someone moves into a creepy small town where everything is just a bit off or eerie. This is the scenario you are trying to avoid.

I have a friend who lives in such a property. Unusual events are so common, it was featured on one of those ghost-hunter shows. Routinely, she is physically attacked by spirits. She will look in the mirror and see marks on her skin, although nobody has touched her. I have been trying to get her to leave the property, but it's been difficult for her to untangle herself from the situation. Anyone who has ever had a bad roommate or neighbor knows that these types of housing scenarios can be a nightmare. It is best that you avoid a potentially bad living situation from the outset by listening to your backside. Sure, the sounds might not be what you want to hear, but neither will the sirens be a welcome sound when you figure out you live next to some form of evil activity. It would have been better to listen to the warning signs in the first place.

One instance where flatulence is your friend is in the morning. If you wake up and toot, it means that good things are in store for you that particular day. There may be good events or happy tidings, and so forth. One interesting instance that Dr. Wu has mentioned is that if you are working out and you have flatulence, it means that you will suffer something bad the following day, but that bad thing will be lessened because it happened during exercise. In this sense, you can say that exercise can ward off difficulties in your daily life. In terms of personal fitness, it is "use it or lose it" when it comes to your health. You might as well get out there and get active. It can only help you ward off the bad stuff in life. From a Daoist point of view, it can do more than increase physical health, due to its interplay with the spiritual warning signs of the body.

One significant differentiation, according to Dr. Wu, is the flatulence caused by some chronic condition, such as indigestion. A chronic gaseous health condition nullifies using flatulence to predict harm. That type of flatulence falls into a different category altogether. If you are experiencing a lot of problems in your daily life, giving your stomach a rest and reset it with fasting might be one way to get things back on track. Of course, when fasting, you should first consult a medical professional to make sure you are healthy enough to do so, but if you are, it could be a way to stem the tide of a bad cycle happening in your life, on an esoteric level, rather than only a physical one.

This concept of the emissions of the anus is relevant within Daoist medicine across a broad spectrum of treatments, including emergency resuscitation. If a person has been rescued from drowning and you are trying to do mouth-to-mouth resuscitation to revive them, Daoist medicine practitioners usually cover the anus of the person. They cover the anus because they think if the person passes gas or urinates during this time, they will not survive. The logic is that when a person dies, they usually lose control of their bowels, so the goal is to prevent the person from losing touch with the motor functions of the body and keep the soul inside the body. This might land you in an odd situation if you were to perform this in the modern era but, according to Dr. Wu, it is the best way to revive someone who has drowned. Keeping this bodily orifice closed is the key to keeping the person alive.

Another interesting bodily reaction is sighing. Just as the anus might involuntarily release its contents or in emergencies even the life force itself, the mouth can do the same in some surprising ways. Sighing is a natural part of life for some but hazardous to health since it destroys good *qi* in the body. It is not good to sign: avoid it if possible since it signals reluctance to move on or suffering in a bad situation. By sighing, we destroy the original *qi* of the body. This makes sense because if you are facing difficulty in life, it is never good to give up. When you just give up, there are many issues that can come about just by you throwing in the towel. If you have come to the point where you cannot help but express your emotional exasperation out loud with an involuntary sigh, your emotions are taking over your entire body. Like it or not, in life, we are to fight off obstacles and hopefully become spiritually triumphant over everything that ails us. If we cannot do this, we may end up having regrets in life.

The Three Elixir Fields

There are three elixir fields: upper, middle, and lower. The upper governs the top, is located at the third eye, and works on anything to do with heaven. In human body fengshui, the different parts of the top of the head are akin to clouds, thunder, and things higher than us. Many practices revolve around this area of the body, as they aim to strengthen one's connection to heaven.

We have to accept that things are not as linear as we would like them to be in terms of understanding the universe. How then does the upper elixir field relate to heaven? Of course it is on the upper part of the body. But when you understand how the body truly functions, it becomes clear how accurate this is. Human beings are the bridge between heaven and earth. There is a deep connection between all three, which is why this system holds so much significance. People have a lot more spiritual potential than they give themselves credit for. It is only due to the culture of our age that most people do not pursue this further.

We all have to think heavily about what we want out of our lives, and for many, a spiritual connection can scratch the itch that not many other things will. This is why opening the upper elixir field is a matter of importance.

The middle elixir field governs sighing. This is because the middle elixir field is near the heart and rules everything emotional. It is also called the valley. Why? Because, in the female body, it is surrounded by the breasts. Daoists also have a phrase that talks about when a baby is trying to reach a mother's breast for milk: it is climbing the mountain. The valley holds the home of all emotions, including frustrations and sorrow. In terms of the body, many parts are compared to mountains: nose, breasts, male genitalia.

A person who sighs heavily should take care of his emotions by washing the chest area vigorously in the shower and by holding the chest forward. This will help with emotional issues, whatever those may be. Another reason to wash around this area is because it is similar to the Daoist practice of soaking the hands in hot water for five minutes upon waking or soaking the feet for five minutes before bed. This has the effect of preventing colds and also strengthens the heart. Why is this? Even Western science has evidence that the heart can release enzymes which kill cancer cells. It also produces these enzymes during exercise, matching the natural way it works to protect itself. This is another of the good and simple Daoist methods for living a healthier, happier life!

The lower elixir field governs base or earthly things. It is akin to the crops in Daoist theory, where the fertility organs lie in humans. The female genitalia are understood in terms of water flow. They modestly call the uterus the "umbrella." They say that after two years, if a woman cannot conceive, it is time to tune up her umbrella. This is also a catch-all term for treating any sort of feminine issue.

According to fengshui theory, the middle elixir field corresponds to the bedroom. The upper one is like the entryway of the house. The lower elixir field is in the kitchen, as it matches earth. These are all essential to recognize, and we should all be aware of the importance of all areas of the house and the body. If something is out of whack, many times we can look to these areas to find the problem area and then work to find spiritual fixes or solutions for it.

Sun and Stars

Why do people live in places like Los Angeles? Well, it is the perpetual sunshine, of course. According to Dr. Wu, sunshine helps to elevate people's moods, so they are going to be happier in places like Los Angeles than they will be in other climates. Places with too much rain generally cause depression. This may seem like common sense, but it is old knowledge in Daoist fengshui as well. We cannot say that there is any magic bullet for mood improvement, but in my experience, mood has a lot to do with the energies around the body. So, if the energy is good in and around us, we will be much happier in our lives. This is a central concept to realize and something that can help us turn the corner to a happier state of mind. The sun is just one example of the simple ways that we can work to absorb more positive energy in our lives. All you need to do to get more sunshine is to live in a sunny climate, a subtle option that we ultimately have under our personal control in life.

We can all agree that sunshine is one of the easiest ways to feel good on any given day. Being outside and moving around is a good way to keep in good spirits and move forward in any endeavor we may have in life. When we imagine an image of depression, we usually think about someone sitting alone in a room or crying. Even though this is not the case and there are obviously many people who are out and about doing things every day who are still depressed. It is just to say that when we think of happiness, we usually think of children out to play in the yard or other images of sunshine and light. That is the closest thought many people have in their minds linked with pure joy. Sunlight is an archetype of happiness that has physical and emotional resonance in the human mind and in human body fengshui.

Just like the sun, the stars have resonance and multiple meanings. Many flags around the world have star symbolism, representing the people of that nation. According to Dr. Wu, the stars twinkling in the sky means change and also represents the passage of time. Daoist monks often go out to gaze at the stars. But really, this is a common activity for many people; lovers and families alike will all go and look up at the stars as a hobby. This serves to help people spiritually, even subconsciously. Especially on the 15th day of the 8th lunar month, during the Mid-Autumn Festival, the Chinese go out to admire the full moon and look up at the stars. This cultural tradition is still very popular today.

Watching the stars helps us understand our place in the greater cosmos. Why is this? Because in a house, the windows are represented by the stars. They are representative of the outlook of a person's life. Clean windows will let in lots of light and tonify the eyes. Sunlight is essential for eye health in general. Even in terms of a vehicle, it is imperative that the windshield is always clean and clear. The side windows may be a bit dusty, but the front needs to be clean, preventing many accidents not just for the obvious reasons of increased visibility, but also due to good fengshui.

In terms of fengshui theory, mirrors are represented by the stars. The stars are mirrors in heaven. Mirrors should always be kept clean and shine brightly. They should radiate light in a home, just like the stars. I asked Dr. Wu about how they used mirrors in fengshui before they invented the modern mirror. He told me that before the modern mirror, they used to polish bronze to a high sheen and that would reflect just like a mirror does today—only with a metallic hue. Many times, mirrors are placed in a particular spot to make up for or fix a fengshui deficiency in the home. In the case of a dark corner or gloomy room, the mirror can sometimes brighten that spot up and make it less of an energy drain. Mirrors also redirect or repel bad energies and bring in good energy, depending on the circumstances.

This is where convex or concave mirrors come into play since they take energy in toward the house, while convex mirrors push it away. These different types of mirrors are used traditionally to attract or repel energy depending on the circumstances happening in the home. But as with anything metaphysical, you should leave the evaluation to a seasoned professional.

Many modern fengshui cures may make a given situation worse if they are not implemented properly, especially if the problem is serious. Even though modern scientists cannot get close enough to a star to take a sample of its substance, they still theorize that they are made up of the same basic elements as the human body. There will be many star discoveries made in the coming years as access to stargazing equipment becomes more and more affordable. Perhaps this age-old hobby will have a resurgence in popularity due to the advent of modern technology, letting average people explore astronomy.

Human beings are accustomed to using symbols that create a form of universal non-verbal communication. When we look at the flags of many countries, their symbols represent the types of people that live in those countries. Of course, even America has had many different flags over the centuries, as have other, older countries. The symbols on national flags often connect to battles in ancient times. The flag is symbolic of the spirit of the people. And although we are all human beings, there are obvious cultural variations that define us as societies, depending on what part of the globe we are born in.

Humans have been using the stars to not only navigate by sea but also to study the internal workings of the mind. Many people today consider astrology a pseudo-science, but in many spheres of influence, it is still popular. Many presidents of the United States have utilized astrology for political guidance. A good example is Carol Ryder, the astrologer for Richard Nixon in the 1970s. Such traditions date back to ancient civilizations where many emperors, kings, and queens received advice or counsel from astrologers. In Daoist terms, this does not conflict with religion, but it may be considered taboo by modern standards. Perhaps new generations will elect a president who accepts such methods again, as astrology is resurging in popularity among younger age groups.

These concepts, while seemingly insignificant, cannot ever be washed out of the human lexicon. They are too thoroughly ingrained and live with us on a deep level. Many people also have a fascination with their own luck and their future. They want to know that some form of progress in life is possible, and the stars can work to prove that to us. Many times, Dr. Wu will go out and find a person's personal star in the sky to see how that person is doing. This is a deep practice, one that undoubtedly takes a special skill set. The trick is for us as practitioners to find our own star.

We also see the importance of torch light as a worldwide symbol of unity. The torch lighting ceremony at the Olympic Games goes back to antiquity. It has esoteric as well as cultural significance, as the Games are a way for many peoples of the world to come together and relate in a way that surpasses standard diplomacy. We also have the term "passing the torch," which means handing wisdom from one generation to another. What we want to accomplish in life usually involves a teacher to make it possible. As such, the torch can also be symbolic of passing this energy on from one person to another. The special part of this concept is that, the brighter we burn as spiritual souls, the more we can help light other people's flames. No matter how we contribute to humanity, it is crucial for us to kindle the flames of spiritual development so that these great practices of old may continue to benefit our culture as a whole. Without balance with nature and within, what do we really have?

Chapter 13

Body Fengshui for Longevity

No two trees are alike, nor are any two humans. Understanding is achieved by careful observation. Daoist knowledge of natural environments, human structures, and system—and especially of the human body—has developed over millennia through detailed observation and data analysis. Such is the evolution of human body fengshui. The eyes represent the windows to the soul as well as to the house. The eyeballs are akin to sun, moon, and stars.

Eyebrows Typology

From this, Daoists have developed specific systems of classification. For example, there are twenty-eight different types of eyebrows. They may look like willow leaves, silk worms, or the Chinese character for "eight" 八. Different shapes indicate various personality traits and spiritual factors. Are the eyebrows thin? Are they bushy? How far apart? Are they at the same height? In this manner, there are many different categories showing opportunities for wealth and success. These opportunities are also indicated by the brow line and the forehead, another aspect of physiognomy that may be presented in future works. In all cases, try not to damage the eyebrows' hair. You can dye them every now and then, but generally try to preserve them. Here are some of the more common traits:

Location

High Eyebrows: People with high eyebrows (far from the eyes) are sweet-tempered, family-oriented and accomplish something early.

Low Eyebrows: People with low eyebrows can hardly retain their composure and are generally insidious and troubled by family affairs. Also, they are realistic and look to immediate rather than long-term interests.

Too Low: If the eyebrows are too low (very close to the eyes), people are usually narrow-minded, like to bear grudges, and inclined to be a voyeur.

Different Heights: For people with eyebrows of two different heights, one of the parents will be prone to accidents. Men with a higher left eyebrow enjoy a high position in the family while those with a higher right eyebrow often abide by their wives; for women, it is the opposite.

Compactness

Compact Eyebrows: Those with compact eyebrows are generally easy-going, especially to their friends, thus have good relations with friends and often get their help.

Loose Eyebrows: Those with loose eyebrows at the tip often become estranged with friends and can hardly depend on their brothers and sisters.

Arrangement

Glossy: People with glossy eyebrows growing in the same direction are lucky and honest.

Messy: People with messy eyebrows growing in different directions have average IQ and reach few achievements. Their words do not match their deeds, and they are generally hypocritical and have incompatible parents.

Broken

If the eyebrow has a break or is thin in the middle, it suggests the death of one parent, brother or sister in early years, or hand fracture and injury. (Yourchineseastrology.com 2014a, yourchineseastrology.com)

Nine Types of Mouths

The mouth is very important in human body fengshui, as it is a key factor in reading other people's feelings. Daoists place a great significance on the study of reading signs by observing the mouth. Dr. Wu believes that this section of physiology can teach us a lot. For instance, the bigger a person's lips, the higher the person's libido. Larger lips have always been seen as sex symbol, as is demonstrated among many celebrities, even in different cultures and eras. A practitioner of human body fengshui should look at the lips and see if they are thin or full and what size they are to determine many things in life.

Not only the shape of the lips, but also the cavity of the mouth is important when examining a person. Is it wide or shallow? Are the lips thick or narrow? In terms of medical diagnostics, the lips of females can indicate many different things about her overall health. A darker color on the lower lip signals that she has regular menstrual cycles, while a darker upper lip indicates that she may have problems with fertility or possibly tumors. In the East, males generally look for thin lips as a sign of beauty, but Daoists look for the opposite. They generally find young women with fuller lips to be better suited for marriage. Another thing the mouth indicates is the size of the genitals. People with bigger oral cavities generally have larger genitals. For males, the size of the nose is another indicator, although the oral cavity is better. There are nine main types of mouth shapes:

Smiling Mouth: This kind of mouth is wide, clean-cut, regular rather than slanting, featuring uniform thickness, rosy lips and slightly upward corners that look like they are smiling. People with a smiling mouth are gentle and love to smile. Good temper and slow coaching are common tags.

Crescent Moon Shaped Mouth: Unlike the smiling mouth, this kind of mouth is naturally upward like a crescent moon. It boasts rosy lips, pretty white teeth, and a slightly thinner lower lip but looks beautiful as a whole. Those with a crescent moon shaped mouth are the born optimists who are capable and experienced rather than slovenly and haggling over every ounce, thus they have quite good relations with people. Born with a silver spoon in their mouth, they are intelligent, fond of study, profoundly learned, well-spoken, emotional, and highly motivated. Rosy and glossy lips suggest better luck in later years.

Reverse Boat Mouth: In contrast to the crescent moon shaped mouth, this kind looks like a reverse boat and features a bigger upper lip. It is dark red, has downward corners, and a tightened and well-defined lower lip. According to face reading, people with a reverse boat mouth are pessimistic, assume the worst, have jitters, and lack confidence. Slow in movement, they have little courage and motivation to move forward.

Round Mouth: People with a round mouth are simple-minded, uncalculating, helpful, easily contented rather than importunate, and accordingly loved by others. They tend to lead a comfortable and peaceful life with high position, great wealth, and many descendants. Being honest and sincere, they are suitable for both politics and business. However, they are self-willed, extremely suspicious, and lacking in security since they tend toward worry and fear, leading to poor communication with the opposite sex and difficulties in relationships.

Square Mouth: With thick and regular lips, this kind of mouth is square and flat, just like the Chinese character *si* 四 (four). The corners are clear-cut and flat rather than downward, making others feel lively and cheerful. Those with square mouth are usually smart, learned, capable, curious about the unknown, and eager to learn. No matter what they do, they are dedicated, decent, honest, tolerant, and trustworthy. They tend to have wealth, rank, longevity, and prosperous offspring, as well as better fortune in old age.

Lotus Mouth: A lotus mouth is flat and long, featuring dull-red and thin lips with slightly downward corners. People with a lotus mouth usually lack sincerity, talk endlessly, and accomplish nothing although they seem to be always on the run.

Cherry/Rosebud Lips: In moderate size, this kind of mouth has slightly upward corners, ruddy and glossy lips, and tidy and white teeth. It looks like a blooming lotus when smiling. In physiognomy, people with this kind of lips are intelligent, gentle, and kind; they enjoy great popularity and always get help from others. For women, the mouth with cherry lips is even better as it suggests nobility.

Blowing Fire/Thunder God Mouth: A blowing fire or thunder god mouth features downward or invisible corners, white yet extroverted and uneven teeth. People with this kind of mouth tend to be alone and helpless, have shortened lives, lack sincerity, stir up enmity, juggle black and white, and lead a miserable later life. Women with blowing fire mouth have bad luck with husbands and children. For men, the situation is not so serious.

Lined Mouth: A lined mouth boasts downward corners as well as thin and lined lips in dark red. In general, older people have wrinkled lips. In younger and middle-aged people, the lined mouth symbolizes a hard life full of busyness and rushing about. Even if they enjoy longevity, they will be lonely, helpless, and uneasy in later years. Sometimes, they attain some achievements but suffer unexpected financial losses. Also, they have poor relations with people and are prone to dangerous things.

Pearl in the Sea: A projecting part in the center of the upper lip marks a mouth that is called pearl in the sea. People with this kind of mouth are arrogant rather than submissive, and their thin upper lip suggests stinginess. If you have such a person in your life, you will get along with them but better do not reveal your inner thoughts because they are Janus-faced, extremely dangerous, and full of nasty tricks. Since they often offend others, they are not suitable for the work related to PR. (Yourchineseastrology.com 2014b)

The Power of Words

While you may think some of the characteristics of the mouth are somewhat trivial, the most significant thing about a person's mouth is that it should say nice things to others. Daoists believe that all disease comes from the mouth. This has never been revealed, but it forms an important aspect in all areas of life. If you say bad things, you attract disease and illness. As, for example, the Complete Perfection Master Wang Zhijin (1178-1263) says,

> Also, do you not know that the mind is the master of the body? If the master is not at ease, the whole body will become disorderly. Have you not heard, as a man of old once said, 'For the mind to be turbulent and the will to be disorderly is the gate to hell'? Thus, you will beckon disasters beyond what was allotted to you. If your mind is in such a state a light illness will become heavy, and a heavy illness will lead to death. This is because your nature has become muddled and disordered.
>
> If you are unrestrained in various matters, you will suffer illness beyond your [normal] share. In this case the disease has been created by you yourself. What you create, you must receive. Who else do you have to blame? Those who exercise the ground of their minds must not be like this. Each of you please keep this in mind. (Eskildsen 2004, 150)

Earlier Daoist thinkers linked illness to poor morality:

> Importantly, illnesses were seen as owed neither to demonic influences (as in exorcism) nor to imbalance of cosmic forces (as in classical medicine), but to moral faults. As part of the healing ritual, an officiant submitted petitions—reporting the petitioner's fault, confession, repentance, and request for aid—to the Officers of Earth, Water, and Heaven, the three main original deities of the Celestial Masters (Tianshi dao). An analogous emphasis on ethics and morals is the main feature of the best-known early Celsetial Masters text, a partially-preserved commentary to the *Daode jing*. (Pregadio 2016; see also Bokenkamp 1997, 29-148)

Yet the direct link between words and disease has never before been revealed to the general public. According to Dr. Wu, disease in the body occurs in two ways—through the food you eat or the words you speak. The analysis of speaking is a study in itself but essentially, without going into great detail, it says that any words we say have a great deal to do with the outcomes of our lives. This may seem hard to fathom, but everything we say does have an effect on the outside world. If we cannot control our mouth, we are not in control of our mind. Laozi also echoes this:

> Watch your thoughts, they become your words; watch your words, they become your actions; watch your actions, they become your habits; watch your habits, they become your character; watch your character, it becomes your destiny. (Goodreads.com)

Communication in itself is an art form, and Daoists believe that phrasing words in a way that does not harm others is essential for one's long-term spiritual growth and personal health. It is also the biggest factor in terms of how one is received in the outside world. Many Daoists practice a form of repentance for ill words they may have spoken in the past by biting their tongues. Sometimes they do this until their tongues bleed. Verbal communication is ninety percent of how you are perceived in the outside world.

Visual appearances make up only ten percent of how you are judged in the public eye. It really is all about words. Communication is an essential component of life, including any form of spiritual study. Many people look plain or ordinary, but they do well in life because they speak well. Dr. Wu has stated on numerous occasions that many university professors are of this ilk. They may dress plainly, but their words propel them to distinction. In modern terms, you could think of someone like this as similar to a YouTube influencer or a Ted X Talk speaker. While these people may not have outstanding merit, their communication style moves them ahead in society.

These communication-based personalities are capable of uniting large groups of people for various causes. The culmination of the art of communication boils down to what Dr. Wu calls mouth morality—the ethics of speech. Is what you say moral, ethical, inspiring, and non-derogatory? This is something extremely simple to change in your life, something you have direct control over.

It may be difficult to reorient your way of thinking overnight. But you can all work to correct speech habits and patterns. When in doubt, do not say anything. We all have heard the saying, "If you do not have anything nice to say, do not say anything at all." Daoists would say that this is a natural form of training from heaven that has been passed down on the instinctive level. Everything we are taught comes from somewhere, and heaven has its own unique way of slipping us enough information to be productive human beings if we choose to listen.

The Buddhist-Daoist Connection

So how did all of this knowledge about the mouth come about? Its history is fascinating. Long ago, Buddhists and Daoists had periodic meetings to discuss different types of spiritual practice. This was a major meeting of the minds, and senior monks would come from all around China, Tibet, and surrounding countries to attend. During these meetings, there were lectures, and participants exchanged information.

The most notable Buddhist in the world is Shakyamuni who reached full enlightenment and became the Buddha Gautama. While sitting beneath the Bodhi tree for forty-nine days, he realized that all human diseases were caused by the mind as expressed in words and lifestyle choices, most importantly food. On the Daoist side, Laozi sat in a solitary cave for an eighty-one-day sojourn of reclusive meditation and discovered that diseases came not only from food but were also driven by words.

Their unique insights into the functions of the mouth eventually gave birth to Five Centers Practice, created to cleanse the body not only of food-borne toxins absorbed during daily meals but also of those associated with the improper usage of words. All food, no matter how organic, contains some toxins in one form or another. If we think about this logically, it is easy to see how a decomposing form of fruit, plant, or animal may be toxic at the root level. This comes back to the fundamental question that asks if something is not alive, how much of its living essence does it retain? But even without this perspective, we can recognize that the things we eat may not always be good for us.

This being the case, Daoists look to medicinal herbs as the best food to ingest since everything contains some form of toxins. Of course, they realize that people need to eat, but there is a difference between eating and nourishing the human body. Some studies have examined how much food one person eats over an entire lifetime, concluding that on average they consume about seventy-five tons of food. The idea is that, after you eat your quotient of food, you are done and will die at that point. Generally speaking, the more you eat, the more likely you are to become sick and die early. To counterbalance this and stimulate the natural functions of digestion and elimination, it is best to practice qigong.

Qigong, then, serves as a valid alternative to eating. Having practiced for years, I can attest to this. Doing lots of qigong will case the appetite to decrease while the energy level remains the same or increases. It may seem odd, but it is in fact the case. Food is more optional than one would think. Of course, it can also be said that food is one of the primary sources of human joy, but at a certain level of development, the joy food provides may subside and a new source of joy may emerge. However, processes like this cannot be done forcefully. Everything should be natural and happen on its own, matching the right timing associated with it. Another dimension of this is extreme fasting, when people eat nothing and, in some cases, even do not take water. Both in China and also especially in

India, such people have been scientifically studied over long periods of time. They do not consume food, and although they may look frail, they are able to function. One example is Prahlad Jani, who has been observed for over two weeks while not eating or drinking water of any kind.

> After fifteen days of observation during which he reportedly did not eat, drink, or go to the toilet, all medical tests on Jani were reported as normal. The doctors reported that although the amount of liquid in Jani's bladder fluctuated and that Jani appeared "able to generate urine in his bladder," he did not pass urine. Based on Jani's reported levels of leptin and ghrelin, two appetite-related hormones, DRDO researchers posited that Jani may be demonstrating an extreme form of adaptation to starvation and water restriction. DIPAS stated in 2010 that further studies were planned, including investigations into how metabolic waste material is eliminated from Jani's body, from where he gets his energy for sustenance, and how he maintains his hydration status. (wikipedia.com)

We can say that an outside, looking inward understanding comes from Daoism and while an inside, looking outward understanding comes from Buddhism. Buddhists discovered that what we ingest (energy going in) causes half of all disease, while Daoists understood that what we speak (energy going out) produces the other half. The true root of all major maladies in the human body is linked to anger of one kind or another. Food transmuted from the external to the internal is a yang transition; words spoken from the internal to the external is as a yin transition. This is a deep concept, but one that makes sense when you think about it. If we cannot control our own emotions as a species, what can we control? If we are consumed by anger, our hearts can never be at peace.

During our lives, inevitably things happen that make us upset. If we do not use our spiritual skills to rid ourselves of these mental hang-ups, we cannot go beyond these issues as the ancients did. Animals, too, if traumatized, often have systemic issues. Horses or dogs that were neglected or beaten are hard to rehabilitate, and many beaten-down dogs react aggressively when meeting new people. To me, humans are similar, many of their reactions coming back to anger.

Without spiritual practices or creative outlets, it can be hard to dissipate heavy emotions. Some traumas come from childhood, but just as many arise from having to bite your tongue in the modern work environments or relationships. We all have to be conscious of the situations around us and the emotions we feel toward these situations. If you want to be in a relationship, you must accept a certain amount of negative emotional behavior to make that relationship work. But when we see communication problems adding up to anger, we must use more caution. Since we may risk more toxins as a result of these decisions, I do not think that there is an absolute right or wrong on many of these lifestyle choices. Still, there should be some thought about the person to whom you give your emotional energy.

Of course, this is where healing work and personal development can come to the fore. They are tools to clear up any lingering issues before they affect us in health or state of mind. These same issues, when brought into the body politic, can also build up and fester. This can lead to things like wars and economic instability. These are important things to realize when we sit and think. Anger is at the root of so many problems in human life. It makes sense that it is at the root of our own health issues as well.

In terms of purification of the human body, ways of detoxification are urination, defecation, and the practice of qigong. Qigong is the premier process as it helps to detox the body on all levels. It is also the only modality we have complete and immediate control over. Dr. Wu emphasizes especially that words are powerful and that all negative things about others have ramifications even if they are not present. Hence, small talk, gossip, and derogatory remarks do not accomplish anything but in the end create hurt for yourself. Silence is another art form, if you look at it from this angle. This may also explain why many spiritual masters may have little to say.

It seems simple and it is the golden rule, but the practice of mindful silence and positive speech is vital for perpetuating one's livelihood. Bad things we say to others will eventually breed disease and cause misfortune in life. Dr. Wu says that saying negative things not only hurts humans in your life, but it also hurts the plant and animal life in the area. This may be why Daoist masters often refuse to comment on certain issues. They know this is a heavenly law and many times do not want to get in the middle of discussions that disparage others unnecessarily. These things must be a central part of living a spiritual lifestyle. We all trust a person more when they are careful and not reckless with words. We all have to do what we can to reform ourselves as we age. Mindful speech is something simple that anyone can practice with a little bit of conscious effort.

Modern science has been catching up to this ancient Daoist concept. Experiments conducted by a Japanese team found that water that was exposed to beautiful words and beautiful music was imbued with mystical crystalline patterns when examined under the microscope. The water that was subjected to hateful and negative things being said had a disfigured crystalline structure when viewed under the microscope.

Dr. Wu also notes that many fruit trees or bushes near a highway are victims of this phenomenon. They consistently yield less fruit, not because of toxic smog but because of the constant car noise they are must suffer. Apparently, large amounts of engine noise equate to negative *qi* in the plant world. This is similar in human housing: anyone who has lived next to a freeway, train track, or airport knows that those are not pleasant places to reside. It is a good idea to remain cognizant of your surroundings and pay attention to where you feel best.

The easiest way for you as an uninitiated practitioner to test the basics of fengshui is to see how you sleep in a certain space. If you do not feel good, the place may have issues. The same is true if children always cry there, so that bringing a child under five into a space you think of renting or buying is an easy way to do you're a small fengshui analysis. If the child is happy and playful, it is a good space, but if he or she starts to cry, is agitated, or upset, it is not good.

In essence, this information is not all that new. Dr. Wu has just taken it to the next level by letting us know that we are all fully responsible for our own health on many different levels. Our words and eating habits have the power to either seal our fate or send us upward. Complaining about others or the vagaries of life does nothing but hurt us in the long run. If you have bad energy around you or in your body, these types of negative activities can seem more attractive. We have the responsibility to know what is most necessary for us to avoid problems in our lives.

Fortunately, qigong presents a viable doorway to self-healing No matter where our spiritual starting point may be, it can help us rectify our past misdeeds and purify our souls. Qigong works to strengthen the stomach and spleen, but it is also the most effective way to eliminate toxins. The movement of *qi* through the organs metabolizes accumulated toxins, both physical and non-physical. Its unique form of breathing meditation is a mental exercise as well, deepening spiritual awareness. As a secondary aid, consuming quality water can help purify thoughts and assist the body in its natural purification process. According to Dr. Wu, this is the essence of why the Five Centers Practice was created: to eliminate bad karma and bad energy from the body.

Spiritually Revered Animals

In the ocean, sharks are often considered the top predators, but Daoists see the giant turtle as the king of the sea. In the spectrum of the five colors, it is characterized by greenish black or blackish green. Turtles represent yin because they can live as long as several thousand years. Modern science has documented turtles living well into their hundreds, but Daoists have tales of revered turtles kept safe in monastic walls for thousands of years. In the animal kingdom, they have the most extended longevity of all creatures. Obviously, sea turtles mostly live in the water, but they also have many lesser-known spiritual functions. Representing deeper meanings, they are seen as the treasured offspring of dragons and can also be viewed as reflecting a person's health. Their key characteristic is being a heavenly yin animal. Incorporating yin increases longevity, which is one reason why human females often have a longer life expectancy than males and today women tend to live seven to ten years longer than men.

All things in this world originally came from beneath the earth. All creatures, human or animal, are born from the females. In Daoist terms, if you search for the origin point, you will find the cause of longevity. This is why many practices focus on returning to an original, more childlike state. Children are energetically pure and do not inhibit their *qi*-flow. They are not merely small people but an embodiment of heavenly principles. This is also echoed in the *Daode jing*. When you look at a child, you will understand Dao, which is the way of all things. Many adults say that they yearn to relive their youth, which Daoists translate into the search for original *qi* as the foundation of spiritual advancement. Children are wise in their own mystical ways. Having been born such a short time before, they still have a connection to heaven.

Wild herbs are most potent when they come from the original plant in the center of the patch. When humans are younger, it is helpful for them to move around a lot. Travelling and experiencing life in different places helps them to live a better life. Yet conversely, trees that move around a lot by being replanted often die. The Daoist takeaway is that if you move around a lot, you should do it before you are forty-five.

After that age, it is best to stay in one primary location. Moving too much in later age can cause premature death. You should strive to settle down between forty-five and sixty. For instance, if you are in a cold place, you should not move to a warm one. Avoid moving from north to south and east to west, or vice versa. This is a key point of longevity among inner Daoist teachings Dr. Wu has passed down.

In the *Yijing*, the number four predicts right or wrong, if something is doable or not doable. One-two-three-four: humans are differentiated from other animals by the number four. They have two knees, two feet, two shoulders, and two hands. The number four, in essence, represents the human body in fengshui study. Turtles also represent the number four, making it another key element of human body fengshui. It does so because its shell looks like the universe, which also made it a key means of divination and the earliest Chinese writing, so-called oracle bone script, which dates back almost 3500 years. Holes would be drilled into the carapace of a turtle, then it would be heated. Cracks appeared that went into certain directions, signifying a positive or negate response to a question asked. Then all this would be recorded in writing on the shell, activating it as a key tool for connecting to heaven

The Rise of the Elements

The interplay between yin and yang is present in all things and should be continually studied to understand the underpinnings and deeper meanings of Daoist worldview. Every day we are subject to the forces of yin and yang, even if we do not think about it. For example, even though flames are yang, they come from earth or wood, which represent the essence of yin. This is most obvious in a simple cigarette lighter: the flame is yang but comes from the lighter fluid inside which is yin. It does not matter whether you were born a man or a woman. In all cases, you were born from a woman, which means form the yin force. It can even be said that, as a species, humans are mostly looking down instead of looking up. Most of our organs grow downward; only the ears grow upward.

Tigers are carnivorous, while sheep and cows are herbivores. Herbivores have more yin essence, and as such tend to be more passive; carnivores have yang essence and are more active and predatory, relying on instinct and aggression. They tend to have shorter life than herbivores, which causes people to avoid eating meat (yang) and become vegetarians or vegans to engage the yin principle.

Daoist's claim that eating animals is toxic because at the time of death, the animal is full of fear and other emotions, which makes its meat toxic as the emotions are transferred through the blood in meat. Plants, on the other hand, also have emotions, but their fruit do not contain their sap, the equivalent blood in animals, and therefore are much less toxic. Japan and parts of China have places where people live the longest in the world, in some areas with populations that are all well over a hundred years old. Most of the people there are vegetarians. Here is one example.

> In 2012, his China-based Mandarin coach mentioned a recent documentary profiling a town with "magical properties" known as Longevity Village. It is called Bapan, located in the southwest of China near the Vietnamese border, and there, nearly 1 in every 100 people is over 100 years old, compared to 1 in 5,780 in the United States. These centenarians, however, are not wasting away, bedridden. They're active, happy, and healthy. (Tucker 2017)

There is new research from Harvard showing that extracted enzymes from fruits and vegetables can prolong life. Scientists have tested this extensively on both animal and human subjects. The head scientist of the team, a professor from China, is forty-nine but reports feeling like he is still in his twenties. The treatment had a rejuvenating effect on old mice, documenting that the consumption of fruit and vegetable enzymes has a rejuvenating result.

Part of the reason is that processed plant enzymes are easier to metabolize than complex animal proteins. But if we look deeper, we realize that the emotions slaughtered animals carry are the real problem. If you are afraid, angry, or sad, how long does it take you to get past this emotion? For some people, a few seconds; for others, a few minutes; for yet others, it may be days. A whole range of stress-induced biochemistry floods the organs and flesh and, even after the main impact of the emotion is gone, the body still deals with the lingering chemical residue.

This is no different for animals, which we consume after the experience extreme fear as they go to slaughter. Not only do our bodies have to process the end result of this emotional stress, but in addition many people eat to cope with emotions. According to Dr. Wu, this is the opposite of what people should do. Eating like this makes the emotional backlog worsen. Spiritually dedicated people are fortunate because they have specific processes to work on themselves and clear emotions. Especially qigong is designed to process both our own emotions and the residue of those of others inside our tissues. Time alone does not have to be our only healer.

From a Chinese medical perspective, it is worth looking deeper into the function of the emotions, the stomach, and the meridians as well as their links to qigong practice. The Conception Vessel represents the yin energy of the turtle, running along the front midline of the torso. It also incorporates the stomach, which looks like a turtle shell and is considered a second brain. Dr. Wu notes that working with Conception Vessel and the stomach is like building a house on a solid foundation. He uses its points extensively, often finding them linked to emotions that relate to the stomach, expressed in common expressions like "I can't stomach this," "I have got butterflies," or "I have a gut feeling."

These feelings are linked with the emotional part of the brain in many respects. If we think about the stomach, we think about things in a different way. It is not about what you think but how you feel or even what your intuition tells you. Many feelings are stuffed into our stomachs, which is why we eat when we are going through emotional or stressful times.

Stress eating is a momentary coping mechanism to calm the body so you can process whatever you are going through. This is acceptable on a micro level, as sometimes we need to take a break and have a nice meal. But when it is taken overboard or becomes chronic, bad energy accumulates. In fact, our bodies do not need much food to operate in the modern world. This is imperative to remember, especially in connection with the Daoist limit of food can consume in one lifetime before we die. Most stress tends to occur during major holidays, when daily patterns are disrupted and seeing family members can cause overeating. Often emotions arise as there is unrest or tension in the extended family. If we are not cognizant of this factor, we may well die before our time.

We all have the ability to process emotions through spiritual practices handed down from ancient masters. They knew that human life is stressful, so they put things in place for people to learn how to deal with stress not only in a spiritual but also in a very mature way. Instead of running away from stress, we can transmute it with spiritual practices. We are energy, and if we do not know how to change energy within ourselves, we will face hardships with no recourse. If we embrace working with the flow of energy, as in qigong, we can transform our lives. It is a blessing to be able to change these emotional reactions in creative and empowering fashion.

The body's main center and back channels should be aligned for best results. Just as you sit centered on a house, it is good to find the middle balancing points on the body. The Conception and Governing Vessels are like measurements on a scale, so when you are looking at a person for treatment or acupuncture, you want to see if these things are lining up. Dr. Wu showed me this in person by looking down the midline of one of his patients. If you look closely, you can accurately see the alignment of a person and tell how their life is going.

This is also why many of the qigong forms involve rotating images of objects in your mind around the center point of the body: this helps clear the channels and keep them straight. If the spine is not straight, usually the internal organs are not in good shape. Similarly, if a tree trunk is straight, its lumber can be used for building a house or other important structures. The spine must be straight and symmetrical to the front of the body for ideal health and life balance.

Anything not in a straight line can represent a different type of condition or disease. When things are out of balance, they can cause untimely or unwanted events in daily life. This is one of the many reasons Dr. Wu usually recommends that people sleep on a hard mattress: it makes the spine stay in alignment. These kinds of small things can make a big difference in life. Anyone who has ever had a bad back will tell you that it is a tough to deal with. Many people with bad backs end up relying on painkillers just to function in their daily life. We have to do all the little things that we can to keep our personal alignment intact.

Central Energy Lines

Any basic fengshui book describes water as governed by yin. Yang creatures, in contrast, are most easily defined by thinking of anything that lives on the land or flies in the air. Flowers, plants, and terrestrial animals all have essence and *qi*, so this is why we should always view them as our brothers and sisters. Whether yang or yin, they are all significant in the eye of heaven. However, some animals are iconic representations of certain finer points of yin and yang. Amongst terrestrial animals, deer are the pre-eminent yang animal, but all two- and four-legged animals are considered yang. Tigers and wolves may be thought of as soldiers who fight in battles, while deer are calm, tranquil animals. They are not contentious, and as a result everyone likes them. They are masters of listening to heaven and hear what is going on around them.

Deer represent the yang channel along the back of the body, just as the turtle represents the yin channel along the front. Throughout history, deer have been thought of fondly for various reasons: they are just like turtles, not bothering anyone else in the animal community. They also have a look of innocence in their eyes and a certain majesty in movement, making them companions of Daoist immortals.

The Sika deer in particular has spots that, according to the Chinese, represent the five lakes and four seas, while their antlers match heaven and the sun and their hooves symbolize hell. In addition, they also have unique ears. Giraffes are similar to deer: they have long necks that can reach up to heaven and obtain information about things, but their bodies do not represent the universe like those of the deer. Among animals, the Sika deer is most representative of the elements, a feature that may also have caused the making of popular movies such as *Bambi*. Deer antlers can be placed in the home to balance *qi*-flow. Chinese medicine uses them to increase life energy and sexual potency, treating impotence and other fertility issues. Herbal formulas that contain deer antler shavings are at a premium, and the antlers are in high demand. This leads to poaching, which causes difficulties and should not be supported.

Then again, deer are linked to the Governing Vessel, which runs along the back of the torso and represents good fortune and potential. If it is not straight, there will be many barriers to success and progress in life, and many yang-deficient patients should take herbal medicines with deer ingredients to balance their energy. In acupuncture, the Governing Vessel (Dumai) is significant because it treats a host of different conditions. Its matching partner is the Conception Vessel (Renmai). It, too, has its own points and is used widely in therapy and self-cultivation.

> The Renmai originates in the uterus in females and in the lower abdomen in males and emerges onto the surface of the body at Ren1 (Huiyin) in the perineum (the center of the pelvic floor).
>
> From there it ascends along the midline of the abdomen, chest, throat, and jaw, ending at Ren24, in the groove just below the lower lip. An internal portion of the channel then winds around the mouth, connecting with DU26 (above the upper lip) and ascending to ST1 just below the eye.
>
> A branch of the Renmai begins in the pelvic cavity, enters the spine and ascends to the base of the skull and lower jaw. This branch that runs basically parallel (if not fully intertwined with) the Dumai points to the mutual interdependence between the Renmai—the most yin of meridians—and the Dumai, the most yang.
>
> The trajectory of the Renmai, along with the midline of the anterior portion of the torso, allow for direct access, via its acupuncture points, to the most important internal organs. Because it traverses the lower abdomen, it also is used (via the points Ren4 and Ren6) to access and nourish the lower dan tian and Snow Mountain, the storehouse of the body's deepest energies. (Reninger 2019, learnreligions.com)

While the deer and the turtle represent the vertical channels of meridian flow, adjusting the body's alignment goes beyond them. Dr. Wu says that the horizontal lines in the body should be aligned as well. Most modern medical doctors will check your height and weight, but Daoists also see if your lines are in alignment in the Chinese equivalent of a routine check-up. In women misalignment is easily spotted: one breast may be lower than the other. But there are also other ways. You can liken this to the wheels on the car needing to be straight to keep you in the lane. Yes, you may make a turn, but the direction of the car should be straight to keep you safe and headed in your chosen direction. Therefore, the mechanic performs a routine tire alignment and adjustment. In qigong, the microcosmic orbit that connects the Conception with the Governing Vessel is strengthened and aligned. The energy rotating within us, as in a gyroscope, needs to flow correctly to keep everything in balance. Many events and potentials in life are linked to the direction that we take.

This is why we have a birth direction and, when practicing qigong, stand facing specific directions at certain times for different purposes. If we do not go in the right direction in life, there will be more problems than need be. We have all taken some trip or vacation that has ended up being not what we had hoped for. These are micro-examples of how correct timing and the right place can be crucial. Yet many people go in the wrong direction in terms of career and love, adding difficulty to their lives. Major life decisions play out slowly over a long time so that people do not notice where they went wrong nor see the connection with their body. In fact, all is intertwined. When we do good things for others and make good decisions, we see tangible positive effects in our internal and spiritual alignment. When we live up to our destiny, good things happen naturally. Such is the nature of the universe.

If you look for a quick-glance cheat sheet to tell someone's fortune, all the fortune and luck you have in your life will also show up on your face. Similarly, when we are looking at the front channel areas in women, we see that the area between the breasts and the belly button can be one way of diagnosing breast cancer. In men, the area between the belly button and the genitals represents marriage or family in life.

The channels associated with deer and turtle are important in healing practice. The one in back, while mainly linked with the deer, can also be considered the dragon, just as the front channel can also be linked with the crane in addition to the turtle. From the center of the chest to the head is thought of as the crane, while the stomach is symbolic of the turtle. When we look at a crane, we can see an interesting comparison to human anatomy. The breast of both people and cranes expands outwards, and the arms are akin to the wings. Our necks can stretch up and elongate and therefore have a crane like nature. Human necks are notable because they are quite large compared to many other creatures. Of course, It is essential for us to make the most our unique traits so that we may expand into our greater selves in the fullness of time.

Life and Spine

he back channel is the dragon column that supports the C1 cervical spine all the way down to the coccyx. It represents a person's life expectancy and health. In terms of symbolism, C1 and C2 are the beams that hold the roof of a house. In this sense, the spine not only has symbolic meaning as the dragon but can also be used as a divinatory tool to examine different periods of life. Thus, it is revered in Chinese medicine and modern chiropractic and massage work. Both modalities place a paramount importance on the functionality, fluidity, and alignment of the spine. Anyone who has ever had a crick in the neck knows just how painful that type of ailment can be.

Daoists have associated each section of the spine with an age in life. The C1-C2 cervical spine represents people up to fourteen years. The section from C3 to C7 shows the next twenty-eight years. Further down, starting at T1, each vertebra represents another seven years of life all the way down to the lumbar segments. Again, C1 and C2 are most critical, also matching the sun and moon.

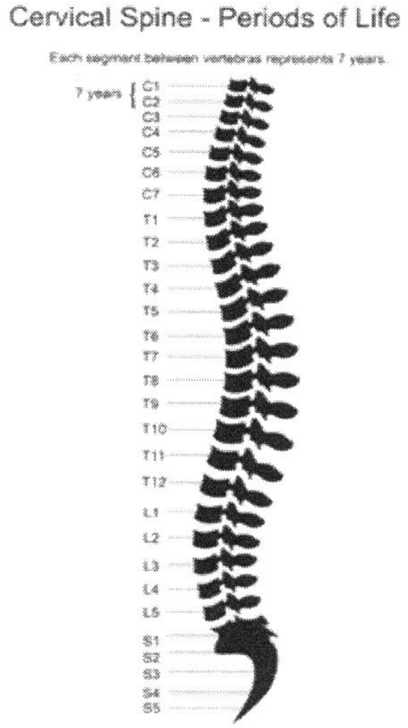

Divinatory practice of examining the spine is known as "touching the bone" or "palpitating the spine." Daoists touch the spine to diagnose a person's life expectancy rather than disease. People today believe that the spine can be manipulated, but in ancient times they would not manually adjust it. To change a person's fortune, physicians would put a towel on their back and light it on fire to extend life and protect against misfortune. Dr. Wu also describes other, more elaborate rituals used to change a person's fate. Sometimes in life, unconventional solutions are the only ones.

This is exemplified by the "Gordian knot" predicament faced by Alexander the Great. For those of you that do not know the story, there was a huge ball of tangled rope in this town in the Middle East when Alexander the Great was traveling along. It was foretold that whoever could untangle the knot would go on to conquer the world. Alexander the Great took out his sword and cut the knot open, indicating his harsh ways of conquest. However, you cannot say that the solution did not work in this instance. Many people would have sat and tried to untangle it bit by bit, but the unconventional solution was the one that worked.

Spirituality can be like this as well. It is a matter of perspective. If we cannot see what is holding us back, how will we eventually solve the problem? Spiritual practices, in this sense, are about gaining the awareness to see what is plaguing or ailing us. Hence, we have terms such as enlightenment. This enlightenment is in fact an advanced form of perception or awareness in terms of figuring out what is causing the things around us on this spiritual plane. When we can see what is going on, we can then craft our solutions in a more unconventional manner. Most people go after the small fish, but some catch the big ones. Why is this? It takes more skill to catch the big fish and the big fish is normally stronger, faster, and harder to tame when catching it. This is the same with spirituality. When we train ourselves, we are training our ability to deal with bigger problems in our own lives and in society at large.

Color by Color

When you combine all of the colors in the world, black is the result. This is why black is not the absence of color, but all colors put together. Another interesting thing to ponder is that black is the color of night. But it is still a color—even in the absence of light, there is color. If we think about it, there is always either some form of light or some form of color in this existence. Perhaps existence itself in this dimension is linked with color. It cannot be said that there is nothing with no color other than air. But even if the deepest realms of space have color, perhaps there is also something there beyond air. Just because we are in a dark room and can no longer see what is in front of us does not mean that nothing is there.

We could say the same for deep space. Things are out there, but due to our perspective, or lack thereof, we cannot see what is there. When I asked Dr. Wu about this topic, he said that cats see well at night because they have their third eyes open. As such, they do not see black in the night sky but white. If the night sky is white, we can begin to understand how in this world, white is akin to yin. Instead of yin being associated with black, as commonly thought, it is white, seen most clearly when looking at the moon. White in color, it is the queen of all things yin. Dr. Wu also said that right before dawn the temperature is at its coldest, then pointed out that all this information is relative or contextual, as there are no absolutes in the universe as documented in the *Yijing*. The key is to understand how yin and yang morph back and forth.

Adepts of human body fengshui have a secret they do not tell outsiders. Black corresponds with yin, which matches the kidneys. Even though black is yin, in the human world, it becomes male. In line with this, when white comes into the human world, it becomes female. Because when you add up all the colors and put them together, they form black. Meanwhile, the absence of any color is white.

This means that a male's life force is judged by the black spots on his body, notably on forehead, thighs, forearms, scrotum, anus, and more. Even though males are considered yang, the root essence of their being comes from yin. Just as in the lighter, the yang flame comes from yin liquid. Even though the natural association with males has traditionally been white, since their yang came from the yin, they are now linked with black. In females, one should look for white spots on foreheads and bodies as well as for a whitish glow. In males, too, one looks for a blackish glow on forehead, neck, and reproductive organs. This coloring is not a tan but subtler. Only one who knows what to look for can read it on the body. This is a more advanced form of Daoist body reading, enhanced by years of qigong training to sharpen the senses.

When assessing the human body for these spots, where should we look? When you are looking for the black or white spots on a man or woman's body, you look at different parts of the body for different ages. From birth to age 28, the key area is the forehead; from 28 to 45, the cervical spine; from 45 to 60, the inner forearm; from 60 to 84, the reproductive organs; and from 84 to 130, the inner thighs.

In terms of longevity, if a female has white inner thighs, she will live to over 90. If body, you see a greenish tinge, there will be health with minor episodes of sickness. Red represents passion, marriage, and friendship. Yellow stands for money and prosperity, especially in the area of the spine. The easiest place to look is the anterior forearm. When there is a fair amount of red, the person will be distraught by emotional events. The forehead in general represents life and death and is a key physical location to give indications about life expectancy. All the five main colors can be found here. The neck governs career issues, while other areas are relevant for love and relationships.

To determine longevity, one way is to look at the hairline, regardless of the amount of hair and whether one is bald or not. The key area is on the outside of the head, the part that shapes the face on its outer edges. This area does not age quite as quickly as the traditional hairline and will stay fixed over years after. Dr. Wu did not elaborate beyond this, so it is safe to assume that this area has certain patterns or characteristics in it that might cause a person to live a longer or shorter life.

Skin color is something that we all have. It is heavily tied to beauty standards that vary widely in different cultures. In America, people like to have a warm summer tan. But in China it is more desirable to remain rather pale, since people with darker skin are assumed to be laborers. Thus, many Chinese women will cover themselves with an umbrella and other sun-blocking accessories when walking outside in the sunshine. According to Dr. Wu, this is in line with *Yijing* and yin-yang theory: women's skin should be lighter than men's. The forehead, however, should be light and bright, indicating good luck, yet some darker or black areas mean extended longevity. A little black in the forehead basically means that this person is healthy and will live to old age. In between the moon and the sun, there are the stars. This refers to the area of the forehead between the two eyes. If it is slightly black, you are healthy; if slightly red, you are popular in romance and have a lot of attraction or charisma. If it is yellow, you will have a lot of money.

This theory also translates into fengshui of the home. If the grass in a person's yard is mostly yellow, the family has a lot of money. If the color in the sky is black above a patch of land, there are treasures underneath such as oil, wealth, gold, and so on. As noted earlier, people can represent mountains and trees. Clouds form around mountain peaks and represent the will of heaven. In *Yijing* philosophy, all things must be approached from the opposing view. When a man is about to die, his forehead turns pale; in a woman, it turns darker. Also, if a man's face is pale, many things will happen; the same holds true for darker coloring in women.

Another area to examine is glow in the pubic area, a feature used traditionally as a form of prognostication and an interesting tidbit to know, although hard to practice these days. More acceptable socially is to examine the overall look of the person and get a feeling of their general vibes. For example, successful women often look more like men—as can be seen in various prominent leaders. Many female corporate moguls and celebrities have more masculine facial structures, body language, or posture. Since celebrities also frequently have pronounced heads or faces, these characteristics can be more widely broadcast to others. Many female celebrities exhibit both kinds of features.

However, there is another type of success woman who has highly feminine characteristics. According to Dr. Wu, this is because the two extremes of yin and yang are both fortunate. This second type is nurturing to her kin and generates a powerful and successful family unit: success manifests in harmony. Yet, there is also a down side in that women may be so nurturing that they neglect their own needs and benefits; others again may be so nurturing to themselves and exhibit such astounding beauty that they betray their own families in a multitude of intentional or unintentional ways.

Men, too, can be feminine and have good fortune and success. If they look or act like women, have this a feminine appearance, they are often accomplished in whatever they do. Examples appear in artists and musicians who are prominent in the world of entertainment as well as in newly arising tech moguls, but there are also many beyond the public sector. These people seem soft on the surface soft but work well with others and succeed through their very gentleness in whatever field they work in. Again, it is the interplay between yin and yang elements in people that spells out their opportunities and good luck.

Beyond the yin and yang traits we are born with, we all have a soul partner who influences our appearance. Another field of study in human body fengshui, the soul partner can be an animal, a plant, or another earth-based creature. Whatever we look like can hold a clue as to what our soul partner is, as this comes through in our own personal appearance.

The highest level of this is reached when a person looks like their Chinese zodiac animal, signaling success on a very high level. For example, former president George Bush was born in the year of the monkey, and he looks just like one. These kinds of designations are dictated by heavenly decree. Say what you will about any political figure, they are in fact predestined for their high positions from heaven. We cannot say that anyone being a leader is right or wrong because these things are determined in advance, a matter of predestination. As discussed earlier, opportunities and prominence require a mixture of efforts from ourselves and prior generations.

By this point, you may be thinking, "Well, shucks, I've searched around and I am not sure I have any of these attributes. Is there anything I can do other than qigong to alter my fate in a positive way?" Yes, of course, there are many things that can be done: burying deceased animals, donating money to worthy causes, feeding and sheltering the hungry and homeless, and assisting in the introduction of couples who will find a loving relationship. Anything that you do in this moment will help you in the long run. The reason why these actions are helpful may seem a little shocking, but in essence, it has to do with other simultaneous realities that coexist with ours.

Most people do not see ghosts or demons because they live in a different dimension. While I personally know quite a few people who can see otherworldly entities, it is generally unusual. Children can see these entities up to a certain age, but adults don't. Beyond the demon and the ghost worlds, a yet different dimension exists, which can be pictured as an inverse mirror image to this one. Many things are happening simultaneously in that dimension, but it is the opposite of what happens here. Fundamentally, when we do good, give to charity, or help souls move on in this world, effects reach the inverse world from where protection extends back to the here and now. By doing good things in this dimension, we create helpers in that other world.

Dr. Wu did not speak on this concept in depth. Suffice it to say that, if we take all things from the perspective of yin and yang, it would make sense that, if we are in the yang world of the living, there should also be an inverse world of yin. People in that world would not be dead, but rather live on a different bandwidth of reality. Many times, it is just good for us to do things that not only affect this world but can also help us build a good reputation in the otherworld. Qigong practice, which helps plants and humans alike, is a key action we can undertake to improve both worlds and our connection with them.

There are many stories of people who do nothing but charitable work and gain prominence as a result. I know several people who have attained high recognition and powerful positions through charitable actions. In addition, there are numerous religious figures who are considered saints or saint-like due to their charity and good deeds. Usually, these people do not have a prominent career *per se*, but the accumulation of their smaller actions over their lifetime ends up bringing them a type of acclaim. This inverse dimension plays a part in this progression in their lives as well. Sometimes the actions we take have immediate and direct consequences. Maybe you do something charitable and meet a person who you would never have met otherwise. Thereby the universe cultivates balance and rewards people based on their merits. The rewards system is two-fold as well, enhancing our advance our position in this life as well as our spiritual legacy.

The Five Senses

When we look at the basics of human body fengshui, we also have to look at the most essential things in existence. To begin, it could be said that heaven has three treasures: sun, moon, and stars; earth has three treasures: fire, water, and wind; and humans have three treasures, spirit, *qi*, and essence. While the moon is the mother of all things, we can say that the sun is the father.

There are many different moons in the universe. There are five billion people and five billion stars. Earth is not the only plane of existence; there is other intelligent life in the universe. There are many different forms of life as well as many different moons, not just one mother and/or one father. According to ancient Chinese myth, there were once ten suns that all came to shine forth simultaneously. An archer with heavenly skills shot and nine of them to keep the planet for burning up. The suns relate to vision, which is a main venue of the spirit, linked with the eyes, and activated through the gaze. The next most important sense, connected to a different form of *qi*, is hearing, which is also linked with a person's ability to smell.

In order of importance in life, the auditory sense comes first, followed by vision, smell, touch, and taste. Dr. Wu notes that aging begins with a loss of hearing. which is yet the last sense to go at death. The senses are primarily for engaging with the world but they also allow us to interact with celestial beings and can be trained for longevity, reaching beyond the biological limit of 120 years to reach 150 or more. Westerners tend to think that the deteriorating condition of the knees is the first sign of aging, In China, the ears and senses are more important matching the belief that, if you start aging prematurely, it is because you have not done a good enough job of protecting your sensory organs. You have to nourish your five senses continually in order to charge your body's batteries and be healthier in every respect.

One of the key dates for qigong practice is the 15th day of the 8th month in the lunar calendar. Practicing on this day or night recharges the batteries and makes them more vibrant for the whole year. Qigong is intrinsically tied to the cycles of nature throughout every single year and also the sixty years of the main Chinese calendar cycle. Practicing with effective timing greatly magnifies the results; some feats can only be achieved when one practices on one special day in a generation. I can personally say from my own experience that, when you practice qigong at the proper times, it is like doing the exercises multiple times since the effects are so much stronger. Some practices cause you to feel sensations much stronger if done on their specific days. It is important to follow the proper guidelines for practice as well as observe any own personal experiences that result from it. In this way, we get the most out of them, garnering healing benefits and spiritual insights.

Movement is always better than stagnation. Sitting in one place for too long can cause stagnation and will eventually lead to aging. Even turtles, the masters of longevity, are continually in motion, even if they move slowly. In fact, they move subtly but constantly and are rarely completely at rest. Encapsulating the essence of the yin and yang, if you want to learn how to be fast in your movements, you first need to learn how to move slowly with complete control.

If we can control our muscles in every movement, we master that movement and then can do it at any speed we want. This is obvious in musicians. Artists, athletes, and others who do things that require a complex sense of muscle interaction based on thoroughly trained muscle memory. They can perform their feats with their eyes closed because they are so at one with what they do and no longer have to think consciously about it. Through numerous repetitions, starting slow and gradually getting faster—like the turtle—they have internalized their art to the point where it is completely part of them.

On the other end of the spectrum from the slow and steady turtle, there are tigers and lions who are explosive with their energy and tend not to attain great longevity. Among humans, marathon runners are like them, tending to overexert their bodies and using too much *qi* so that they run out of energy in the long term. Yet oddly, we can see that mailmen and college professors attain longevity. Why is this? It is because they have a steady, routine lifestyle and do a lot of walking and standing as part of their jobs. Dr. Wu also suggests that mailmen live longer because they deliver messages to people, which is a form of doing a good deed, and thus accumulate lots of merits. If we think about it logically, society cannot function properly without messengers bringing important news on time. This is something quite interesting to sit and think about. In life, many times the small things matter most.

Why, then, can Daoists attain longevity? They do not walk all day long nor do they deliver mail. Rather, they boost their senses of hearing, seeing, and so on, move about slowly and maintain a routinized lifestyle. In addition, as Dr. Wu recommends, they eating little at night so they sleep well and harness the overall amount of food assigned to them for their lifetime.

Sensory Perception

The sense of hearing is primary for longevity. Listening to natural sounds, such as wind, water, and animal noises, helps to tune up all the vital senses. Nature strives to keep things in order and balance, applying many different systems that people may never fully understand. Balance can only be achieved through utilizing both yin and yang, essences that originate from the sun and the moon. Listen to all kinds of sounds and achieve balance within your life. All of us instinctively feel better when we are listening to the songs of birds and crickets, sounds with frequencies that not only allows us to tune up our own senses but also destress our system.

Many scientific studies have been conducted on this level, but it is pretty obvious to most people that they feel relaxed after spending time in a forest listening to the wind in the trees or by the ocean listening to the waves. It is not only the *qi* of these things physically affecting our body, but also the auditory sensation we feel. Hearing, moreover, relates to the kidneys, the root of vitality and key storage center of essence. Training hearing and enjoying beneficent sounds thus also enhances the kidneys.

This means that you should listen as much as possible to various noises and sounds. What do they tell you? Well, Daoists listen to natural sounds and use them as alerts to different events in the universe. For example, the rooster's crow alerts them that it is time to wake up and proceed with the day, providing a biological clock that should be followed so one can attain longevity. Dr. Wu also notes that listening to music you like is gives a massage to the brain, and activities that involve sound attune the senses and enhance perception and acuity. The same idea is behind the practice of many grade school teachers who play classical music in classrooms while their students work, creating harmony and increasing intelligence.

Qi, a light breeze, and oxygen are all air, taken in through the nostrils and relating different kinds of information. This allows you to exchange information about the interior and exterior *qi* flowing in and around you. Some smells are pleasant while others are not. People may also experience phantom smells due to fluctuations in hormone levels or certain health conditions. The link between the sense of smell and the emotions is a strong bond that has been further pushed into the spotlight since the Covid-19 pandemic. Maybe there is something to be said for stopping to "smell the roses," as they say.

All the different things we do and interact with during our lives help us grow. This is the key concept to take away from this for personal cultivation. When we are born, we are an amalgamation of all of our experiences. This is why Dr. Wu insists that the first seven years of life are the most formative. Root experiences frame a large part of our life at this time, allowing us to absorb energy from the things around us as well as have experiences with nature and receive different influences that end up shaping us. This form of sensory usage is part of our growth process as well as of longevity. This is a serious thought, because it highlights how our spiritual efforts and connection to nature are important for the growth of society. Given this information, it is obvious that societies with a deeper connection to nature will also support longer lives.

Dr. Wu also talked about touching, listening to, smelling, and even tasting some ancient artifacts to enhance our longevity in the long term. This can also be done with a cell phone, making it possible to always find it if it goes missing. Perhaps by doing this, we develop a psychic link with that object, not unlike the experience of sudden awareness when family member is in trouble. I know that many times my mother sensed when things were amiss with me. She would call and say she had a bad feeling or something else to that effect. Our ancestors had to rely on their five senses to function safely in the world. We still have those abilities now and it is up to us to use them for guidance in a world that increasingly relies on artificial technologies.

The life force of the body rests in the uterus. As we know, the uterus can produce life. Then, we can ask, what is a flower? A flower is like the metamorphosis of the uterus. The uterus itself is like the bulb of a rose. So, by smelling flowers, it can reinforce the energy of the uterus. It will allow you to absorb that particular type of *qi*. You can also practice particular qigong forms in front of plants to absorb the *qi* that way. In Daoist theory, they say you should eat different types of *qi*. This means absorbing them through all of your different senses. During periods when flowers are in bloom, you are subconsciously harnessing their *qi* to aid you in your quest for longevity. That is another key example of human body fengshui.

Chapter 14

Endings Are Beginnings

Human body fengshui explores humans and their environments, both artificial and natural, and how they meet in the middle. Plants and animals act as intermediaries between heaven and earth. Anything alive between heaven and earth is a medium of expression and a way for things to communicate back and forth, etc. As I have said before, heaven faces earth and the two generate yin and yang. Clouds, in this sense, complement rain: they are yang as rain is yin. Still, the act of rain falling is yang while the process of it evaporating is yin.

Females are yin, males are yang. But in terms of their make-up, females are two parts yin and one part yang, while males are one part yang and one part yin. This is different from what modern science says about the X and Y chromosomes which are evenly matched. The yin-yang pattern manifests when determining a baby's sex. One method is to have the woman walk along a path, then call out her name. If she turns to the right as she looks back, the baby will be a girl; if left, a boy. Similarly, in one experiment in China, a thousand expecting mothers were asked to walk around a park with a dividing trail. Those who were carrying boys gravitated to the left, while those who were had girls moved right. This may seem a bit crazy, but it has been documented quite widely. Another related feature is the phenomenon, found in China's gynecological hospitals, of streaks in birth patterns, meaning that either boys or girls will be born in a row, rather than alternating. Staff know to expect this and make according preparations. It may seem insignificant or coincidental, but yet shows another way the yin-yang pattern manifests in life.

Without patterns like this, Dr. Wu says that there would be no reason for religions since they study and document the manifestation of spiritual phenomena in the material world. Without structure in the universe and a higher sense of being, how could we have order in human culture? While things are always changing, there is still constancy in terms of how material existence operates according to key principles such as yin and yang. Without these, why would people need to spend time implementing, documenting, and developing strategies to harmonize life?

Dr. Wu also notes that the *Yijing* is a major method for understanding the meaning behind the patterns. He says that scientists may study their whole lives, but only a few high-level *Yijing* practitioners will ever truly understand it. If you want to appreciate the world, you must first realize the root principles of its operation, otherwise you will not be fully integrated as a living and spiritual being. The same also appears in the face that the first records of humanity were about divinatory functions, giving rise to methods of writing and greatly advancing culture.

Even though much of human history and its knowledge has been lost over time, we still have a lot at our disposal. We just have to want to learn from it. If we do not take the time to understand our environment and the principles of nature and the human body, we will suffer from a lack of knowledge. Of course, if something bad is going to happen, you want to know about it so you can try to avoid it, right? People may not think about this on a conscious level, but we all do want to know the hard truth many times, even if it goes against what our ego feels should or might happen. The *Yijing* presents an answer to the mysteries of the human condition, and as such, there is always more to learn in this respect. Without an eternal sense of curiosity about life, it is hard for us to remain open to the new experiences that we will have day-to-day.

Yijing Concepts

Approaching the concepts of the *Yijing* requires you to think outside of the box. In the light of today's common knowledge, they may not make any sense and grasping them is challenging. This does not mean that you are not intelligent if you do not understand them. Rather, the difficulty lies in breaking through your accumulated assumptions about reality, just like going against muscle memory built up over a lifetime. It means retraining the brain to see things with a different perception. There may be much initial confusion because the concepts and the theoretical discourse are so alien. You have to come at it from the angle that this is a spiritual language that nobody is teaching outside of a few select places.

In terms of *Yijing* cosmology, if you are having difficulties in your life, you should use the principle that you have to harness "that which cannot be changed" and, at the same time, you need to change your surroundings as well. The philosophy here is "adapt to survive," but not in a brutal way of "kill or be killed." It is more "adapt to what happens so that you can move with the tide of things as they come." As such, there is a serious emphasis on this phrase: "Use the unchangeable to change everything else." What is unchangeable? You could say nature itself is unchangeable, but there are other elements as well. This is just something interesting to meditate upon and reach your own conclusions.

Some things cannot be changed. In this context, Dr. Wu speaks about harnessing the energy of mountains, air, sun, and moon, but also extols the principles of integrity and purpose that continue to exist. Life is interesting in that sense. When we think about things that have an extremely long life, such as a mountain, we normally would not think of it as alive. But if plants grow on a mountain, how can we really say that it is dead? It is vital to reorient your ways of thinking when you look at the *Yijing*, as a lot of times it starts to present a line of thinking that is not linear by modern culture's standards.

Of course, as humans, we only want to hear positive news or learn about what sounds good. But the true nature of *Yijing* is based on sometimes difficult truths. This type of reverse philosophy cannot be accepted by many people, because we want to think about our surroundings positively. But say, for instance, you are married to someone in this life. From the *Yijing*'s perspective, in a past life you were mortal enemies and now you have come together as spouses to achieve a counterbalance. We may think that a child is the culmination of a couple's love, but the *Yijing* will say that parents in a previous life were in debt to the person who is now their child.

It takes a hundred years of previous connection for people to meet in this life, and it takes thousands of years of cultivation to have a romantic relationship or even a date with someone. Let us say you get along well with your spouse; then the *Yijing* would say your previous hatred and entanglement has now been resolved in this life. This is another reason why they do not believe in divorce, if it is possible to avoid it. Divorce can sometimes have unintended consequences beyond this lifetime, if that anger or hatred for one another is still unresolved from that past life issue you two had.

Cultivating spirit and soul only happens through this line of reverse thinking; or, more accurately, it only happens when we calculate the happenings of things according to the *Yijing*'s wisdom. Just like when you reach an apex of happiness, there may be some misfortune waiting. And then, when your misfortune reaches its apex, fortune will start coming again. This system of good fortune and its reversal is the cycle of life for all creatures, not just human beings.

Your parents represent the sun and moon in this lifetime because they are not just your parents but also your gods. They were the ones who brought you to life, so they deserve to be admired even if they may fall short in one area or another. Of course, there are extreme cases where parents do terrible things, but on the whole, this is the *Yijing*'s take on the subject and should be followed if possible. It takes the sun and the moon to come together and create things in the universe, and as such, your parents represent this for you.

Changing Fortune

Many times, people want to change their life trajectory and ask Dr. Wu how they can do so. Everything in the universe requires effort. One way to increase longevity is to save the life of another being, resulting in up to seven years' extension. Even saving a fish will help build wealth in the form of business success, while saving a bird will increase opportunities and good fortune. Heaven is always in favor of saving life. Maybe reading this will inspire you to go and take a basic first aid course and learn to help someone who is choking, just in case you are ever in a situation to help someone in need.

Other ways to change fortune involve practices performed in the right circumstances and by the right people, rituals that cause heaven to take notice of your good deeds. Even though heaven sees everything, it does not put you under a spotlight without some practices being performed for you. Daoists would tell people to save a life and then come back so that they could perform a fire dragon ritual for them but setting parts of their back on fire. It a similar way, the emperor in ancient times would venerate heaven, making sure it continued to bestow blessings. Some practices may seem merely ceremonial, but they accomplish certain things and can be very effective.

Heaven is present in the body from the Baihui point on top of the head to the upper lip. Working with this area can increase good fortune and multiply opportunities. The area from the lower lip to the sternal notch represents the first seventy-one years of life, followed by the space between the second notch to the middle of the chest, which represents the remaining time until death. You can also view the chest area to see what your children's careers will be like. From the chest to the belly button is the wealth area. From the belly button to the genitals is marriage. A person's life partner as well as offspring are represented here. Everyone has a line that is apparent and which you can see that runs down the middle channel of the body.

Traditional people did not believe in what we call retirement today but thought of death as the ultimate retirement. They also did not see life as linear but understood it to run in cycles. Rather than a single lifetime, it involved several lifetimes, on some cases understood as happening concurrently, a feature Dr. Wu will elaborate more on later.

He describes the curve in the middle of the yin-yang or *taiji* symbol (as seen on the right) as representing the life of a person and notes that a similar understanding is also present in other religions such as Christianity, Hinduism, and Judaism. At the same time, the larger circle on the periphery of the *taiji* symbol represents the vision of seeing the universe as one whole, notably found in Daoism.

The yin and yang sides can be seen as fish and birds. The white yang side marks one's career, while the black yin side shows wealth. In addition, the central line also matches the spine in the body, which also relates to the dragon in the greater world. According to Dr. Wu, some dragons are lying down while others are standing up. In nature, those lying down are akin to the mountains in Malibu, while those standing up are more like peaks in Las Vegas. Anyone can learn to see these mountain phenomena for themselves with a little effort. It is also known that certain points are always an outlet to the bay if the mountain range is by the ocean, because this is where the dragon drinks water. This outlet point will usually be at the head of the dragon etc. These are interesting points as these places will usually feel good and calming as they represent the best type of fengshui that a person can acquire in this world. This place represents the perfect mixture of yin and yang.

A spot like this exists in Malibu and businesses there are thriving. It is also interesting to note that the Native Americans in the area hold festivals at that location as well. Perhaps they have their own form of fengshui analysis as well that led them to that spot.

But why do we bring up mountains now? It is because a person's life is like a wheelbarrow, pushing from the bottom to the top of the mountain. (This mimics the life-long journey age-wise from the lumbar up to the cervical spine.) This line of thought says a person goes from the bottom to the top during their lifetime. Your life is an uphill battle in this respect. It is hard to push. If you are careless in your efforts, your cart collapses and you die or lose. As long as the cart does not collapse, your job is to push it up till you cannot push any further. When the cart is stuck or a large calamity falls upon you, you should stop for a minute. Dr. Wu notes that you could stop for as long as you wanted, such as a day, a month, or a year. It is what you think will do you the most good. During this time, you can either join a spiritual retreat or do good deeds. You can find dead birds and bury them or buy living birds and turtles and release them.

Pushing forward during these times is risky, so they do not usually advise this. Some people are successful at pushing through these difficulties, but it depends on the person's character. Some have the strength to break through that hurdle by charging straight through it. Conversely, they ask that you use time to heal things. Time in itself can heal many wounds. We have to be cognizant that in this reality, nothing lasts forever. We will always be able to overcome our difficulties if we have enough patience with our personal approach. This is where we can learn from creatures such as the turtle: it lets things happen naturally and makes no fuss. It is always moving forward silently through its own form of spiritual practice. It can reclusively meditate anytime it wants in its shell.

The Power is Yours

What can be done to help a person's life go more smoothly? According to Dr. Wu, if you have undesirable physical traits, you can consider plastic surgery to alter your fortune a bit. He says it is not the worst thing in the world, except when it comes to nose alternation, which is bad and can negatively affect your life expectancy. A broken or crooked nose indicates issues difficulties or misfortunes, and even though surgery may make it appear straight, you had to undergo breaking the nose in the first place to perform the operation. Other types of plastic surgery are acceptable. For women, it is better to have larger breasts, which are like mountains in the body and ease life. Perhaps this is why so many women underwent breast enhancements in the later 20th century, when they were also entering the workforce at a greatly accelerated rate and starting to have an impact at the highest level of corporate and political influence.

Many people feel uncomfortable with surgery, but for some it seems to work out. It depends on the type of person you are and your goals in life. It seems excessive to think changing your body could affect your fate, but it is hard to argue with the results of certain people who have done it. It is a "to each their own" process and an individual choice. Of course, Dr. Wu is not trying to glorify the superficial aspect of society, but is strictly speaking from a human body fengshui perspective. He has sometimes said that having foreign objects in the body is not good, so there are health trade-offs to certain cosmetic procedures. But to summarize, nose surgery is bad and can affect one's life expectancy, but other than that, it is up to you what you do within this sphere.

It is key to know that learning anything esoteric is a serious, high-level commitment. While many may want to learn things such as the *Yijing*, only a few have the patience. Dr. Wu has talked about this in the past and continues to stress the pre-requisites for learning and lengthy years of study. Everything we do in our lives is a process, but learning the *Yijing* would be a process that few choose to take due to the length of time involved.

He described learning studying the *Yijing* as like learning a foreign language. While many people might want to learn it, they give up when they understand the difficulties involved. It is interesting and easy in the beginning, but it is supremely complex to be able to calculate correctly. One in a million may be able to master it. One must have an interest in it as a hobby or a motive for studying it. A seeking spirit. You would need a motive to want to understand it and a reason to dig deep. These are all, of course, based on the dreams of the individual. In terms of the *Yijing*, a lot of people know a little bit about it, but most will never truly become transformed by its mastery.

Mock Death Practice

From the beginning, humans have been mortal. Certainly, this is a difficult subject, one that depresses many people today, feeling that their time is limited and they have no real purpose in the world. This book provides a wide range of tools for growth, good health, and spiritual evolution, culminating in this final chapter dedicated to teaching a physical practice that will renew one's attachment to life through facing death. This serious and risky procedure is best used when people faced extreme circumstances. Masters act as guides, leading the suffering individual through a mock death, an experience with a new significance in modern times that utilizes visualization for healing the mind and presents a new technique to combat apathy and depression. You undergo it to free your soul, allowing it to leave the body long enough to alleviate sorrow and put a new perspective on life.

Mock death practice also connects to the Buddhist concept of emptiness. If you are truly empty, you can leave this world peacefully because you no longer have any attachment to it. Some people face such extreme pressures that they think of harm themselves or ending their lives. Thinking like this may provide a temporal sense of relief, but it is not a valid solution or option, no matter what cultural values one has. Instead of suicide, there is this rebirth practice which allows you to die and return.

Daoists believe that the universe is both limitlessly vast and infinitely small. As you expand something and make it bigger, the other side of that object grows ever smaller. This is yin and yang at work. For something to expand, something else must contract. This is essential to internalize, mind, body and soul, if you are to understand the concept of yin and yang.

All known information within the universe can be held within one grain of rice. The concept of yin and yang's simultaneous expansion and contraction is how this is possible. We are seeing this concept growing in acceptance, even in popular culture, where more than a few movies present superheroes trying to save the universe, which is minute or microcosmic compared to the realms that they were able to operate from.

Although this combination of expansion and contraction may seem intellectually perplexing, deep meditation will help you realize that all size is relative to the person who intentionally chooses to experience either end of the spectrum or both states at the same time. What we cannot accept rationally is not difficult to imagine not only in the mind but also as a physical sensation. This fundamental perceptual duality we have lived with from the moment of birth.

What is big? What is small? These are manmade concepts regarding matter. Infants may know they are small relative to their mother who is large, but Daoists know that we are all half a star on earth plus another half beaming to us from deep space. Wouldn't that other half have to be huge to be so bright and felt clearly? We have never physically travelled to the stars from earth, but we do know they are real, complete with their size and physical presence, massive enough to shine brightly in the sky.

If our star out there is only one half of our soul, what we have within, our sense of self on earth, must match it, this huge burning ball in deep space. If we are willing to believe that our soul is a real, energetic force big enough for this star, we can let go of our physical sense of proportion and get past our everyday perception of and connection to our bodies. We can also overcome the pain and suffering in our minds. In this dimension of philosophical imagination, we can unite contradictions and release ourselves from our most mundane assumptions and perceptual expectations. Physical size becomes irrelevant. In fact, we can show how big an illusion size is. As big as you make your problems, that's how big they can become in the real world. If you are ok with making them as small as your mind and body wishes, you can release your problems from the hold they have on your physical life.

Buddhists value emptiness, while Daoists honor nothingness. This is one of the core differences between the two systems. But if we think about this from a simplistic view, if you have nothing, nobody can take anything from you. If you do not exist, how can anyone bother you? These are simple reductions of complex concepts, but they shed light on how achieving a state of nothingness can have its advantages in both the spiritual and physical sense.

When we think of religious figures, we may have the sense that none of them exist on the earthly plane anymore. Many religions have a basic teaching that their holy leaders are not here and will only return one day in a messianic future. Why is this? Where did they go? Have they all become immortal? Or have they disappeared into a state of nothingness? This quest for nothingness may present a valid explanation as to why we feel that there are no spiritual prophets anymore. Could it be that the quest for nothingness was at the root of what made them so spiritually enhanced that massive religions were able to form around them? It is hard to say which masters have achieved transubstantiation, nonbeing, nothingness, or any other term one might use, but Daoists would say that this is the ultimate aim of spiritual cultivation and call it the attainment of the rainbow body.

Many people in today's society are asking themselves how to drop out of the rat race in a meaningful way. States of total emptiness and pure nothingness represent a deep subconscious yearning that is more biologically based than we might realize. Even in mainstream society, where traditional religious practice has been dropping for generations, we are still yearning for these states on a subliminal, often inchoate level. Perhaps tuning into this ingrained connection to emptiness and nothingness presents a road to salvation for those weary of the grind. That our society has become more complex or technologically advanced is no guarantee that we will become spiritually wiser. A Daoist would say that the more complex our lives, the more we crave nothingness. If we are meant to return to nothing, perhaps it does not matter what society around us has accomplished or values, as long as we work on ourselves. There are many ways of looking at all of these concepts, but if we do not look for our own road to enlightenment, it is good bet we won't find it.

Preliminaries

Before outlining the actual practice, we have to discuss some of the root principles involved and why they achieve the effects they do. Daoists believe that smelling something good can act on the body like a form of anesthetic. If the fragrance is intoxicating enough, it will help put you out. On a physical level, a strong smell with highly positive associations can be powerful enough to override our other senses. For a Daoist, the smell is also what causes your soul to start to levitate. Good-smelling things are lighter, while bad smells are heavy in terms of their energies and their interaction with human perception. Another fundamental is the recognition of bird song as a form of universal language. Birds chirping help in leading the soul to heaven after it is levitating. Why do we need to levitate?

Well, that one is easy—heaven is above us. This bird song musical principle is also important because sound is what leads us back to the heart.

An emotional soundtrack opens our hearts enough to care about the words being spoken in our favorite movie. It is common to see people weeping from sheer emotion at magnificent operas, choirs, or even national anthems during sports events. Music is the key that unlocks the heart. As such, the songs of birds are some of the most appealing and subconsciously powerful sounds. They are heavenly music, which, along with a fragrant aroma, can lead the soul where it wants to go. This also relates to *Yijing* calculations, which are not as simple as it would seem from how they are currently made. In the public, 99 percent of calculations are being done with the wrong methods. This is because the starting point, before calculations begin, is wrong, without observing birds and listening for their calls.

If you do not have the right appreciation of birds and fish, you are starting out wrong. Dr. Wu has gone to great lengths over the years to stress this appreciation, because if they are our true origin, we should have a deep respect for them as our cosmic ancestors. We had no choice to be born as human, nor was our family a choice. We were sent here to do something and therefore we must honor the wisdom of the birds who know the heavenly edicts of our missions in life.

It is also interesting to note that, with advanced levels of perception, it becomes easier to experience different aspects of synesthesia, such as seeing pictures that speak to you in sound. If you have the skill, you can hear the image, not just look at it visually. Hearing is the most advanced of the human senses. Humans exhibit these unique hearing abilities because we hear in the womb before we can see. Our hearing thus has been developing even before we were born. Spiritually, it is our most valuable resource. Many studies have shown that by twenty-four weeks, the fetus can recognize voice patterns and also recognizes music. It is postulated that a baby's way of learning through osmosis stems primarily from the sense of sound. But the Daoist belief is heavenly *qi* plays a part in young infants' unusually advanced level of cognitive development. The vibrations from this heavenly *qi* are discerned through our special hearing abilities, which qigong seeks to train and refine.

Certain practices can be considered odd or unconventional. Intriguing, they tend to easily dismissed as impossible. Why is this? It is because we are taught many things about the spiritual realms from an early age, but not all of them are hard and fast laws, even if they are trained into us as such. We are generally taught that our spirit cannot leave the body to go to any other realm before we are dead. This is not entirely the case. Long ago, Daoists knew that there would be certain periods in life where flux or chaos would be heightened. These could be due to an individual's circumstances or could be broadly imposed on entire populations due to global events caused by either human or natural acts. During these times, more extreme methods would need to be prescribed in order to fully allow people to rise past the difficulties that surround them and help them gain an overarching sense of clarity of how to proceed. This is why these death and rebirth practices were developed over many generations and perfected by the monks of the White Cloud Monastery.

The ceremonial mock death allows practitioner to ascend back to heaven in their soul to gain greater awareness of their purpose in life. It can also help people understand the trials they go through on the path to living out their destiny. This experience can reveal insights from beyond our physical lives, like areas where their ancestral fortune was hidden from past family members, and obstacles that they will face during this life from any people surrounding them who may try and block them and halt them from their purpose. Many of us, unfortunately, will face hidden enemies. This practice unlocks an awareness that frees the intuition so that we may understand what lies beyond the lowest points of our lives. It is no in conventional terms t a practice that can be considered safe. To attempt it comes with warnings and requires a master to act as a guide. But some people are willing to take risks in consciousness in order to gain a greater understanding and possibly a way out of whatever is currently befalling them in their quest.

Dr. Wu does not recommend that anyone take on the challenge of pseudo-death without his help. Even the most seasoned Daoist practitioners generally thought of this practice as dangerous because the soul will, in fact, leave the body. If the person does not approach in a judicious manner, strictly following each step with profound humility and reverence, there is a chance that their soul will leave the body for good. That does not mean that you will physically die, but it does mean that, without a soul, you will have inadvertently created an entirely different set of problems. As such, if you want to do this practice, you should contact Dr. Wu directly and ask for him to oversee your attempt. These practices were brought forth to ease extreme times of crisis in society and allow an emergency option to gain a greater awareness of one's purpose and the blockages that must be removed to create this drive to serve within the balance of the universe. In this sense, one does not need to act out the ritual to benefit from the inspiration and insight that can be achieved simply by learning about it and accepting its symbolic potential to empower one's life.

This practice is designed to help a person feel reborn. Your soul will still be your own, yet it will be different after it returns from its journey through heaven. With this newfound knowledge and wisdom, it might never be the same, but even profoundly changed, it is the same soul you were born with that has returned to your body. This reawakening to your potential has deep benefits whether you study the practice and contemplate its symbolic significance or are brave enough to attempt it physically with Dr. Wu as your guide.

The practice takes a lot of patience to accomplish, as it is a rather laborious process to coax the soul out of the body. It feels strange when the soul is leaving, as in many ways it does feel like you are dying. As such, it is important to renounce fear and just calmly allow the soul to go out without being afraid of actual death. The good news is that we can also get some of the same effects of this practice by just doing the first steps of its qigong exercises, without the ritual portion where the soul leaves the body. These initial stages allow us to open up our "*Tai*," roughly translated as the gods or masters within the body. To open the Tai is to reopen our mind, body, and soul. We can so easily lose touch with our intuitive guidance that is innate, instinctual, physical, emotional and spiritual. It can close up due to many kinds of shock and trauma, and we can also build up walls around their messages to us as protection against the world if we go through intense struggles at times in life that challenge our ability to stay open and flexible. This is an energetic defense mechanism that can be involuntary or conscious, and we may have attracted bad energy and difficulties through our choices and actions as well against our will. This practice can help us to get our mind, heart, and soul balance back in balance and operating again as our clear and conscious guides. The tapping section of the practice in particular allows a new flow of enhanced abilities and vivid perspectives to open up within the mind.

Many people in this day and age suffer from a host of debilitating conditions, from PTSD to addiction, to nameless despair. These conditions, while not necessarily life threatening, can be incredibly incapacitating. The stress and tension can make you feel as though you cannot breathe. You might not feel like yourself, or may feel like you just do not know where to go. Things happen in our lives that, in many cases, are beyond our ability to cope with and recover from. This is why Dr. Wu has released this singular practice in this time and place. There are many obstacles that force us to step outside of ourselves in order to regain our equilibrium and sense of perspective. If we do not understand the spiritual goals in our lives, it is hard to know which direction to head. Daoist cosmology has always recognized the fundamental struggle of human existence and here provides a solution for these most extreme sets of circumstances.

Dr. Wu highly recommends that he first draw a particular talisman on the individual's forehead before anyone attempts to begin the ceremony. This talisman is drawn near the third eye. This talisman is a particular type of spiritual protection talisman so that the person can recover their soul after releasing it from the body.

The Yin-Yang Cycle

Dr. Wu has pointed out that in all cycles of life, there is a dark point and a high point. The dark point is indicated by the lowest part of the diagram right before it turns back into white. He notes that at this point in life, every last thing can go wrong and you will feel pretty rough. You may be broke, in bad health, abandoned, and more. One can imagine any amount of negative human conditions.

When people have reached rock bottom, their luck starts to change. This pattern is significant because the same thing can happen at the other end. If a person is on top of the world, they may have a great fall. This can be prevented, according to Dr. Wu, by being humble and gracious about one's position and not seeking additional wealth, fame, love, etc. when you know that everything is as good as it can get. If you can be a good person and act graciously at the top of the luck cycle, you can avoid great calamity in a fall from grace.

This cycle is also why hubris is so dangerous. No earthly creature is beyond feeling the wrath of the yin-yang cycle. No matter what happens in your life, there is no good that can come from forgetting that there must always be a balance in all things. No one person can have it all forever, and I feel this is what was illustrated by Dr. Wu's example.

Life is illusory in the sense that false security can lull us into forgetting our need to constantly discover ourselves. If everything were perfect on the outside, we would never begin our inner quest to find our true sense of self. That sense of self is what will keep you not only sane but, in fact at peace and content, even when the external world goes haywire. Daoists know that all things change in time, so they do worry about the frivolous fancies of the world. This is a principle that will always put you to the test because, in reality, it takes a noble spirit to know when enough is enough in life.

Being in a pinnacle state can be addictive, so it takes a strong spirit to accept and let go when needed, to keep safe for the next cycle of fortune. The public sees this so many times with celebrities. How many celebrities have had a fall from grace? Countless. We should always realize that the potential is real for anyone to fall victim to imbalance if one ignores the changes as life turns.

This practice is high-level. According to Dr. Wu, it is a fifth-level Daoist cosmological practice. To the layman, this means that it is rather advanced and was only able to be released due to a unique set of circumstances happening within his clinic.

1. The first condition of this practice was met when one patient came in with a serious relationship quandary. This relationship problem was life-threatening. A patient's son had been left psychologically paralyzed after his much beloved fiancé vanished out of the blue. Being the center of his world, she left him with nothing to keep him spiritually grounded. This was unfortunate for him and also for his mother, who was in a different country without much recourse. She turned to Dr. Wu for help and he calmed the young man's emotions and got him back on track.

2. The second condition was met when a monk arrived who had come from Tibet and was in a quandary as to how the Tibetan Buddhist lineage should move forward. He was fraught and confused. He wanted the lineage to go forward, but did not know how to proceed. He sought out Dr. Wu, knowing that he came from a monastic background like himself. At that point, Dr. Wu started thinking of ways to assist.

3. The third condition was met when an overseas person appeared who had severe turmoil in his life and did not want to continue living. Hardworking and smart, he had a daughter and many natural skills, but nothing he did was working. He did not feel motivated to find a partner, felt isolated from friends and

coworkers, and generally did not enjoying life. This, of course, translated to a difficult headspace to live with. Dr. Wu took him on and began to work with his issues.

These three circumstances happening in conjunction fulfilled the prerequisites necessary for Dr. Wu to release this practice in public. It encapsulates the 5th level of the nine palaces teachings and forms the 4th class in that series, but we are able to jump ahead and introduce it to you without prerequisites because of the three men coming into Dr. Wu's life.

Human Conditioning and Natural Flow

Another thing we must cover are the concepts of human conditioning (*tai*) and natural flow (*shi*) and how they form an integral part of this death practice. They form the framework that allows us to walk through life in accordance with nature's principles. Natural flow is the ongoing pattern of things that cannot be changed by man. The sun rises in the east and sets in the west, and there are the four seasons. There are mountains and oceans, rain from the skies, wind, and all that's part of nature's flow. Human conditioning, on the other hand, includes everything manmade or involves the human will to have things a certain way. For instance, the way we perceive things such as elections and voting are part of this as much as anything motivate, or accomplished by, humans.

Try as we might, we cannot change things in the category of natural flow. Even though there is a storm, we can try to disperse the clouds with technology. That is a man-made action, but it is only temporary. It can be explained simply. Let us say when you see a person, there is a sense of déjà vu, like you know that person, that is part of nature's flow; it could be that in a previous life you were friends. Let us say you see a person at the grocery store who reminds you of someone, but you have never met. In actuality, this is not uncommon. This belongs to the natural flow of things.

Between people, love is part of the natural flow; because you love someone, you want to make sacrifices. According to Dr. Wu, making a sacrifice is the truest form of love. He said that the act of wanting to hang out with someone, in terms of wanting them around for your own purposes, is a form of human condition. It is wanting to control when they are around you or how they interact with you. True love for people is about helping make a sacrifice for others. This is crucial in the context of a monk-like life and philosophy as well.

People attaining spiritual understanding are helping all of humanity to grow, through the efforts of their individual good deeds during their lifetime. This is a key point for us to take away and to personalize with serious reflection. When we try to cultivate ourselves, we must realize that we should work on changing the three types of human conditioning. After we achieve that, we can try to enter and immerse ourselves in the natural flow of things. Because when spirit emerges, it belongs to the natural flow of things; it is not manmade. When you are born, half of you is lingering in heaven. Through cultivation, we are trying to find and align ourselves with this other half in heaven. That half will rotate and change, and then your human-half will descend back into your body. It is like recharging the battery. That is why this practice is so impactful; to change the various forms of human condition, we must review the following points

First, conditioning of the heart. In your heart, you must have love. With the force of love, there is nothing that cannot be conquered. Only through love will your soul have spirit. It does not matter how you were before. With the right heart condition, when you yell out by letting the soul leave the body, it echoes back. Similarly, when you have love, the love will resound and bounce back. So, first you must have love. Love belongs to the heart.

Second, conditioning of the physical body. This governs our clothes and attire. As we all may realize, your clothes will bring out your figure in terms of your day-to-day look as a human. For women, makeup changes the contours of the face and high heels change the walk and add the appearance of height. All this belongs to physical conditioning. Because our physical appearance is significant, we should walk with our chest raised and our head level. One simple way to improve is to envision yourself lifted by a string attached to the top of your head. This motion serves to form a triangle from the two shoulders and the top of the head, lifting yourself as if hanging from the ceiling.

Third, visual conditioning. That means training the eyes as well as the hands. Dr. Wu has taught these types of movements in various classes, for visual powers working with rotating the eyeballs fifty times clockwise and counterclockwise.

The best analogy for doing this practice is changing the engine in a car. If you replace the engine, it may be the same car, but it will not drive the same. After you replace the soul, you can use ancestral energies and memories to help you, to help your health. It will change you and help you to see things differently. You are going in dead and, when you come out of it, you come out living alive. That is why this information is deep and difficult for people to understand. It is only taught internally at the White Cloud Monastery, not introduced to the outside world, because the instructor must contain and control everything to make sure it comes out right. To do this, you mix and take realgar wine and Eaglewood on the summer solstice, the winter solstice, or your birthday. This will secure the best possible results.

If you toss a pebble into a pond, the water will ripple. The same happens when you scream loudly into a canyon; the echo will bounce back. Similarly, when your soul goes out, it travels the universe. You can look at this as being similar to you bringing a crystal ball to wash it in the ocean; it will resound and eventually bounce back like that echo. You can't see it, but you can experience it through cultivation. The ripples of a stone thrown into a pond appear to fade, but they are, in reality, bouncing back. When you yell a name, the echo fades, but it is bouncing back to you at the same time. This brings us back to the fact that our auditory senses are more sensitive than our visual senses in many ways as well.

In an effort to help all those involved in his own personal way, Dr. Wu taught the release of the soul practice for the first time publicly in over 200 years. The steps of this unique form are outlined below. We are humbled by the opportunity to study this knowledge.

I. Changing Heart Conditioning

1) Create a three-layer trigram image at the third eye point to open the heart. The trigram is specific to you: think of your favorite plant coupled with your Chinese zodiac image and the zodiac animal of the year.

a) First envision a tree or plant you have an affinity for. Place it at the third eye point, on the brow between the eyes.

b) Below the plant, place the image of your Chinese zodiac animal.

c) On the bottom of the trigram stack, place the image of the zodiac animal of the current year.

d) Fuse these images together so that they form one unit, about the size of a quarter.

2) Cycle the three-layer image.

a) While inhaling slowly through the nose, using the diaphragm and kidneys at your back, move the image down the center front of the body to the genital opening point at the front of the groin. Hold there for three seconds while continuing to inhale.

b) Continue to circle the image down and around to the anus and hold for 3 seconds, while continuing to inhale.

c) While exhaling slowly through the mouth, circle the image up the center of the back to the Baihui point at the top of the head and hold there for 3 seconds, continuing to exhale.

d) Circle the image down from Baihui back to the third eye point and hold for 3 seconds, continuing to exhale the whole time. This is one cycle.

e) Cycle for a total number equal to your age, ending at the third eye point.

This movement is performed to help open up the heart Tai in preparation for the soul to leave the body.

II: Changing Physical Conditioning

1) Strike the Knees

a) Form the hands into loose fists.

b) Bend at the knees and lean forward slightly with your back straight.

c) Strike around the knee caps, at the three "elephant eyes" or indentations at left, right and top of the knee caps, and also down the "elephant trunk," from the point at the bottom of the kneecap down the center front of the leg. Strike using the flat pinkie ends of the fists.

This is done to release the good fortune from your ancestors. We all have good deeds built up in our lineage, not necessarily from deeds we have done but from deeds that our parents, grandparents, great grandparents, etc. have done. These deeds can be released through the striking of the knee. Patting different parts of the knee (or Elephant head) corresponds to different areas of fortune. One is health, one is luck and the last is financial fortune.

d) Strike the area for a total equal to your age or at least 50 times if you want to make changes. Strike all the points mentioned as needed as part of this total number.

2) Massage the Abdomen

a) Place left hand over right, palms on top of the abdomen covering the navel and below.

b) Massage in a circle, clockwise up and around then down, around and up, for a total of your age. Basically, circling around the navel.

c) You can massage counterclockwise if you want, but massage in only one direction per day.

3) Massage the Lower Back

a) Form hands into loose fists and bring to the back over the kidneys on the muscles to either side of the spine. Backs of the hands are against the back.

b) Use the ridge of the knuckles to massage this area up and down or in and out.

c) If you are feeling stuck in difficulties and adversity, you can instead dig into the muscles with the knuckle ridges and push the flesh upwards, while leaning forward onto the balls of the feet, lifting the heels up. This is to generate more motivating, forward momentum energy for your body.

d) Do either Step B or Step C, depending on your needs, for a total number equal to your age.

4) Massage the Chest and Correct the Posture

a) Place hands palms down at the inside/top of the pectoral muscles.

b) Massage up from the center, out and around in circles, while retracting the scapulae, straightening the shoulders and back and opening up the chest. Bring the shoulders back and down as you massage.

c) Do the number equal to your age.

This helps posture and inspire a sense of self-confidence. If someone has good posture, they are usually more confident than a person with poor posture that is not as good and as such, end up being more successful in life as a result.

III: Changing Visual Conditioning

1) Rotate the Eyeballs

a) Start with the left eye.

b) Rotate clockwise, which is starting from the inside corner up, out and around, 50 rotations.

c) Then rotate the left eye counterclockwise, which is starting from the outside corner, up and around to the inner corner, down and around, 50 times.

d) Repeat with the right eye.

Eye rolling has many meanings in qigong, but it has traditionally been used to prevent any long-term heart conditions. It also carries the meaning of being able to see through things in your life; to see if they are good for you, or if they are illusory.

2) Strike the Drum

a) Place the palms over the ears, with the fingers pointing back, wrapping around the back of the skull and the thumbs pointed down.

b) Tap the sides of the occiput, the soft spot right under the base of the skull with the fingers, or you can flick a finger off the rest of the fingers to strike the area with extra force.

c) Strike 9 times.

This movement is done to train a specific part of the brain on the backside of the head to awaken a part of the brain and stimulate it.

IV: The Cicada Shedding Its Skin

1) Face Your Birth Direction

a) Spring = East, Summer = South, Fall = West, Winter = North. You should find this date using the Chinese calendar, not the Western calendar, as they have different timings for spring/summer fall, etc. Spring starts on Chinese New Year and lasts 3 months. Lookup your date based on that timing, not Western calendar timing.

2) Pre-Shedding: Heaven Position

a) Lift the arms up over the head in a rounded manner, so that the fingers are facing each other and the palms with their central Laogong points (CV-6) are in line with the closed eyes down below.

b) Hold this position, feeling the *qi* from the Laogong points shining into your eyes.

c) Hold this position 1-3 minutes, until the forehead area feels a heat sensation, which will help your shed. (This movement is done in order to heat up the forehead in preparation for the soul exiting the body. It is important that you can feel a sensation of heat on the forehead, and as such, you should hold it until you feel such a sensation.)

d) Then open up the palms and wrists so they are facing out from the body, and with the arms still raised, turn slowly from the waist from side to side. Bend the leg on the side you are turning toward to distribute the weight and force of the movement, as if your face is a flower and your arms and hands are the branches and leaves.

When you open up, you become a flower. Try not to envision yourself as a large tree but as a small plant, even a blade of grass. If you envision yourself as a large tree, lightning could strike you or a typhoon blow you away, but a blade of grass can withstand everything. This is reverse psychology, thinking the opposite way. When you envision yourself as small, you can grow to be big and strong. You envision yourself as something small and fragile, so there's a lot of potential to grow into something big and strong.

e) Turn from side to side as much as feels comfortable, to recharge the Lao-gong points. Repeat at least 9 times.

3) Pre-Shedding: Human Position

a) Bring the rounded arms down in a barrel shape with the palms facing the chest at the line of the nipples. The fingertips are pointed toward each other but not touching. The thumbs are held relaxed and down.

b) Hold in this position, either clawing all the fingers toward you, or flexing individual fingers to help a specific person: index finger = mother, middle finger = father, ring finger = family, pinkie = friends.

c) Hold until you feel a strong sensation and heat connecting the fingers.

d) You can move the hands out and in, as if pulling taffy, to increase the sensation between the fingers, as needed.

4) Pre-Shedding: Earth Position

a) Move arms into the next position: One arm is held outwards with the forearm up and the hand gently cupped, as if you were holding a baby facing you. The other arm is at the waist, held loosely with the elbow bent and the palm gently cupped and facing up.

b) In this position, you are going to gently sway side to side from the waist, as if you are rocking and lulling the baby. Use a couple of gentle waist movements like this to end with a gentle jolt or outwards expression from the waist movement from the side/front of the waist and abdomen that corresponds to the upraised arm all the way into the raised cupped hand and arm, like a light crunch that pumps energy all the way into the hand and fingertips.

c) Switch arms and repeat, gently and fluidly. This is one set.

d) Keep switching from arm to arm, side to side, for at least 9 sets, to lull the baby to sleep with a loving feeling.

When you "take care of the baby," this helps to prevent misfortune from striking you.

5) Shedding the Old Skin

a) Hold arms straight out in front of the body, with the palms down. Keep one arm stretched out further and held a bit higher and the other arm is held below, with the elbow more bent so it is in closer to the body. The elbows and shoulders are held nice and loose.

b) With a motion that circles up from the waist, allowing the arms and palms to slightly circle to get connected, build up some momentum, and then express it outwards into the hands and fingertips, shaking and vibrating the whole body as part of this strong jolt, to shed the body's shell.

c) Switch hands and repeat. This is one set.

d) Switch from side to side until you feel you have loosed and shed this skin, at least nine sets.

This movement series is done in order to symbolically shed your skin like that of a snake. Dr. Wu said that a snake's shedding is painful for the snake, but it must do it, as it is part of their natural cycle of life and growth. While doing this movement, you may feel slight shifts in the spine or as if your *qi* is being jolted around the body.

Soul Death Practice

WARNING: This practice should only be done within fifteen days of the summer or winter solstice. This practice also cannot be done outside of the direct supervision of Dr. Wu, as he must apply a specific talisman in order for it to be safely attempted. After all, the soul will be leaving the body; it is not something to be done flippantly or pridefully. It is important that the talisman be drawn with a very specific type of wood from the *Chenxiang* tree, *Aquilaria agallocha*, known as Chinese eaglewood or agarwood tree. This tree's bark is worth more than gold on a per ounce basis, and as such, is exceedingly hard to get a hold of, if you can even find it.

Also, Dr. Wu has many years of experience with drawing talismans, so even if you had the correct wood, it may not be as effective without a qualified qigong master drawing it. When Dr. Wu draws the talisman before the practice, it creates a special energy field for the practitioner. This happens because of the Eaglewood, which has its own powers, and the realgar wine, used to dip the wood into, as if it was a brush dipped in ink. It consists of a special formula of minerals and spirits that must be made in advance by Dr. Wu under specific conditions. Having these two elements combined generates a field of protection for the person, to make sure the practice goes smoothly. Sometimes, when practicing these profound forms, you have to take many special precautions. When doing this for others, Dr. Wu will dip the wood in the wine and draw the talisman on your head and will also teach you the method to practice.

To perform the practice, complete all preceding practices first at some point close to the time you have set to do the soul rebirth process.

1. Prepare a space on your bed or on the floor if you are in good health and face your head toward your birth direction (mentioned in step 1 above). Before you lie down, you will put pillows around you in four directions (North, South, East, and West). Underneath each pillow, you will put seven grains of rice. Before you practice this, you can act as if you are about to die. How do you do this? First, put on your best clothes, the clothes you would like to be buried in, and have a nice bite to eat or a glass of wine. This will help you relax and prepare for the practice. You can also write out a last will and testament and place it beside your bed or on the floor near you.

2. Lie on the ground and imagine the sound of birds chirping. Dr. Wu notes that this part is important because the sound of birds will help the soul find its way back to heaven. Birds being messengers of heaven, this makes sense if you think about it

3. Imagine you smell your favorite scent. It could be food or pretty much anything delicious to you! Dr. Wu says that this part is done because the *qi* of good-smelling things is light, so in this instance it will lighten the soul and help it to levitate up and out of the body.

4. Feel like you are turning into a fish. He said that in certain instances, you might feel like you are turning into a bird instead of a fish. This relates to the previous idea of all souls originating as either birds or fish. This may take a moment, so be patient. This requires a bit of relaxation and trust in the process.

5. Still feeling like a fish, listening to the birds chirping and smelling that delicious smell, start to move your soul (located between the third eye and the middle of the brain). Move it back and forth from the middle of the forehead to the top of your head (Baihui). 200 times is one set.

6. Continue doing this until you do feel the soul start to move. It will feel like you are dying, so just try to relax.

Practice Effects

This form is a Daoist way to help people overcome serious problems in life. This can be a single problem that finds you and just sticks with you, then causes a domino effect of one major bad event after another. To break this chain, you have to adopt the pose of a stubborn mule in the qigong form. This is because a stubborn mule on a mountain trail needs one person pushing from behind and one person pulling it from the front to make it go.

It can be equated to dealing with a coworker who you just cannot see eye-to-eye with, no matter how you try to explain things. As such, you have to come up with a creative way to convince them. This could be done by pretending you are sick, so the other person will feel like obligated to take care of you, or pretend you're going away on a trip, so they appreciate you more when you return. In terms of the *Yijing*, it is believed you can only change yourself. The underlying principle at the root of the *Yijing* encourages you to find solutions on your own.

This breaks rank with traditional Western theories. Western people may say you should talk to others about your problems. And certainly, there are times when that is appropriate, but talk as we might, other people may never understand our lives as deeply as we do, so perhaps their solutions may not be right for us. It is also interesting to note that even Western psychologists have done studies showing that talking to other people about your problems can make you feel worse.

So, it is just something to be careful about. I do feel like the *Yijing* encourages this type of mental independence because it is pretty much what animals do in nature. They do not sit around and chat about their problems; this is a human behavior that has its advantages and disadvantages. Maybe this Chatty Kathy attitude holds us back on some levels, especially if it gets in the way of other modes of observation, reflection, and action. We want to move forward, not trap ourselves in a loop of old habits and traumatic memories.

Daoists also suggest that a person who can't move ahead in life should light their finger on fire, as this will help them to make this change in themselves. It certainly would be a shock to the system. But it is unnecessary. In qigong practice and for legal reasons, we do not recommend it. The pushing motion in the qigong form should enable you to achieve the same results. If it still does not help, ask Dr. Wu for help.

We have not talked much about the knees in terms of the human body, but they represent the elephant. If you look at a knee from the front, you can see the shape of an elephant's head around your kneecap. The eye at the top of the knee is related to health, particularly cancer, and to the emotions. You want to strike the emotions to achieve a good balance with the meridians, according to Dr. Wu's calculations.

Sharks do not get cancer. They are big, strong, and self-confident, often hailed as the kings of the ocean. They are not scared of anything, and if the cancer cells became any bigger, they would just want to eat them. The more aggressive and stronger the animal, the less likely it is to contract cancer; the more fearful the organism, the more susceptible it is. Pounding and striking is like ringing a gong; through the vibrations of force and sound, you diminish fear. You pound the knee, representing the biggest, strongest land animal.

Practice this exercise right before you go to bed. Through striking, you can elevate happiness, career, and relationships. This is the reverse thinking of the *Yijing* at work again—by striking, reversing old patterns, and breaking them up, you can bring out new and better ones. Strike the eyes of the elephant if you are having trouble visualizing with the third eye as well. Martial artists practice breaking tiles with a knee, but they are really trying to change their destiny and fortune by doing so. When you look at a bronze statue of Guanyin, think how it has suffered thousands of strikes to be formed. The same thing can be said for striking your knee. It is hard to understand this type of thinking without personal practice, but give it a try as a part of this rebirth practice.

Daoists have studied how to create different numbing and anesthetic states. Imagine that smelling your favorite scent plus hearing the bird's chirp is a natural way to achieve this numbing state, born from a combination of mind, body and emotion. As it comes from your own effort generating a targeted brain chemistry response, especially when compared to modern recreational drugs or alcohol, the sensation is incomparable and very clean. Love in itself is also considered numbing in a way because of sacrifice that comes along with it. Of course, many people have said that love, itself, feels like a drug.

When you smell something sweet and then lie down, you will join nature to the point that you become one with it. This operates on the total body in ways similar to some of our most primal life experiences. Holding a baby simplifies your life as you return to nature. This happens because when a child is born, it is like a clean slate or a blank piece of paper. The way you educate the child is how it will develop. Try to see how you can understand the situation from the Daoist perspective.

In Daoism, love is a color. When you put all the colors together, they merge into black; conversely, when you take all the colors away, the result is white. Thus, there is yin-yang differentiation, also manifest in love. In one sense, love can be considered selfish and is categorized as yin. However, it must transform from yin into yang because the other part of love is sacrifice. Fish live in water and when they swim, they create movement. Such is the metamorphosis from yin to yang. From an *Yijing* perspective, love is to give out and to sacrifice. Good things will happen to you when you do good deeds and abundant acts of charity.

What's in a Dream?

Dreams are a reflection of a person's reality. Everything should be reflected in your reality, and you should act accordingly. I was curious one day as to whether babies dream and what they would dream about, so I asked Dr. Wu. He said that babies do dream, but their dreams generally reflect the maturity of the brain. A baby's dreams are usually a response to his or her mother's experiences, emotions, and the like. For this reason, you should never argue with a pregnant wife. This will keep their mood stable. A baby's dreams are generally positive. The babies will dream about what they want to become, or see later that day, etc.

Dreams are quite important in terms of a person's life because they are a direct connection between us and our spirit in many ways. Of course, it is almost curious that we call our goals "dreams." Maybe that is one way to look at spirituality in that sense. When we evolve to a place where there is little difference between our dreams and our waking reality. Of course, while we are in this world, nothing is ever going to be perfectly smooth in terms of our progression through it, but they can end up manifesting in harmonious and beautiful ways given the right amount of effort.

In life, we go through different phases. According to Dr. Wu, these phases can vary, but they generally go along the same type of path. First off, we have the dream stage. This is the prenatal stage when we are still in the womb. After birth, the next phase is the toddler phase, which lasts from birth until we are six years old. Then we have the young adult stage from 6 to 14, the teen stage from 14 to 18, the adolescent stage from 18 to 27, the mid-adolescent stage from 27 to 46, the adult stage from 46 to 60 the elderly stage from 60 to 90, and the end-of-life stage from 90 to120. By practicing qigong, one can not only lessen any karmic pitfalls we may have during these times but also work to align ourselves with the stars.

According to the *Yijing*, these stages have a lot of depth in them, but it is interesting to note that our parents are technically responsible for our behavior, according to Dr. Wu, up until we reach the age of forty-five. This is when we step into adulthood, according to him. This makes a lot of sense when we look at the average psychological development of people within modern society. Many people do remain semi-adolescent until later in life; this makes more sense to me than the things we are taught. Of course, this also depends on a lot of parental and societal factors, but the bottom line is, the sooner we learn that hard work is the most significant element in our lives, the faster we can get on track to becoming a successful human in whatever capacity we would like to thrive in.

The difficulty in our lives is just in understanding the meaning behind our trials, and this is why human body fengshui in conjunction with some *Yijing* knowledge is so powerful. When we can see the pattern, we can let it go and also be one with it. The pattern isn't what's holding us back; it is our own inability to understand where the pattern is going next that causes us to falter and feel self-doubt. Someone in tune with themselves and nature would really, truly have no need for worry or dismay. They would take everything as it is and not be caught up in changes over which they have no control.

All forms of life are competing for resources: human, plant, animal, and more. We just have to view the system for what it is. We cannot be too quick to dismiss other human beings if they do not meet our expectations. As soon as we cast these other souls aside and label them as a lost cause, we are throwing out some of our greatest opportunities. Good or bad notwithstanding, human life is immeasurably precious and entire societies can change in the blink of an eye. Just because a particular country acts one way one day does not mean that they will act that way forever. Think about how people act today versus even twenty years ago. Our lives are totally different, so why should we not be optimistic in our outlook? All creatures deserve the benefit of the doubt, humans included. We just sell ourselves short due to our lack of understanding our role in the greater scheme of things.

The Lifestyles of Humanity

No matter what type of lifestyle you pursue, difficulties will eventually come your way. You may be more equipped to deal with them if you have money and good people around you, but there is always the chance that there is nothing to help at that point. Spiritual training is there to help you. As any good spiritual teacher will tell you, if you work hard on your spiritual path, you can achieve great things.

Yet many people start on a path like this and then abandon it. But the calling of human body fengshui is the calling of the eternal quest of the soul. We all have to be prepared to understand what we are here for. Eventually, we all want to pursue the quest back to our home star in the sky. During this lifetime, some of us are destined to be great parents, others become career moguls, yet others rest in between lifetimes of strife and struggle. But when we think about vocation, it usually revolves around the question, "What can I do for the world that nobody else can do?" As Confucius has said, "One in three people can be my teacher." So, in essence, an amazing number of people on this planet have the capacity to reach insane spiritual heights. They just do not utilize this capacity.

Some people will look at this and say, "That's crazy! I have to spend my life doing qigong and a lot of things introverted or meditative!" But I feel like every spiritual path has a way of keeping you engaged with activities that work for your particular style, hence it never gets dull. There is always something new to learn or some new challenge to master, be it offered by a spiritual teacher or encountered on your own.

Mastering spiritual disciplines takes patience, but for those looking to accelerate their quest, there is no other way to go about it. The practice known as *gongfu*, which literally means "effort" or "work," has a close relation to time. It indicates that everything that we embark upon in this life will take some time and a process to master. Dr. Wu notes that there is no real word that means "practice" but only ways of saying "grind it out," marking a different kind of thought process. It makes sense if we think about it logically because, if we carry heavy energy from the past, we can do nothing but grind away at it until it is gone.

It is an odd quirk of fate that many people will not willingly look for the truth behind their spiritual existence. They only start searching for it because the pain of reality is pointless or there is some burden they must eliminate. Sadly, many people choose to end their lives because of this. Spiritual disciplines such as the mock death practice can alleviate the weight of these spiritual burdens. If more people in the world knew that they could change their fate with little effort, I do not think spirituality would have such a bad rap. Every day we are alive, there is a new quest. We are looking for mastery over something; it just depends on what we choose to make that quest about. It is only through spiritual development that life as we know it can stay fresh and new every day.

The truth of the matter is that your own personal suffering and lack of change end up bleeding out into the world. If you are sad all the time, you may end up bringing other people down. Spiritual training, on the other hand, presents a way for you not only to raise yourself up but also help the people around you become more spiritually buoyant. It helps human beings accomplish their dreams even if they have no idea how they come to fruition.

When you break through fear, you discover the reality of yourself. That is the essence of human body fengshui: understanding your place in, and unique contribution to, the universe. You may ask yourself, "Wait, is it my job to even do any of this?" As Laozi states, "You want to improve the world? I do not think it can be done." If we cannot change the world, what are we to do? Are we to merely move in harmony with it, or just change ourselves? Or both?

This is a decision that you alone must make. No one can tell you what to do with your life, or if it is your responsibility to fix anything you see. Your quest is your own, and if you work hard enough, you will find its meaning. But until then, it is nobody's job to make up your mind for you. You are the only one who can decide to be great, to climb, to attempt the impossible. You are the one who can take the truth and run with it. If you do not, there is nothing anyone else can do for you. Generally speaking, at some point in your life, you will be given the gift of personal insight, but you have to choose to see. And this seeing should not jade you or close your heart. Evil forces will always work to hide the meaning behind spiritual development: it never serves dark aims.

Dr. Wu and we all sincerely hope that the information in this book brings you a sense of fulfillment, enrichment, purpose, and clarity. In a world that can be difficult, any spiritual tool is helpful. Having existed for eons, the tools presented here come with a great deal of gravity. We are all here on earth for a limited period of time and might as well make that time the most meaningful we can. I hope you join me on a journey to the center of your being, a happy place where you can see the purpose of your life and your efforts add up to something uniquely amazing.

Bibliography

Anderson, Troy.2014. "Why Negative Ions Have a Positive Effect on the Human Body." *Airtamer.com*, 15 November 2014. https://www.airtamer.com/negative-ions-positive-effect-human-body/#:~:text=The%20most%20important%20benefit%20of,mold%20spores%2C%20bacteria%20and%20viruses. Accessed 7 March, 2024.

Arain, Mariam et al. 2023. "Maturation of the adolescent brain." *Neuropsychiatric Disease and Treatment*, 9:449-61.

Bradley, Scott. 2012. "Fulfill Your Destiny." *Ramblingtaoist.blogspot.com*, 17 November, 2012. https://ramblingtaoist.blogspot.com/search?q=fulfilling+destiny. Accessed 7 March, 2024.

Bui, Peter. 2021. "Trees are a little like humans." *Interstem.us*, 3 April, 2021. https://www.interstem.us/2021/04/03/trees-are-a-little-like-humans. Accessed 7 March, 2024.

Cohen, Treasure. 1994. "Tree-Planting Ritual." In *Lifecycles: Jewish Women on Life Passages and Personal Milestones*. Edited by Rabbi Debra Orenstein. Woodstock, VT: Jewish Lights.

Coitir, Niall Mac. 2023. "The Plants and Animals Associated with Holy Wells in Irish Folk Tradition." In *Holy Wells of Ireland: Sacred Realms and Popular Domains*. Edited by Celeste Ray and Finbar McCormick. Bloomington: Indiana University Press.

Coveville.com. 2022. "When Do Men Stop Growing?" *Coveville.com*, 30 November, 2022. https://coveville.com/men-stop-growing. Accessed 7 March, 2024.

Emoto, Masaru. 2006. *Love Thyself: The Message from Water III*. Carlsbad, CA: Hay House.

En.daoinfo.org. 2009. "Daoist Funeral Rites." *En.daoinfo.org*, 7 November, 2009. https://en.daoinfo.org/wiki/Daoist_Funeral_Rites. Accessed 7 March, 2024.

Eskildsen, Stephen. 2004. *The Teachings and Practices of the Early Quanzhen Taoist Masters*. Albany: State University of New York Press.

Goodreads.com. "Quotable Quote." *Goodreads.com*. https://www.goodreads.com/quotes/8203490-watch-your-thoughts-they-become-your-words-watch-your-words. Accessed 7 March, 2024.

Graham, Sarah. 2002. "Scientists Sequence Rice Genome." *Scientificamerican.com*, 05 April, 2002. https://www.scientificamerican.com/article/scientists-sequence-rice. Accessed 7 March, 2024.

Grant, Richard. 2018. "Do Trees Talk to Each Other?" *Smithsonianmag.com*, March, 2018. https://www.smithsonianmag.com/science-nature/the-whispering-trees-180968084. Accessed 7 March, 2024.

Japanese Mythology & Folklore. 2014. "The custom of planting a paulownia "princess tree" at the birth of a baby girl." *Japanese Mythology & Folklore*, 14 December, 2014. https://japanesemythology.wordpress.com/2014/12/ 07/the-custom-of-planting-a-paulownia-at-the-birth-of-a-baby-girl. Accessed 31 January 2024.

Karsen. 2018. "Do Fish Bite More on Sunny or Cloudy Days?" *Mountaintrailsfishing.com*, 2018. https://mountaintrailsfishing.com/do-fish-bite-more-on-sunny-or-cloudy-days. Accessed 7 March, 2024.

Law, Sung Ping. 1986. "The Regulation of Menstrual Cycle and its Relationship to the Moon." *Acta Obstericia et Gynecologica Scandinavica*, 65.1:45-48.

Littlejohn, Ronnie L. 2019. *Historical Dictionary of Daoism*. London: Rowman & Littlefield.

Nall, Rachel. 2018. "What Are the Benefits of Sunlight?" *Healthline.com*, 01 April, 2019. https://www.healthline.com/health/depression/benefits-sunlight. Accessed 31 January 2024.

Ott, John. 2011. "About Dr. Ott." *Scienceoflight.org*, 2011. https://scienceoflight.org/ott-index/dr-john-ott. Accessed 7 March, 2024.

Papazian, Sjur Cappelen. 2019. "T / D (S) – Dingir, Dyeus, Tian, Shen." *Aratta.wordpress.com*, 22 May, 2019. https://aratta.wordpress.com/2019/05/22/t-d-s-dingir-dyeus-tian-shen. Accessed 7 March, 2024.

Perry, Philip. 2016. "Plants and Trees Communicate Through an Unseen Web." *Bigthink.com*, 26 August, 2016. https://bigthink.com/surprising-science/plants-and-trees-communicate-help-each-other-and-even-poison-enemies-through-an-unseen-web. Accessed 7 March, 2024.

Pregadio, Fabrizio. 2016. "Religious Daoism." *Plato.stanford.edu*, 19 August 2016. https://plato.stanford.edu/entries/daoism-religion. Accessed 7 March, 2024.

Prettydarkhorse. 2012. "Lucky and Unlucky Numbers in Chinese Culture." *Discover.hubpages.com*, 09 December, 2012. https://discover.hubpages.com/holidays/Lucky-and-Unlucky-Numbers-in-Chinese-Culture. Accessed 7 March, 2024.

Reninger, Elizabeth. 2019. "Introduction to the Ren Meridian Conception Vessel." *Learnreligions.com*, 3 March, 2019. https://www.learnreligions.com/introduction-to-the- conception-vessel-ren-meridian-3183062. Accessed 7 March, 2024.

Sun, Jiahui. 2015. "The Chinese Mermaid." *Ecns.cn*, 26 August, 2015. www.ecns.cn/learning-Chinese/2015/08-26/178755.shtml. Accessed 7 March, 2024.

Suwandy, Iwan. 2013. "The Chinese Imperial Ceramic Artwork Found in Indonesia (Continiu)." *Driwancybermuseum.wordpress.com*, 28, June 2013. https://driwancybermuseum.wordpress.com/2013/06/28/the-chinese-imperial-ceramic-artwork-found-in-indonesia-continiu-13. Accessed 7 March, 2024.

The Professor. "Nine Star Astrology." *Mantakchia.com*. https://www.mantakchia.com/nine-star-astrology. Accessed 7 March, 2024.

Tucker, Reed. 2017. "The Secret to Living Past 100 Can Be Found in This Remote Chinese Village." *Nypost.com*, New York Post, 3 July, 2017. https://nypost.com/2017/07/03/the-secret-to-living-past-100-can-be-found-in-this-remote-chinese-village. Accessed 7 March, 2024.

Wikipedia.org. *En.wikipedia.org*. https://en.wikipedia.org/wiki/Prahlad_Jani. Accessed 7 March, 2024.

Wong, Tony. 2003. "Of Wives, Concubines and Mistresses," *Scmp.com*, 06 July, 2003. https://www.scmp.com/article/420753/wives-concubines-and-mistresses. Accessed 7 March, 2024.

Wu, Baolin, and Jessica Eckstein. 2000. *Lighting the Eye of the Dragon: Inner Secrets of Taoist Feng Shui*. New York: St. Martin's Press.

_____ Brent Christopher Wulf. 2022. *Dog Mother: World Culture and Dog Qigong*. St. Petersburg, FL: Three Pines Press.

_____. 2024. *Rousing the Rabbit: Qigong for Opening the Occipital Third Eye and Foreseeing Destiny*. St. Petersburg, FL: Three Pines Press.

Yourchineseastrology.com. 2014a. "Face Reading Eyebrows." *Yourchineseastrology.com*. https://www.yourchineseastrology.com/face-reading/eyebrows. Accessed 7 March, 2024.

_____. 2014b. "What Your Mouth Shape Says About Your Personality?" *Yourchineseastrology.com*. https://www.yourchineseastrology.com/face-reading/mouth/shape.htm. Accessed 7 March, 2024.

The Authors

Dr. Baolin Wu is a senior master of Daoist taijiquan, Chinese medicine, and *qi* cultivation. Born in China, he now heals and teaches in Santa Monica and is widely recognized as an authority in Chinese medicine and the martial arts. He is also the author of *Dog Mother* (2022), *Rousing the Rabbit* (2023), *A Bright Light in the Darkness* (2024), and various other works on qigong, longevity, and health. For more, see https://beijingchinesemedicalcenter.com/

Austin Lane Muhs is a career tarot reader, astrologer, and author based in Santa Monica. Born in Dallas, he brings many years of qigong training, community service, and reform work to his written work. He is also known as an authority in the fields of national disaster response and animal rescue.

Kevin T. Hill is a student of Daoism, Chinese medicine, the *Yijing*, and *qi*-cultivation under Dr. Wu Baolin. Born and raised in Santa Monica, he holds a liberal arts degree from Santa Monica College and has studied and practiced martial arts, philosophy, and meditation for over twenty years. With Dr. Wu, he has co-authored *A Bright Light in the Darkness* (2024).

Jessica Eckstein has been Dr. Wu's student in qigong, fengshui, martial arts, and *Yijing* for thirty years. She is co-author of *Lighting the Eye of the Dragon*, voted one of the ten best Fengshui books in English, *Qi Gong for Total Wellness*, a classic on the essentials of Daoist qigong, and *Qigong Journey* (2021).

Michael McBride, a Los Angeles native, has studied with Master Wu for twenty-four years, working in qigong, taijiquan, swordplay, and medical massage. He has traveled extensively in China for over two decades. With Dr. Wu, he has co-authored *The Eight Immortals' Revolving Sword* (2012) and *The Soul of Taiji* (2020).

Paulina Wierzbicka, originally from Poland and now residing in Los Angeles, began her qigong studies with Dr. Baolin Wu in 2023. Her journey reflects a deep commitment to integrating the healing practices of qigong into daily life, aiming to foster well-being and balance within her community.

Brent Christopher Wulf, a California native, began studying qigong under Dr. Baolin Wu in 2006 and has since studied other Daoist arts such as taijiquan, swordplay, and medical massage. He also earned a Master of Science degree in Acupuncture and Oriental Medicine in 2019. With Dr. Wu, he has co-authored *Dog Mother* (2022) and *Rousing the Rabbit* (2023).

Index